Also by Judith Viorst

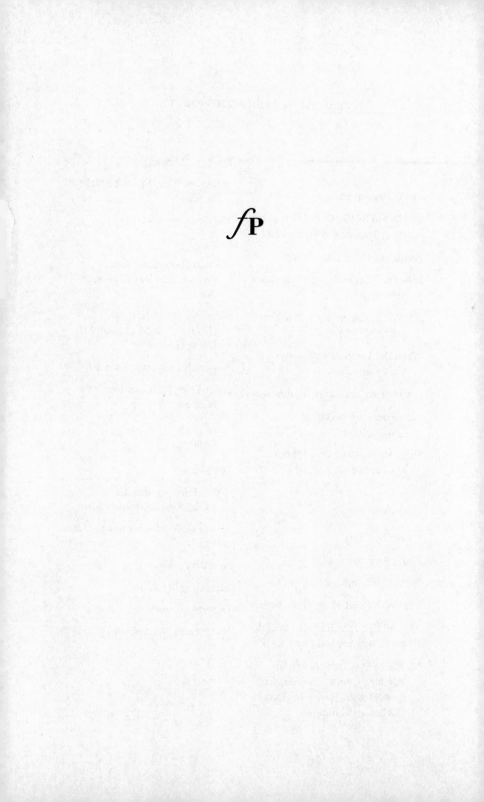

JUDITH VIORST

Grown-up Marriage

What We Know, Wish We Had Known, and
Still Need to Know About Being Married

THE FREE PRESS
New York London Toronto Sydney Singapore

_f_P

THE FREE PRESS
A Division of Simon & Schuster, Inc.
1230 Avenue of the Americas
New York, NY 10020

THE FREE PRESS and colophon are trademarks
of Simon & Schuster, Inc.

For information regarding special discounts for bulk purchases,
please contact Simon & Schuster Special Sales at 1-800-456-6798 or
business@simonandschuster.com

DESIGNED BY LISA CHOVNICK

Manufactured in the United States of America

1   3   5   7   9   10   8   6   4   2

Library of Congress Cataloging-in-Publication Data
Viorst, Judith.
Grown-up marriage : what we know, wish we had known, and still need to
know about being married / Judith Viorst.
p. cm.
Includes bibliographical references and index.
1. Marriage. 2. Man-woman relationships. I. Title.

HQ734 .V484 2003
306.81—dc21

ISBN 0-7432-1080-8

this book is for

Miranda Rachel Viorst

Brandeis Lowell Viorst

Olivia Rigel Viorst

Nathaniel Redding Gwadz Viorst

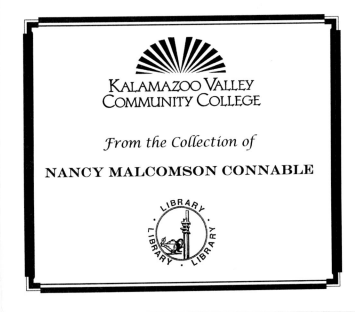

CONTENTS

. . . I tell you now,
in every house of marriage
there's room for an interpreter.

—Stanley Kunitz, "Route Six"

INTRODUCTION

ALTHOUGH MARRIAGE IS for grown-ups, very few of us are grown up when we marry. Growing up takes time, perhaps a whole lifetime, and getting there—if we get there at all—is hard. But marriage, which can be the most vexatious of human relationships, can also be the engine of our growth. For in making some sort of peace with the disenchantments, demands, and astonishing complexities of ordinary everyday married life, we can create—and no, this isn't a contradiction in terms—a grown-up marriage.

In a grown-up marriage we understand that we aren't, and shouldn't be, each other's teacher, parent, editor, supervisor, or home-improvement project.

A grown-up marriage allows us to find a balance between autonomy and connection.

In a grown-up marriage we gradually acquire a rueful tolerance of each other's limitations and imperfections.

In a grown-up marriage we do not keep score—at least not out loud.

In a grown-up marriage we recognize that we don't always have to be in love with each other. In fact, we are well aware that we couldn't possibly always be in love with each other. But a grown-up marriage enables us, when we fall out of love with each other, to stick around until we fall back in.

A grown-up marriage involves a tricky combination of honest and polite.

In a grown-up marriage we're able to apologize when we're wrong and not gloat when we're right. We can also accept an apology that falls short of total abasement, but not too short.

In a grown-up marriage the laughter exceeds the regret.

In a grown-up marriage we've learned to forgive and forget. Well, maybe not forget.

In a grown-up marriage we know how to communicate with each other and know when the only and best thing to do is shut up.

In a grown-up marriage we recognize that marriage will not give us a real identity, or keep us safe from the sorrows and pain of life, or even protect us forever after from loneliness.

This is a book about the possibilities and difficulties of being truly and well and enduringly wed. It's about what one married friend of mine calls "the wonderful, knotted, tangled, loaded, complicated joining of two lives." It's about the triumph—and when marriage works, it is indeed a triumph—of creating and sustaining that joined life. It is a book about having a grown-up marriage.

I've written this book for married people who, though they sometimes—maybe more than sometimes—hurt, enrage, and disappoint each other, want to stay married. It's intended both for the newly wed and for those who, like me, have been at it a long, long time. I'm speaking to, and about, middle-class heterosexual couples because theirs are the marriages I know best. I'm speaking to couples who already are, or ought to be, aware that marriages are rarely made in heaven, that sometimes they include a few seasons in hell, and that if a husband and wife can finally manage to get marriage right, the hell part is worth it.

In preparing this book, I've looked at the collision between expectation and reality. I've examined the issues we struggle with in our journey from "I do" to "till death do us part." If I sometimes find marriage funny, that is because what goes on in a marriage is, at times, more ridiculous than sublime. And if, in this age of divorce, I sound quite hopeful about marriage, that's because I am.

I've drawn, in this book, on my own forty-plus years of marriage, on interviews with women and men at every different stage of married life,* on case histories provided to me by several couples therapists, and on the wisdom I've found in the works† of psychologists, novelists, essayists, and poets, as well as on the stage and in the movies. Here is the core of what I've been thinking about and writing about for as long as I have been a married woman. Here is what we know and wish we had known and still need to know about becoming grown-ups in a grown-up marriage.

JUDITH VIORST
Washington, D.C.

---

* Names changed and identifying details altered.

† See the end notes and bibliography for information on all of my source materials.

CHAPTER ONE

Why We Get Married

*The dread of loneliness is greater than the fear of
bondage, so we get married.*
— Cyril Connolly, *The Unquiet Grave*

M O S T   O F   T H E   W O M E N   of my generation probably married too young to have grown acquainted with the dread of loneliness. Most of us were taught, however, before we left our teens the dread of unmarriedness. One of my aunts, who remarkably got a Ph.D. in physics at a time when most of her peers went no further than high school, was perceived by my mother and father and other relatives as our family's tragic failure because she never achieved a husband and kids. Another of my aunts, who was seen as a lesser tragic failure because, although divorced, she at least *had* been married, was still an object of pity because she needed to earn her own living instead of being supported by a man. Earning a living was something a woman aspired to be relieved of. A solid middle-class marriage was a marriage in which a woman did not, thank God, have to go out and get a job.

So we married because, for a woman, there was no higher attainment. And we married to be taken care of financially. We also married in order to have safe sex, which—had we been pressed—we would have defined as sex that wouldn't make getting pregnant a vast catastrophe. We also—most of us—married to get pregnant and raise a family. Of course what we said was that we married for love.

As for the men who married us, why did they do it? Why in the late 1950s were men, at the average marrying age of twenty-three, in a rush to become our economic providers? Part of the answer, I think, is that they were brought up in a culture that equated becoming a man with settling down. Maybe no one whispered words like "breadwinner" or "responsible" in their ears, but most of them knew what they were supposed to do. "A young college-educated bourgeois male of my generation who scoffed at the idea of marriage for himself . . . laid himself open to the charge of 'immaturity' . . . ," writes Philip Roth in *My Life as a Man.* "Or he was just plain 'selfish.' Or he was 'frightened of responsibility.' Or he could not 'commit himself' . . . to a 'permanent relationship.'"

And so these young men committed themselves, receiving in return the approval of society plus—very important—sex on a regular basis. Of course what they said was that they married for love.

We all meant it—well, most of us meant it—when we said we married for love, and we knew what kind of love that ought to be: Romantic love. And lustful love. And tender love. And giddy love. And you are my one true love, my destiny. And love-song love. And movie love. And happily-ever-after love. And baby, baby, you belong to me, so let the beguine begin because I've got you under my skin. Dreamy, steamy, now-and-forever love.

We all married—well, most of us married—for love, for some version of Sinatra and *Casablanca* love, for a love that would light up our lives and cast out fear, for a Romeo and Juliet love (except with a better ending), for a love that the poet John Donne once wrote "makes one little room an everywhere." And if our feelings were, as they doubtless were, a bit naive, a bit adolescent, I don't intend to disparage them, for there can surely be nothing sweeter than a man and a woman marrying for love.

And most of us did. But whether we consciously knew it or not, most of us also married—let's be honest here—for the sex, the kids, the security, the approval of our community, and marriage's other pragmatic benedictions. There were plenty of reasons to marry back in my day. But that was then. Why get married now?

Now that the state of unmarriedness isn't the disaster that it used to be. Now that women are raised to be economically independent, and actually want to go out and get a job. Now that unwed sex and unwed living together seem to be widely tolerated, and even unwed parenthood no longer shocks. Now that two people who love each other can freely, and some would say fully, express their love without doing something drastic, like getting married.

Why not simply live together as long as love survives, without insisting on "always" and "forever"? Why accept the constraints, the obligations, the routinization, the rut of marriage?

Especially when so many marriages fail.

Certainly, with 45 percent of first marriages ending in divorce, marriage today is a high-risk occupation. For those who have divorced once and those whose parents have divorced, it is even riskier. Divorce, the experts tell us, occurs more often in second marriages than in firsts—the current figure is 60 percent of the time—which surely says something dismaying about our ability to learn from past experiences. Even more dismaying are the statistics on children whose parents have divorced: compared to the children of parents who have not, the chance of their marriage breaking up is currently said to be two to three times greater.

Some of these children of divorce are, not surprisingly, wary of getting married.

"I want to be sure we won't mess up the way you and Mom messed up," Don explains untactfully to his father, who has asked him why he hasn't yet married the woman he has been living with for five years. She is a perfectly lovely woman, Don says. She is everything he wants, but how does he know if he's always going to want it? Living together until he feels 110 percent sure seems to him more prudent, right now, than marrying.

Even without the shadow of divorce in their personal history, those now considering marriage seem a lot more cautious than my generation was. (*The New York Times* reports on a wedding in which the vows excluded "till death do us part," on the grounds—the bride explained—that "we didn't want to make any promises we couldn't keep.") That caution may help explain, in part, why the median ages for marrying today are the oldest that they've been in American history—twenty-seven for men, twenty-five for women. Maybe people are trying to wait until they harbor no doubts, until they are 110 percent sure.

Sure that what they want now they'll want ten years from now. Sure that their differences aren't irreconcilable. Sure that there aren't any deep, dark secrets. Sure that this is love, not infatuation. Sure that they won't—like their mothers and fathers—be stuck for life in an inert, juiceless marriage. Sure that, good as this seems, they won't be missing out on something even better.

Christy, pushing thirty-five, has been telling me about Benjamin, a man she describes as pretty close to perfect—warm and smart and funny and reliable and crazy about her and just as eager as she is to start a family. The trouble, Christy says, is that while she's very fond of Ben, she isn't what she'd describe as madly in love, though the men she's been madly in love with had no interest in getting married and would have made really rotten husbands and fathers. Ben, she's completely confident, would make a great husband and father. And her biological clock is ticking away. Isn't it time for her to say that this is maybe as good as it's going to get? Isn't it time to stop holding out and get married?

I didn't know how to answer her, although I was tempted to say, Marry the man today and start a family. I didn't know if not being madly in love was code for he doesn't thrill me in bed. I didn't know if, by letting Ben go, she'd miss out on motherhood and always regret it, or if, by marrying Ben, she'd miss out on passionate love instead and regret that more. I once watched a woman decide to marry a man with whom everything worked except the sex. She believed they would figure that out eventually. But they wound up getting divorced because she solved the problem with sex by engaging in adultery. Then he found out. And when he told her, It's either your lover or me, she chose her lover. And married him, and lived extremely unhappily ever after because he was a rotten husband and father.

Maybe we simply have to hold out for Ms. or Mr. Right. Remember that Neil Simon movie *The Heartbreak Kid?*

The heartbreak kid is Lenny, who marries Lila, goes off to Miami Beach on their honeymoon, and falls madly in love—on their honeymoon!—with the girl of his dreams, a golden goddess named Kelly. "I've been waiting for a girl like you all my life," Lenny tells Kelly. "I just timed it wrong." But he doesn't let bad timing stand in his way. Instead, while still on their honeymoon, Lenny tells Lila they're wrong for each other and that he thinks they ought to get divorced, after which he pursues and woos and succeeds in marrying the glorious Kelly. At the end of the movie we see Lenny on his wedding day. He is looking rather uneasy. He is looking much less than 110 percent sure. Has he or hasn't he finally picked the right woman? How do people know if they've made the right choice?

———————

Perhaps if we find it so hard to decide if we're making the right choice, we ought to commit to something less binding than marriage, some sort of legal arrangement that provides us and our partner with certain protections without signing on until death does us part. France, for instance, now offers a civil solidarity pact—*Pacte civil de solidarité*—which was intended for same-sex couples but has been seized upon by marriage-shy heterosexuals. It establishes for both partners of the PACS, as it is known, a number of marriage-like obligations and rights.

Because it's dramatically easier to dissolve a PACS than it is to end a marriage, this arrangement appeals to those who wish to formally acknowledge their relationship while avoiding the terrors of making a lifetime choice. It is definitely more serious than the low-commitment arrangement known as "sex without strings, relationship without rings." It is definitely more serious than living together with no sense of obligation. It is definitely more serious than living together with some sense of obligation while refusing to put any promises down on paper. But it's definitely *less* serious than marriage.

So what is it called if a woman and man decide to be legally bound without being married? What is it called to be sort of, semi, married? Some call it hedging your bets or fear of commitment. Some call it half-assed, halfhearted, or half-hitched. Actually, the Germans have a name, a very, very long name for it. They call it *Lebensabschnittgefährte*, which means temporary partners or companions through a slice of life.

The women of my generation were looking for lifetime, not slice-of-life, companions. We were looking for a strings-and-rings relationship. We wanted to know, for the next fifty years, exactly who our New Year's Eve date would be. We wanted to be not semi, but totally, married.

Indeed, I suspect that my friends and I, had the option been available back then, would have signed on eagerly for the "covenant marriage," which requires premarital and predivorce counseling, as well as—in Louisiana, one of three states that now have covenant marriage—two years apart before a marriage is terminated. The point of the covenant marriage is to make divorce much harder, to intensify the commitment of husband and wife, to give them the opportunity to choose "marriage heavy" over "marriage lite." The point of the covenant marriage is "to lock in forever and throw away the key."

I married, of course, believing that I had chosen marriage heavy, that I had locked in forever and thrown away the key. I certainly never dreamed that I would divorce.

I was still in my twenties when my brief first marriage came to an end in the late 1950s and on my own for the first time in my life. A single woman living in Greenwich Village, I was only just beginning to become acquainted with the dread of loneliness. On her visits from New Jersey, my mother would often reassure me, as she fluffed up my hair and proffered a darker lipstick, "You're a nice-looking girl. You'll get yourself a husband." But I knew that she was worried about my matrimonial future. So was I.

Will I ever get married?
Is the end of my searching in sight?
There are lamps that I'm waiting to light,
Waiting to light them together.

Will I ever get married?
There are secrets my heart yearns to speak
To that someone who seeks what I seek,
And wants to seek it together.

The world is full of short-term lovers
Who don't even know your middle name.
I want to cuddle under the covers
Year after year after year after year
With the same . . .
With the same man.

Will I ever get married?
Will I ever be somebody's wife?
Making dinner, love, babies, a life,
Making a life together.

Then one night the telephone rang. It was Milton.

My first husband and I had agreed that we would wait to file for divorce until one of us decided to remarry. I decided, in 1960, to remarry. But when I went off to get my divorce, I fell into a panic: Ending a marriage was horrible. I never wanted to go through this again. How could I be sure that I never would? Why was I, a woman who loved the great indoors and obscure poetry readings, planning to marry a man who loved to ski and canoe and go on camping trips? Surely Milton and I were irredeemably incompatible. Surely it was best to break this off now and avoid the grief of a second divorce.

I called him up and broke it off. He told me we needed to talk. And after we finished talking, and hugging and kissing, and going out shopping to buy me a wedding dress, it was back on.

What is the lesson here? If I had listened to my panicky inner voice instead of listening to Milton, we would not now have been married for forty-two years. But should everyone beset by you're-making-a-really-big-mistake fears simply ignore them?

One young man, a few weeks before he was due to say "I do," had a powerful wish to flee his fiancée. He felt that his marriage was already doomed, but persuaded himself to stay by telling himself that "although there's a lot about her I just don't like, I'm twenty-seven years old and almost all my friends are married, so maybe the problem isn't her but me."

A twenty-four-year-old woman, only a week before her wedding, decided that although her husband-to-be was a man of many fine qualities, he was also a workaholic and undemonstrative and "I didn't think I'd be happy living that way." She wanted to call off the wedding, but her parents gave her Valium and told her that everything would be okay, that she was simply suffering from normal premarital jitters.

"I don't think I love her," Rick told his dad about his bride-to-be. His father quickly replied, "Oh, you'll get over that."

"There's too much we don't agree on," Mary Ellen wailed to her mom, who said, "No, there's not."

And Maggie, who informed her mother and father the day of the wedding that she wasn't good enough to marry Scott and therefore she wouldn't, was informed by her mother and father that she was plenty good enough—and therefore she would. She was also informed it was normal, if you really took marriage seriously, to find yourself with a case of premarital jitters.

That's what Jeffrey tried to tell himself too.

For Jeff had looked at Annabel and decided that, since their engagement, they had been going down two very different paths. He knew in his gut, he said, "that she wasn't the one." But they now owned a dog and a house, and they had a wedding coming up to which three hundred people had been invited, and "the train was in motion. I couldn't stop it. I couldn't stop that train. I was just too much of a coward to try to stop it." Embarrassed at his change of heart, Jeff didn't breathe his secret to a soul. Instead, he kept reassuring himself, "We'll find things to talk about, things to do with each other." Pasting a happy smile on his face, he walked into the church on his wedding day, saying—or maybe praying—"It will work out."

So Jeff and Annabel, Maggie and Scott, and the other couples got married. Then Jeff and Annabel, Maggie and Scott, and all the other couples got divorced.

Perhaps these jittery people should have bravely postponed their weddings until, with counseling, they had explored their concerns. Indeed, some experts have argued that marrying couples, whether jittery or not, should attend premarital education classes, which teach them how to listen, praise, deal with conflict, and fight respectfully, and which sometimes recommend a compatibility quiz. For those who prefer to skip the quiz, Todd Outcalt's book, *Before You Say "I Do,"* supplies an exhaustive list of questions that couples, prior to marriage, are urged to explore:

Like how many kids do you want? And how important is religion in your life? And what do you call a clean house? And are you in debt? And how close to your folks do you think we should live? And do or don't you like animals? And what big secrets haven't you told me yet? The questions cover hopes and dreams and values and work and sex and money and family and household chores and personal history, although the usefulness of the answers depends on the answerer's honesty and self-awareness. For couples who set a wedding date without ever asking each other the most basic questions, this Q&A may be a revelation. But sometimes almost a decade of knowing each other will still not provide enough information to guarantee a woman and man that their marriage will last.

For marriage, as Ted and Nancy learned, can provide a whole different kind of information.

Ted and Nancy met in their sophomore year of college in southern California. They were living in the same dorm and became close friends. They took classes together, studied together, and hung out a lot together before, in their senior year, falling deeply in love. After graduation they temporarily put their relationship on hold while they each went off "to do stuff on our own," then after two years of separateness, they got back together, moved in together, and lived together for four mostly pretty good years.

"We believed that we loved each other and were meant to be with each other," Nancy told me, although there were some tensions that arose, what with Ted becoming something of a free spirit who couldn't be bothered with paying bills, and Nancy becoming "the stabilizing force, the administrator, and sometimes the nag." Nevertheless, she says, they were very committed to the relationship. "We thought," she said, "we were building a shared life." So when Ted began behaving less free-spiritedly and declared that he wished to be married and have a family, they decided that the time was right to get married. Five months later, in a state of panic and confusion, Ted stunned Nancy by saying he wanted out. He couldn't stay in the marriage, he told her. He needed to be free. He wasn't, he explained, the person he'd claimed he was (and maybe had hoped he could be), a person who wished to be married and have a family.

Nancy, who had known Ted as her friend and classmate and roommate and lover for nine full years, didn't know the confused and panicked Ted who'd become—and did not want to be—her husband. She was astonished, *astonished,* she said, and then repeated the word again, astonished to discover she didn't know him.

Couples who think that living together allows them to learn the "truth" about each other may also assume that knowing this truth enables them to make a sounder marriage. But in *Should We Live Together?* a review by David Popenoe and Barbara Dafoe Whitehead of recent research on the subject, the question of whether cohabitation before getting married is helpful to the marriage is (you may be surprised to hear) answered no.

Consider this: Between 1960 and 1997, the number of cohabiting couples—unmarried sexual partners sharing a household—grew from less than half a million to four million. Consider this: More than half of all first marriages today, in contrast to almost none at the start of the twentieth century, are now preceded by cohabitation. And consider this: Almost all the research on the subject finds that marriages preceded by living together have a greater chance of ending in divorce.

If you want a figure on this, it's about 46 percent higher than for marriages not preceded by cohabitation.

Alhough this finding doesn't apply to couples who've already planned to marry and are simply cohabiting briefly before they do, it's a blow to those who believe that living together will help them get to know each other, thus helping them decide if they *ought* to get married—and inoculating them against getting divorced.

So how come it doesn't?

The most common explanation is that people who choose to live together are less traditional than those who don't, and that the same untraditional outlook that allows them to cohabit allows them to divorce more easily. Studies also find that cohabiting couples, compared to couples who are married, display less of a commitment to the relationship, along with a greater insistence—in matters like money and social life—on individual autonomy. "It is reasonable to speculate," concludes the *Should We Live Together?* report, "that once this low-commitment, high-autonomy pattern of relating is learned, it becomes hard to unlearn." Add to all this the studies suggesting that living together itself negatively affects the way that partners value the institution of marriage, and we've got some persuasive theories of why the married state may be riskier for those who, before getting married, have first cohabited.

Ian, age thirty-six and married for the second time, offers his thoughts on the subject. "I lived with my first wife for two years before we got married. Although I don't have any religious or ethical objections to living together before marriage, I would now advise against it. The problem is that, once you live together for a significant period of time (say, six months), you . . . do not have reasonable middle ground or neutral corners if differences arise. You're essentially faced with either getting married or ending the relationship."

He concludes that "if you have doubts about your partner, it is unlikely that living together will clear anything up."

I respect what Ian is saying, and yet there are still, in my view, some good arguments for cohabiting. Even if living together doesn't ensure a successful marriage, it does weed out clearly poisonous relationships. (Indeed, I've known a few parents who've urged their children, "Don't be rash! First live together," hoping they'd see the error of their ways.) It also allows men and women who are too young or not yet ready to be married to become somewhat more responsible and mature. And of course, it enables those who do not wish to be celibate to have regular and safe unmarried sex.

———

Eventually, however, the issue of marriage will arise. Indeed, it will arise if a couple is only seeing each other, not living together. The reason it will arise is that marriage remains, for most women and men, a desirable goal. Although cohabitation is increasingly becoming a marriage alternative, although the rate of marriages has declined, although a mere 23.5 percent of American households are currently composed of nuclear families, and although (as one report puts it) "marriage . . . no longer looms like Mount Everest in the landscape of the adult life course," the vast majority of women and men still intend, and still are going, to get married.

Why? Let's hustle past wise-guy replies, such as, to get all those presents, to get on her health insurance, to save my mom from committing suicide, and consider the deeper reasons why men and women today continue to want to marry: Because it provides a greater degree of emotional security. Because it's "a permanent sleepover with a best friend." Because it creates a stable framework in which to bring up children. Because it's a vow to share a future together. Because it alters the way they are seen by their family and friends and colleagues and by all the institutions of society.

Here, from some of the many young married women and men I queried, are a few more becauses:

FROM DEB: "Because I wanted to get to hang out with my best friend for the rest of my life with everyone's blessings."

FROM OLIVER: "Because the difference between living together and being married is like the difference between eating at McDonald's and eating at a five-star restaurant. Both satisfy your hunger, but only one of them is a real meal."

FROM WILLIAM: "Because with family and friends and work constantly pulling at us, it was our way of saying—to ourselves and the world—that we're the most important thing in the world to each other."

FROM TOVA: "Because I met, at the right time of my life, someone who was totally what I was looking for, and getting married meant more to me than just physically putting two people under one roof—it meant making a real agreement to try to work together to be together forever."

FROM DAN: "Because marriage has a religious significance to me, and it was important to me that our marriage be recognized and blessed by God."

FROM HEATHER: "Because I did and do adore him; there isn't a moment of my life I wouldn't prefer to be with him; and marrying him seemed the best way to make sure that we would spend a lot of time together."

Marla, who lived with our youngest son, Alexander, before they got married, offers this response to my question, Why marry?

She says that, after a while, living together without being married starts to feel "like you're holding out for something better." She says that if marriage represents a greater commitment than living together, then "that's the commitment I want to give and to get from the person I love. I want the whole thing." She says that marriage, much more than living together, "entangles you, making you responsible to this specific person and this life." She also says, "I was drawn to the *romance* of marriage, to becoming part of something that was so much bigger than the two of us."

Alexander adds: "Getting married was making a public statement that she's mine and I'm hers and we're going to build a life together."

Even a seemingly untraditional woman like Marjorie Ingall, a self-described "purple-haired, tattooed, nose-ringed feminist," wants to acknowledge publicly, in a religious wedding service, that she plans to spend her whole life with the man she's been living with. "I want to say," she writes, "in front of everyone that this is holy and legally binding, and I care enough about this person to enter into a very ancient covenant with him."

It's the public aspect of marriage, the entering into a covenant sanctioned by society, that makes it feel so different from the strictly private arrangement of living together. It's the public aspect of marriage, fortified by the law, the service, the family, the rings, that makes it feel like a much, much bigger deal.

But marriage isn't only a much, much *bigger* deal, argue sociology professor Linda J. Waite and Maggie Gallagher, director of the Marriage Project at the Institute for Family Values. It is also, as they exhaustively document in *The Case for Marriage,* a much *better* deal. Says Professor Waite, "We have looked at well over 1,000 studies that overwhelmingly show the strong and consistent relationship between marriage and well-being." Here's what they've found:

Compared to cohabiting couples, married couples seem to be blessed with better sex, greater happiness, longer lives, shorter hospital stays, more money, and less anxiety and depression. In addition, married couples get to live a more settled existence in better neighborhoods and have children who are less likely to drop out of school. Furthermore, being married can benefit physical health, while unmarriedness may actually be more life-threatening than heart disease or cancer. And if you consider that married people enjoy, in addition to all these other advantages, more sexual fidelity, less alcohol abuse, and a stronger sense that life has purpose and meaning, "Will you marry me?" can start to sound like one of those offers you can't refuse.

It's unlikely that many couples depend on social-science research to persuade themselves that they would be better off married. Some couples, in fact, need no persuasion at all. In contrast to those who agonize over whether or not they should go for it, there are some who, like Christopher Marlowe, ask, "Who ever loved who loved not at first sight?" and make their decision to marry with awesome alacrity.

Like Cynthia Heimel, who three weeks after she met her "wonderful dream man," said, "Yes, oh, absolutely yes," to his marriage proposal because "I fell in love with this man all the way to my reptilian brain."

Like Cal Fussman, who loved his wife at first sight because "I'd been traveling around the world for ten years and had seen about all there was to see. My instincts knew she was perfect before I could blink."

Like Al Gore, our former vice president, who met his wife, Tipper, when he was seventeen and says he knew almost immediately that he wanted to be with her for the rest of his life.

And like Jessie, my friend Jackie's daughter, who called up her mother from Vermont and breathlessly said to her, "Guess what I found today?" Her mother, bemused, pointed out that her answer could range from a five-dollar bill to . . . virtually anything, and that maybe she could use a little hint. "Just think about what I've been looking for, for almost my whole life," Jessie hinted. "The man of your dreams?" asked Jackie facetiously, not exactly prepared for Jessie's fervent answer to be "That's it!"

Two days later Jessie again phoned home and announced their plans. "It's all settled. We'll get married, have kids, and live here in Vermont, as soon as I finish up my master's degree." Two years after their fateful meeting, with undiminished love and certainty, Jessie and the man of her dreams got married.

For those who believe in love at first sight, in a match made in heaven, in soul mates, such certainty seems a sufficient basis for marriage. But cooler heads will argue that falling in love is a state of temporary insanity and that deciding to get married requires careful consideration and rational thought. Indeed, the extremely rational and meticulous Charles Darwin, in an act of scientific deliberation, preceded his decision to marry by drawing up two lists under the headings "Marry" and "Not Marry," mustering the arguments for (a "constant companion," "charms of music and female chit-chat," "better than a dog") and the arguments against ("forced to visit relatives," "anxiety and responsibility," "less money for books"). He finally concluded that "one cannot live this solitary life . . . friendless and cold and childless" and that, although being married might enslave him, "there is many a happy slave."

But deciding in favor of marriage isn't enough, the cooler heads tell us. We must also assess our chances of succeeding at it. We can't confuse alluring with enduring. We can't trust the feelings sweeping us away. We cannot be so blinded by love that we aren't able to see the person we're marrying. We cannot be so bedazzled that we ignore all the reasons why this will never work out.

Ellie, while still in college, was introduced to Norman by a mutual friend who cautioned her, "This will never work out. This will be going nowhere. He's not your type." A few weeks after they met, they decided to marry. On their fiftieth anniversary Ellie teased her friend, "Are you still convinced that Norman's not my type?" "Absolutely," her friend replied, adding cheerfully, "which only goes to show you that being somebody's type isn't everything."

Looking back on a long and remarkably happy married life, Ellie asks herself, "How did an unworldly twenty-year-old, who had never bought a pair of shoes without her mother, do so well in making this critical decision?" The answer she gives to her question is "Dumb luck." I think she is right and would add that her answer applies not only to her but to all of us who are basically happily married, to the women and men of my generation who married back when I did, and to the women and men who marry today. For even with premarital living together, and even with should-we-marry questionnaires, and even with marriage counseling and a lifetime supply of how-to-do-it books, married couples need a lot of dumb luck.

The dumb luck has to do with picking a partner who suits us—not perfectly, but sufficiently, suits not only the person we are when we marry but also the person we turn out to be. The dumb luck has to do with being compatible in ways that compatibility quizzes may fail to reveal. The dumb luck has to do with being well matched enough to be able to deal—as partners—with life's seismic changes and unexpected blows. It has to do with choosing—when we're way too young and dumb to know what we're doing—someone that we want, and keep wanting, to be with, even if we're not each other's type.

In the white heat of love, young lovers might not notice they hold different views on quite crucial matters, or might not worry much about whether their lover will be a good partner, good parent, good person five or ten or twenty years from now. But if we have dumb luck, there'll be something between us that will bind us over the decades, even when love falters and times are tough. There'll be something between us, and maybe we'll never quite figure out what it is, that becomes the glue that helps to hold us together.

So we'll need to have some luck when we choose a partner. But we'll also need to be prepared to work. Although work won't be enough unless we're lucky in what we're working with, luck won't be enough if we don't do the work. "There is scarcely anything more difficult than to love one another," writes the poet Rainer Maria Rilke. "That it is work, day labor, day labor, God knows there is no other word for it."

This labor, this work, demands vast stores of patience. It requires paying attention, more attention than we've ever paid before. It requires compelling ourselves, when we are sick and tired and ready to slam the door, to nonetheless leave the door just slightly ajar. The work includes not only the work we must do on the relationship but also the work we must do on ourselves.

In working on the relationship, I think it helps to see it as an entity greater than the sum of its parts, an entity that's been described as "bigger than both of us" and that I have taken to calling the "third thing." A thing with its own existence and its own rights. A thing to which we owe certain obligations. A thing on whose behalf we will, at least some of the time, have to transcend our individual needs. And so, in the fall of 2000, when the intensely autonomous Nick married his intensely autonomous Marya, I sneaked in a little advice for our middle son and his beautiful bride in a sonnet I composed for their wedding day:

> There's you and you, and then there's this third thing
> Which is the marriage. To it may you bring
> The finest strivings of the human heart.
> The "I," the "me," the "mine," the self apart
> Must yield some portion of its separateness
> And say a risky but unguarded yes
> To this third thing, this marriage you create. . . .

The outer work we must do on behalf of our marriage, our relationship, our "third thing," is deeply intertwined with the inner work we must do on our "I" and "me" and "mine." That inner work involves making peace with compromise, ambiguity, contradiction, and many, many different shades of gray. It demands significant self-examination. It requires us to revise and reshape our earlier expectations to meet the changing realities of who we are and where we are today. It means giving up. It means shaping up. It sometimes means shutting up. And it means growing up.

Rilke puts it like this: "For one human being to love another:

that is perhaps the most difficult of our tasks, the ultimate, the last test and proof, the work for which all other work is but preparation." Love, he tells us, "is a high inducement to the individual to ripen . . . ; it is a great exacting claim upon him, something that chooses him out and calls him to vast things."

A doctor in his midthirties, when I asked him why he got married, said that "after all these years and years of impersonating a grown-up, I wanted to become a full-fledged adult."

Getting married will not guarantee this, of course, but it will provide the opportunity. For marriage, if we are lucky and if we are willing to do the hard work, can help us to become full-fledged adults. And becoming full-fledged adults can help us create, and help us sustain, an enduring, satisfying, grown-up marriage.

CHAPTER TWO

The First Shocks of Marriage

Marriages, after all, begin in delusions, in the drug of
love, in a lie, if not knowing who you are and who the
other one is can be called a lie.
— Lynne Darling, "For Better or Worse"

WE MARRY without really knowing ourselves or our mates.
We marry without much awareness of the fears and expectations
we bring into marriage. We marry unprepared for the discontents
and disappointments, for the hassles and hurts—for the shocks—
of married life.

Even those who have lived together before the official "I do's"
find that matrimony is not only a whole other state but a whole
other country. And even the closest of live-in lovers might not be
prepared for what they become when they become husband and
wife. Perhaps they refrained from exposing the less-lovely parts of
themselves until their status moved from contingent to permanent.
Perhaps they did not feel entitled either to make or to refuse certain
demands, at least until their union was legalized. Perhaps they
could endure their partner's unendearing habits until getting married made them realize that they might be enduring these habits
forever and ever. Perhaps they needed the license and rings in order to believe that rehearsals were over and show time had begun.

My friends and I didn't live with our husbands before we married them, with the exception of one audacious couple—audacious, that is, except when Joan's mother and father came to town and Paul had to clear every sign of his presence out of their shared apartment and stay with a cousin until her parents left. Not living together, we found married life to be filled with constant and often unpleasant surprises, which started as soon as the honeymoon was over.

> The honeymoon is over
> And he has left for work
> Whistling something obvious from *La Boheme*
> And carrying a brown calfskin attaché case
> I never dreamed he was capable of owning,
> Having started the day
> With ten pushups and a cold shower
> Followed by a hearty breakfast.
> (What do we actually have in common?)
>
> . . .
>
> The honeymoon is over
> And we find that dining by candlelight makes us squint,
> And that all the time
> I was letting him borrow my comb and hang up
>   his wet raincoat in my closet,
> I was really waiting
> To stop letting him,

And that all the time
He was saying how he loved my chicken pot pie,
He was really waiting
To stop eating it.
(I guess they call this getting to know each other.)

Getting to know each other, we get to know each other's irritating habits in dozens of daily living-together matters: Like his failing to close dresser drawers and mayonnaise jars. Like her keeping the lights on in every room of the house. Like his never replacing the roll when he's used up the toilet paper. Like her leaving him the car without a single goddamn drop of gas in the tank.

Getting to know each other, we learn how much we're invested in our own way of doing things and how difficult, infuriating, impossible it can seem to live with a spouse who does these things a different way, a way that (in our opinion) is clearly wrong or absurd or embarrassing or insensitive or peculiar or downright dangerous. So although, in the days of our courtship, we agreed on the major questions, such as is God dead and who should be our next president, we may become fiercely polarized over such mundane matters as the minimum number of dishes that there ought to be in the dishwasher before it is okay to turn it on. Or the minimum sum of money that must always remain untouched in the bank account. Or whether or not he's setting us up to be robbed and maybe murdered when he leaves the door key under the welcome mat.

It was only after we married that my husband and I discovered just how deeply we disagreed about exactly how far in advance one must leave for an airport, since he prefers to board a plane seconds before it taxis down the runway and I prefer to be there dramatically sooner. I have pointed out to my husband, many times, that he should care about my happiness and that among the happiest moments in my life is reading a book at the airport some two hours before my plane is due to depart, secure in the knowledge that I won't miss my flight. Until heightened airport security made everybody get to airports early, Milton and I had major when-to-leave battles every time we flew anywhere together.

Along with information on each other's wrong ways of doing things, marriage also presents us with a cold, clear view of our spouse's unadorned self: What she looks like without the eyeliner and the blusher. What he smells like before he's showered and brushed his teeth. How unwilling she is to talk before she's had coffee. How testy he is when he hasn't had enough sleep. How badly he behaves when she forgets, yet again, to give him his telephone messages, and how badly she behaves when he forgets, yet again, to wipe the mud off his feet instead of tracking it all over the hallway.

In addition, being married can provide us with in-depth insights into some of our mate's more subtle psychology. We discover that when he's not in control, he tends to become overbearing, and that when she gets really scared, she tends to withdraw. And that after he fights with his supervisor, he always wants to make love, and that after she fights with her mother, she always doesn't. And that every time guilt is called for, she's excessively, and he's insufficiently, guilty.

Furthermore, married life supplies us with all kinds of information on many hitherto unrevealed aspects of character, on everything from is she polite to the trashmen, to does he tend to pad his expense account. One wife was stunned to find that, while hosting a dinner party at home, her husband served her and himself a pricey red wine while pouring a cheaper brand for their friends, on the grounds that they would never know the difference. And one husband was just as stunned to find that his wife didn't change the bedsheets in between houseguests. "What kind of person does such a thing?" groans the wife. "What kind of person does such a thing?" groans the husband. What kind of people are they married to?

Yes, those of us who didn't live with our spouses before we married them were in for a multitude of surprises and shocks that—or so the theory goes—premarital living together protects against. But even those who figured that married life would bring no new news because they already knew about things like unchanged sheets and undelivered messages may not be prepared for how differently all that information sits with them *after* marriage.

Indeed, no matter what any of us may know about our partner before we're married, it very often feels very different after. Before is when we good-naturedly say, "He's such an incredible cheapskate" or "She pitches a fit if I'm thirty seconds late," pleased we're prepared to frankly face up to one another's flaws and secretly convinced we'll be able to change them. Before is when we tell ourselves that of course nobody's perfect and that love will help us accept what we don't like. Before is when we agree that, although we will often disagree and often fight, we will always have great respect for each other's differences. Before is when we tolerate, laugh off, or try to ignore what we realize only after will be driving us nuts the entire rest of our lives.

We may be shocked to discover that marriage can give us a new perspective on a wife's or husband's uncongenial qualities. We may be shocked to discover the many ways in which married life breeds discontent.

"Shortly after the wedding—on honeymoon, at home, or when the partying has to stop—comes a wonderful clarity when man and woman know they are wretchedly human and have been caught in a wheel of sentiment and circumstance which propelled them away from truth . . . ," writes Kathrin Perutz. "The clarity is frightful, like hallucination. Am I mad? Is something wrong with me? There must be, or I never would have chosen this one, never have agreed to marry."

Wendy, a textbook editor, hasn't read Kathrin Perutz, but she echoes her point of view as she looks back with a sigh on her five years of marriage to Roger.

"I got married at twenty-seven," she says, "and none of my close friends were married yet, and so I found myself in this all alone. You know, your parents throw you great parties and buy you a gorgeous white dress and a new blender, but they don't tell you anything about the reality."

The reality, Wendy says, is that "it's not fun every day, it's not easy every day, that sometimes you really don't like him—in fact, you hate him—and that sometimes you look at this person in the middle of the night and wonder, 'Why did I marry you? What am I *doing* here?'"

Furthermore, she adds, no matter how much you've been together, "there are zillions of things that you don't know about him, things that are the results of his life experiences and all of his weird genes." So sometimes, she says, he'll do something strange—like lining the bathroom shelves with aluminum foil—"and I'll stand there asking myself, 'Who *is* this person?'"

Wendy was stunned to discover that sometimes she hated the man she loved and wished to be married to, stunned to discover how difficult the marriage she cherished and wished to remain in could be. "Nobody ever tells you," she says, "that it's sometimes okay to wonder, 'Who *is* this person?' Nobody ever tells you that it's sometimes okay to wonder, 'What am I *doing* here?'"

Nobody ever tells you that a marriage can be a basically good marriage and still be a breeding ground for discontent.

———

A possible source of discontent is the old sales ploy known as bait-and-switch—displaying, before marriage, certain irresistible qualities (the bait) that turn into something quite different (the switch) after marriage. This can lead to significant disillusionment.

Some couples hope to avoid this kind of postmarital disillusionment by insisting—as Joy and Andrew did—on "telling each other, on our second date, the worst part of us and our earlier life experiences." Or as another woman straightforwardly put it, "Our shit was pretty much on the table long before marriage." Nonetheless, although my kids' generation may be more forthcoming than mine was about unattractive aspects of themselves,

I've encountered bait-and-switchers of every age. As Cathy observed, "When men come a'courting, they know how to hide their less desirable traits. And women do too."

A drastic example is Audrey, who in the years she and Sandy were courting, took an amused and tolerant view of his shortcomings, making him feel that he could bumble, mess up, and even fail and that she—indulgent and loving—would continue to find him adorable and acceptable. Since they've been married, however, Audrey—no longer indulgent and loving—has adopted the role of poor Sandy's in-house critic, sighing and scolding and shaking her head and making it painfully clear that he is inadequate. She is constantly disapproving of—never amused by, never tolerant of—his shortcomings. And he is constantly wondering what happened to his adoring, accepting Audrey.

As for the bait-and-switch tactics of men, the one that I most often hear about has to do with their workaholic ways. Some men who were quite available during the halcyon courtship days seem to be relieved that they are now married and therefore freed of paying their wives so much time-consuming attention. "As soon as he had me nailed," says Elaine, "my can't-get-enough-of-you husband was back to fourteen hours a day at the office." Baiting his hook with attentiveness, he switched to unavailable after she bit.

Benjamin Franklin, writing his "Reflections on Courtship and Marriage," addressed the bait-and-switch problem all the way back in 1746. "I must affirm it a most dangerous Folly, an Imposition highly culpable, to mask our *Tempers*, and appear what we really are not . . . in order to win the Affections. . . . Is this laying a Foundation for our future Happiness? Monstrous! But this is sometimes, too often, the Case with both Sexes."

Denouncing the practice as stupid, shocking, and shallow, he indignantly asks, "Can we think the Cheat will lie long concealed in a Society so intimate? When Time and Experience unmask our *assumed* Appearances, show us in our *native Colours,* and *expose* that Reality we so industriously laboured to *cover,* can we expect Love & Esteem from any One whom we have so *shamefully over-reached* and ensnared? Surely *no.*"

Ben Franklin notwithstanding, I don't think that baiting and switching is always a cynical ploy designed to trap a credulous partner into marriage. Some women, especially those of my generation, were raised to be amenable, to please. And maybe some of the Audreys truly feel amused and tolerant—at first. Certainly most women and men, hoping to beguile a future mate, don't rush to reveal the worst about themselves. If we appear more wonderful than we turn out to be, it's not always because we intended to bait and switch.

Helena, for instance, who married twenty years after she had divorced, was as stunned by her transformation as her new husband was. "I was a totally competent person—I drove fearlessly on freeways, I bought and sold houses, I lifted heavy loads. I did it because I had to, but when Harry came along, I guess I suddenly felt that I no longer had to. Neither of us expected that the independent woman he had married would become, after marriage, so dependent on him."

Whether it's the switch after baiting, or some other unwelcome news about our mate, we may find ourselves living with someone we hadn't quite bargained for. These shocks of married life can make us feel we've been bilked and betrayed, seduced and abandoned. These shocks can make us feel that the person with whom we've signed on for life has done us wrong.

When we sign on for life, we carry with us many expectations, about the person we married, about being married. The expectations we bring into our marriage can set us up for serious disappointment.

One woman told me that what she expected from marriage was nothing less than "love, adoration, companionship, physical intimacy, emotional availability, accountability, respect, humor, and tolerance." Another woman told me that she expected "everlasting romance and passion." Other women and men said that they expected to be the center of each other's universe, to be more important to the person they'd married than anything, or anybody, else. And one man said he expected his wife to respect his need for autonomy and "to give me plenty of room to do my own thing."

Most of us expected that we'd cherish each other's virtues and accept with good grace each other's imperfections. That we'd give (or try to give) each other joy. That we'd do our damnedest to understand each other. And that, above anything else, we'd make every possible effort to spare each other pain.

But marriage teaches all of us that we won't get all we expected—some of the time, most of the time, or ever. It teaches us that, unless we're incredibly lucky, we're going to have to work hard for what we want. We learn, as Emily put it, to stop "expecting to get 100 percent of my needs met by my husband. That's what my sister and my girlfriends are for." And we learn how much damage our dearly beloved, our nearest and our dearest, inadvertently—or deliberately—can inflict on us.

High on our list of expectations is that the person we married will always, unconditionally, be on our side. Our model for this could be Matt, who says that if his wife told him she had killed somebody, his only question would be "What did he do?" But not every husband or wife is going to be that supportive, even of lesser infractions, like, for instance, making a world-class fool of ourselves. Instead, we may hear, as Val did when she told her husband she'd acted like a jerk, "You certainly did." And when she continued, moaning to him, "And everybody saw it," he unfeelingly observed, "How could anyone miss it?" And when she pressed on, hoping to salvage some comfort from this exchange, with "Maybe by tomorrow they'll have forgotten," he replied by reassuring her, "They won't be forgetting that one anytime soon." Then we'll ask ourselves, as Val did, what happened to our dream of a safe harbor? Where is that consolation, that immediate support, that we expected marriage to provide?

That support is not always there. Our mates, we will learn, may not invariably be on our side. Sometimes, in fact, they will be on the opposite side. Says Dorothy of her husband: "I expected, when we married, to be part of a team that confronts the world together. But I often feel that we are less of a team than we are competitors—an Agassi-Sampras-type situation in which you need the other to play, yet you are in battle."

Those of us who expected that we would always be a team confronting the world together soon learn the many ways we can be divided. One of these ways is by temperament, as some of us have discovered to our sorrow by picking a marriage partner with a temperament quite different from our own. Although well aware of this difference, we may choose to ignore its potential for divisiveness, hoping that our mate's temperament will complement ours and offer our life some balance, and cheerfully noting that opposites attract.

Sometimes it works.

"I have a tendency to think so much about the future that I forget to enjoy the present," Rachel says. "And Gil is thinking so much about the present that he forgets to plan for the future. So he reminds me to be in the moment, to pay attention to what's going on in front of me. And I take care of making sure we actually get tickets to the shows we want to see or for the trips we want to take."

Among the couples I've heard from, at every age and stage of marriage, there are many combinations of complementarity: He likes routine. She likes adventure. He's a homebody. She's gregarious. He's laid back. She's more of a type A. He takes forever and ever to make a decision. She comes to a decision right away. He's a saver. She's a tosser. He holds everything in. She lets everything out. He is self-effacing. She is bold. He's generous, open-handed, a big-time spender. She's afraid that if they don't watch every single penny, they'll end up in the poorhouse when they're old.

Maybe the notion that opposites attract is more viable in theory than in practice.

Most of us see our differences as both positive and negative, as sometimes valuable and sometimes irritating. We may, on occasion, find them amusing as well. We may even hope that those qualities we particularly admire will rub off on us. But some of us, sooner or later, may come to resent, resist, reject, or out-right loathe qualities we initially embraced, a dramatic change of heart that is yet another of the shocks of married life.

When Hubbell (Robert Redford) marries Katie (Barbra Streisand) in that memorable movie *The Way We Were,* there are many significant differences between them. The most obvious is that Katie is, in her words, "a loud-mouthed Jewish girl from New York," while Hubbell is, in her words, a "gorgeous goyische guy" from a ritzier milieu. The deeper difference between them is that Hubbell is a far less serious person—far readier to accommodate, even sell out—while idealistic Katie is uncompromising and sometimes scolding and humorless. Although Hubbell is often infuriated by Katie's intemperateness and self-righteousness, he also is powerfully drawn to her deep-down decency and her passionate faith in him. He marries her, in spite of the fact that she pushes and pushes and pushes "every damn minute," because he knows that what she says is true: that he'll never find anyone else who loves and believes in him as much, and that "you'll never find anyone as good for you."

But Hubbell cannot become the person that Katie believes he can be, and Katie can't stop pushing him to be it. Despite their love for each other, the way they were will not survive their divisive differences.

In the pioneering study *Marital Tensions,* British psychoanalyst Henry Dicks says that complementarity can add a great deal "to the possibilities of psychological cross-fertilization and growth." But complementarity, Dr. Dicks notes, can also be a source of marital difficulties, because husbands or wives "may persecute in their spouses tendencies which originally caused attraction."

In other words, a woman who is an expressive emotional type may marry a cool and calm, unruffled man, only later to decide that, rather than cool and calm, he's a cold-hearted bastard. Or a nonconfrontational man who once delighted in his fiancée's bold assertiveness may be cringing—after three years of marriage and several scenes in restaurants—at what he now sees as high-decibel aggressiveness. Or a path-of-least-resistance Hubbell gets tired of always failing to meet his high-standards Katie's impossibly high standards. In the cold light of married life, what looked like laid back may start to look a lot like lazy, detail-oriented may look like obsessional, and adventure-loving may look like just plain reckless. In the cold light of married life, we may find that what looked like complementary is starting to look a lot like incompatible.

"Nadine thrived on defiance," we're told in Joanna Trollope's novel *Other People's Children*, "defiance of the orthodox, the traditional, the accepted way of thinking and behaving. It was this defiance that had attracted Matthew to her in the first place. . . . Nadine had seemed like someone flinging open a window to let great gales of wild, salty air into the confined stuffiness of Matthew's life, and he had adored her rebelliousness. But then in time it drove him mad."

In psychologist John Gottman's book *Why Marriages Succeed or Fail*, he quotes Dwayne and Rita on the shocks of marriage:

DWAYNE: People told us when we were going to get married, "Oh, your first year is going to be rough." And we said,

"Oh no, we love each other." We thought everything would be just great and dandy.

RITA: Yeah, we thought, "We love each other; we won't have those conflicts. Love conquers all." Well, it doesn't. Getting married was like, "Welcome to the real world." It really took us by surprise.

I don't know if Dwayne and Rita lived together before they married, but maybe it wouldn't have made that much of a difference. Dr. Dicks tells us that "all hell may . . . break loose" when cohabiting couples make the move into marriage. "I am discussing couples," he writes, "who would be called deeply committed lovers . . . who had already experienced each other in such humdrum, sobering roles as shopping, house-cleaning, etc., during their 'illicit' cohabitation. Why should these free, socially emancipated people fall into mutual recrimination . . . now that they are respectably married?"

The answer seems to be that, whether consciously or unconsciously, we always ask more of marriage than marriage can give us.

We idealize the person we marry, no matter how certain we are that we're seeing clearly. We bring our secret hopes to the married state. We aren't prepared for the harm we can do to each other. We aren't aware that love does not preclude hate. And when the idealizations collapse and the secret hopes are crushed under the inescapable weight of reality, we may very well find ourselves asking the same questions that Wendy asked: "Who *is* this person?" and "What am I *doing* here?"

And if we decide that what we're doing here is staying married, we must figure out how.

So now the work begins, the work of: Accepting the flawed,

imperfect person we've married. Reconciling some—not all, but hopefully enough—of our difficult differences. Coming to terms with what we cannot get, and never are going to get, from each other. Creating, we two together, our "third thing."

Such a creation takes time, however, and meanwhile we may wonder where is the partner we hoped our partner would be and where, particularly, is the deep companionship we hoped marriage would provide. In the reality of married life, she sees his eyes glaze over when she talks, as she loves to talk, about her work. And he sees her eyes glaze over when he explains, as he loves to explain, about Yugoslavia. And he tends to turn the music down low while she's listening to the glorious *Jupiter* Symphony. And she tends to turn the Cuisinart on while he's reading aloud a great story about Michael Jordan. Sometimes it is very difficult not to be anxiously wondering, "What do we actually have in common?"

But the life couples make together, the third thing they create together, will be composed of many common experiences— shared friends, shared children, shared movies and meals and vacations and troubles and pleasures, shared days and weeks and months and years and decades. And sooner or later, although she'll continue to wish he cared more about real-estate law and Mozart and he'll continue to wish she cared more about world affairs and basketball, these disappointments will move away from the center to the periphery of the marriage. Sooner or later, the what-we-share will become, if they help it along, far more central to their life than the what-we-don't.

As a couple endeavors, together, to create a shared life, the third thing, they will have to deal with some serious marital shocks. And so, along with the other work they're doing, they need to figure out why this work is worthwhile.

What is the worst thing your husband or wife ever did to you? Gabrielle asks in Neil Simon's marital farce, *The Dinner Party*. And what is the best? she asks her dinner guests next. In contemplating the complex realities of married life, it's important not to forget that second question.

For just as we may be shocked by what we start learning about each other almost as soon as the honeymoon is over, so may we also be happily surprised. We may find that marriage reveals in our spouse, in addition to the not-too-terrific news, quite unsuspected reservoirs of tenderness, generosity, strength, compassion, honor, patience, or good humor.

"She is," says Lyle of his wife, "much wiser than I thought she was, and much more giving than I had ever imagined."

"He has," says Dru of her husband, "the kind of courage I never dreamed that he possessed."

"I didn't know, until he was my husband," Tova says, "how easygoing and flexible he could be."

Even Wendy, who, as we've seen, has complaints about the shocks of married life, offers this story about its sweet surprises. Soon after she got married, she was fired from her editing job in an extremely unfair and ugly way. A short time later her husband, Roger, came across her former boss on a golf course. Although Roger is not a menacing man, he turned into one that day, marching up to the former boss and saying to him, "You owe my wife an apology. And if she doesn't get it, I am going to wrap this nine-iron around your neck."

Wendy was astounded to receive an apology from her former boss. But she was far more astounded—and also tremendously touched—by Roger's wild and loving act of chivalry. So when she complains about discovering that Roger can be "impossible," she remembers that he can be "my little hero." Furthermore, she has gratefully learned that "whenever I am sick, he is a saint." In the middle of the night, when she is wondering, "What am I *doing* here?" as she contemplates his rigidity, his workaholism, his mother, his aluminum foil, she temporarily may forget these virtues. In her better moments, however, she finds them tipping the balance when she weighs them against her marital discontents.

───────────

"Any marriage worthy of the name," writes psychiatrist Peter Kramer in *Should You Leave?*, "entails repeated remarriage"—to the same partner—"active choices to stay on in the face of new perspectives on self and spouse." It also entails the brave, hard work of transforming these new, and sometimes shocking, perspectives into something expansive and creative, into an opportunity for a husband and wife—and a marriage—to grow up.

CHAPTER THREE

Marriage and the Families

If . . . I quit inviting Louise with the giggle, and
He quits inviting Jerome with the complex, and
We avoid discussions like . . .
Does his mother really love him, or is she simply one of
    those overpossessive, devouring women who can't let go,
Maybe we'll make it.

—Judith Viorst, "Maybe We'll Make It"

IN A NOVEL I recently read, a newly wed husband says to his
wife, "We're not marrying anybody but us." That isn't quite so. For
when we marry each other, we also marry Louise with the giggle,
Jerome with the complex, and a wide array of friends and relations, including a mother-in-law who may or may not turn out to
be an overpossessive woman who can't let go. Family and friends
are part of the dowry that each of us brings to the marriage. Family and friends add pleasure—and complications. In figuring out
the place of these people in our married life, we must renegotiate
our obligations, reconsider our loyalties, relinquish old dependencies, and establish ourselves—within an intricate web of other
relationships—as a special, separate entity, an "us."

The claims that we allow others to make on that "us" are
sometimes fitting and sometimes excessive, the consequence of

our pity or fear or helplessness or guilt or needy love or a power-ful sense of indebtedness—especially toward family—that makes us feel that we owe and owe and owe. And if we haven't, as yet, psychologically separated ourselves from the family we were born into—our first family—now is the time to take that crucial step into adulthood or to pay a price in our marriage for remaining, first and forever, our parents' child.

How do a husband and wife remain attached, but not too attached, to their mothers and fathers? How hard is it to persuade their mothers and fathers that, though they love them, they must pull away? How far from their mothers and fathers do a husband and wife have to go in order to separate? And how close, if they want to separate, can they stay?

———————

When our son Alexander told us that he and Marla were thinking of moving back to Washington, D.C., where Milton and I live, I came up with all kinds of reasons why the move would be a marvelous decision. I reminded him of the beauties of the city in which he'd been raised, pointed out all the exciting career opportunities, and assured him—and asked him to assure his wife as well—that we wouldn't be making annoying parental demands on them.

"You won't be expected to drive us to airports or pick up our mail and newspapers when we're away. You won't be expected to come on a regular basis for dinners on Friday or brunches on Sunday. We'll never ask you . . ." and on I went, promising him that we wouldn't be pesty parents, that indeed they'd hardly notice that we were here.

"Mom, Mom, wait," Alexander said. "I don't think you understand. Marla and I have these lists of the pluses and minuses of moving back to Washington. And you and Dad—we've put you in the *plus* column."

I guess I didn't understand because, when I married Milton, I worried a lot about parents making demands on us. So even though I was sorry to leave my beloved Greenwich Village to join my husband in Washington, D.C., the good news was that we wouldn't have to make command performances at weekly dinners and brunches in northern New Jersey. Both Milton and I were actually quite fond of our mothers and fathers, but we knew that they—his particularly, since he was an only child—could be a little more clutchy than we were comfortable with. We wanted—I particularly—to be an exclusive twosome, to be clearly and definitively unentangled with them.

One couple, after marrying, moved clear across the country, from Chevy Chase, Maryland, to San Francisco, because—as they both agreed—they wouldn't have made it living in the same town as her folks. This was not because her parents were difficult people. They both think her parents are generous, sensitive, warm. "But," the wife explained, "what with them getting us tickets to the ballet and the opera and inviting us to dinners to meet some people who'd help us find the perfect jobs, we'd have been smothered. They would have loved us to death."

It isn't just geography that determines our entanglements with our families. If we haven't established enough emotional distance, it won't matter how many miles apart we are. Indeed, some family therapists have observed that our guilty sense of obligation may *increase* with every mile we put between us. On the other hand, if we've made a sound psychological separation, we can maintain it even at close range.

Shortly after Alexander and Marla moved to Washington, a friend of mine sent Alexander a gift. I wanted to be sure she was properly thanked. So I telephoned my daughter-in-law and asked her if she'd please remind my son to write my friend a thank-you note immediately. Instead, I got a call from my son immediately, letting me know that I had a crossed a line. "Never call up Marla again," he said sternly, "and tell her to tell me how I ought to behave. And besides," he added, his voice just a little softer to show he forgave me, "you taught me ages ago about sending thank-you notes."

And *he* taught *me* that day that there would have to be some respectful distance between us, even though we lived in the same area code.

As much as a husband and wife may love the families they were born into, they need to insist upon a respectful distance. As psychiatrist W. Robert Beavers, a couples therapist, points out in *Successful Marriage,* establishing a married life "requires leaving home, a clear renunciation of being a child in the family of origin, and becoming an adult in a new household."

This is a process that Anna began soon after she married Wayne, when they ran into a problem with their car insurance, and Anna picked up the phone to call her dad to ask him to help them solve the problem. Before she could reach him, however, Wayne took the telephone from her hand, gave her a kiss on her forehead, and gently said, "No, don't call your father. We'll handle it ourselves. We're grown-ups now."

But sometimes we're not. When Tracy, for instance, got sick during her honeymoon with Silas, they didn't fly back to their New York City apartment. Instead, they agreed she should move back "home" to her parents' house in Connecticut, where she could be taken care of by her mother. Unlike Wayne, neither Tracy nor Silas (nor her mother and father) believed that they could handle things themselves.

Handling things ourselves may also require saying no to parental stipends, especially if the money that parents give to their married children undermines their need to work, to live within their means, to be self-supporting. Says one young husband, "I love that big check my folks give us every Christmas. We use it for things we could not otherwise afford. But my wife and I have to know that the basics of life—like rent and food and such—are being paid for out of the money that *we* earn."

There are many young married couples who are grateful to their parents and their in-laws for their kindness and generosity, for their "accepting, approving love," for the pleasure of their company, and for being great examples to them of "feminism" or "zestiness" or "dignity" or "aesthetic awareness" or "guts." Separating from them has nothing to do with not loving them or being ungrateful. It has to do with trying to become a grown-up partner in a marriage.

The struggle to establish and maintain separateness as a couple may occur at many stages of married life, but it is of special importance early on because the structure of the new family will be threatened, Beavers writes, if the ties to the former families are too strong, particularly in families in which "loyalty to one's parents seems to require remaining a child."

Sometimes husbands or wives continue their ties to their first family by trying to reproduce their parents' marriage, although they might not be aware that they are doing so. Mina, for instance, who married at twenty-five after knowing Bertram for eight years, including two years of living together, astonished him on the first Sunday of their legally married life by asking, "When are you going to get the cold cuts?"

What was she talking about? her new husband wondered. In their many years together, she'd never shown any serious interest in cold cuts before. Why was she expecting him to walk out the door and find a delicatessen? Where, he asked Mina, was this strange request coming from?

Mina explained to me that she thought for a moment and then realized "that when I was growing up my father went out every Sunday morning and brought home cold cuts. And I guess I had the notion, somewhere deep in the La Brea tar pits of my mind, that this is what a husband's supposed to do. So now that Bert was finally my husband and it was Sunday morning, I thought that he ought to go get cold cuts too."

We come to marriage with many notions garnered from our first family about what spouses do. Not all of them are as benevolent as Mina's. Indeed, family therapist Carl Whitaker warns that unless young partners "emotionally grow up and appropriately divorce their parents and leave home, they will bring into their marriage the same problems that Mom and Dad had." For example, a woman whose mother "got whatever she wanted to get from my dad" by sulking may use sulking in order to get what she wants from her husband. A man who grew up in a family in which "the way my folks discussed things was to yell at each other" may see nothing amiss about yelling at his wife. And women and men who learned from their mothers and fathers that wives treat husbands as helpless babies or that husbands are supposed to dominate wives or that it's okay to embarrass a spouse in public may replicate or accept this kind of behavior because it feels normal and familiar, because it is the way that things were done.

But we needn't be mindlessly trapped into repeating the way things were done. We can, with some effort, make choices and make changes. By identifying the origins of marital his-and-her roles, we can discover we needn't keep reproducing them. By understanding that being different isn't being disloyal, we can go our own way. By recognizing that what is familiar is not necessarily "normal" or okay, we can pick other paths. And by separating ourselves from our father and mother's definitions of what a husband and wife are supposed to be, we can begin to define and create our new family.

In creating a new family, a husband and wife have to negotiate both the extent and the limits of their family ties. How often will they see their parents or talk to them on the phone? With whom will they celebrate the major holidays? Will they take vacations with them? Take money from them? Go to them for advice? How closely involved should they be in each other's lives? Husbands and wives must deal with what their spouses expect them to do with and for their families. They must deal with what those families expect from them too. And they often must deal with parents who still feel compelled to guide and instruct their married children on where to live, what house to buy, whether they ought to switch jobs, and when they ought to start trying to have a baby.

Another issue a couple may need to negotiate is how honest

they can be with each other regarding their not-so-nice feelings about their in-laws. A friend of mine has an interesting insight on that. "Early in our marriage," he said, "when I'd criticize my wife's folks to her, she felt she had to defend them, no matter what. But I noticed that when I stopped bad-mouthing them and stopped making her so defensive, she felt free to complain about them to me."

Some husbands and wives may have to deal with the fact that they come from such drastically different families that each regards the other's as extraterrestrial. Take Mort, whose parents live a life of bohemian, good-natured chaos, in which meals are never eaten together, nobody ever gets to a plane on time, and plans for major family events are generally made on the morning of the event. He is married to Candy, whose parents actually send a multi-page memo before she and Mort go off on foreign trips—and I thought she was exaggerating until I took a look at one of these memos—which provides a list of books to read about the places they're visiting, lists of the clothes they should pack and the shots they should get, information on whom to call if they lose their money or tickets or credit cards, and even (I swear!) what steps to take if, God forbid, they fall so critically ill that they need an air ambulance to fly to a hospital.

Although Mort and Candy developed a great affection for each other's family and a great tolerance for each other's family's style, many husbands and wives must struggle to work out a cordial relationship with in-laws whose way of doing things, whose politics, religion, manners—you name it—are utterly alien to them.

Figuring out our relationships, as a couple, with our parents and our in-laws can be challenging even when there's goodwill on all sides. But plenty of couples must figure out these relationships under considerably less than idyllic conditions.

Wendy, for example, drew her husband, Roger, a diagram—"Roger," she explains, "works well with diagrams"—to demonstrate her view of the relationship of their marriage to everyone else. The diagram showed a circle, inside of which were Wendy and Roger and their puppy ("when we have children, they'll be inside it too") and outside of which, revolving around the perimeter, were tiny circles that represented her family, his family, friends, and professional colleagues. "These people," she told Roger, "are part of our life. They're important to us. They're very important. But," she added firmly, just in case he hadn't quite grasped her visual aid, "they do not get to be inside the circle."

Wendy believes in being clear about what she needs and expects—"I try to get on a very basic level"—and she's made herself exceptionally clear in talking to Roger about his difficult mother. This is a woman, Wendy complains, who routinely asks her son to do things like come right over and change a lightbulb. She's an unhappy, self-pitying woman about whom Wendy says with a sigh, "Before we were married, Roger's mother was Roger's problem. Now she's *our* problem."

Like it or not, Wendy's marriage includes Roger's mother.

But one of their larger problems is that Roger's mother has trouble including Wendy and can't bother to say hello to her when she calls him at home and Wendy picks up the phone. "I told her that she either has to acknowledge me or call her son at his office. She calls at his office."

So much for the popular phrase "I didn't lose a son; I gained a daughter," which family therapists Ivan Boszormenyi-Nagy and Geraldine Spark, the authors of *Invisible Loyalties,* somewhat cynically characterize as "more often a wish than a reality." Indeed, they say, some families see a daughter-in-law or a son-in-law as a rival for their child's support and affection and may therefore target that in-law's "value system and way of life" for "attack, depreciation, or rejection."

Most of the parents I know have lovingly welcomed their daughters- and sons-in-law into their family, but I've known some unwelcoming mothers and fathers too. Wendy says Roger's mother sees Wendy's family and way of life and point of view as targets for attack and depreciation. She also concedes to me that the feeling is mutual.

Wendy explains that she made Roger promise, the day before they married, "that she'd never spend one *night* with us, no less live with us." On the other hand, in spite of the hostilities, Wendy would never ask Roger to break with his mom. At the moment the mother-marriage issue is fairly well under control, but perhaps not for long. Wendy foresees all kinds of new problems when she and Roger have kids because, she explains, "I couldn't leave our child with Roger's mother. I just don't trust her to respect my wishes."

Roger isn't an only child, but he is the most available child because he and his mother live in the same city. Furthermore, he feels sorry for her because she has endured a difficult life. He seems to be trying his best to do right by his mother and by Wendy. So far he has managed to more or less keep his filial obligations in balance with his wife's legitimate grievances.

On the other hand, other husbands and wives may be so tenaciously tied to their mothers and fathers that they accede to even their most outrageous demands. Both of Gary's parents, for instance, opposed his marriage to the delightful Anita, probably on the grounds that only royalty would be good enough for their son. For the first two years of that marriage, they refused to see their daughter-in-law but expected Gary to pay them—and, indeed, he continued to pay them—regular visits. Gary assured Anita that eventually his parents would come around, asking her in the meantime to please be tolerant of his—yes, neurotic— failure to say to them, "You don't get me without her."

Anita was able to wait it out, and Gary's parents did indeed eventually, sort of, grudgingly, come around, though this wasn't the last parent compromise she made. Their marriage, bumpy but still intact, has lasted but sometimes she wonders, Was she a fool or really mature to have stayed?

———

Guilt and pity in Roger's case, something darker in the case of Gary, bind them—in different ways and degrees—to their parents, making them choose between conflicting loyalties. Such conflicts are discussed in *Invisible Loyalties,* in which the authors present the view that "marriage represents an encounter between two family systems," thus placing "demands on both spouses to balance their marital loyalty against their loyalties to their family of origin." Ideally, a husband and wife should "form a solid loyalty team to support each other in responsibly emancipating themselves from their families of origin," but often this doesn't happen because of the powerful tug of first-family loyalties. And so, say the authors, once the initial sexual excitement has simmered down, "many married persons discover their inability to form loyalty ties with their spouses."

Like the man who can't find time for his wife because he's spending most of his evenings and weekends helping out his father with his restaurant business.

Like the woman who is unable to spend any time alone with her husband without feeling guilty for not including her mother.

Like the man who, despite his wife's urging, has refused to take a great job in another city because "it would kill my mother if I moved."

Like the man who works and lives near his folks up in Boston during the week and sees his wife in Atlanta on the weekends, discouraging her from quitting her job and joining him up in Boston because (though he doesn't put it this way to her or to himself) her presence would intrude upon the primacy of his relationship with his parents.

All of these married people believe—sometimes consciously, sometimes not—that they owe their primary loyalty to their first family.

Loyalty to the first family may be directed as well, or instead, to brothers or sisters, who have been in a married person's life much longer than a spouse and who (unlike a spouse) are flesh-and-blood relatives, and who therefore are entitled (so the emotional logic of some married people goes) to first claim on one's allegiance and money and time. And so Sonny lends his brother a hefty $14,000 without bothering to check it out with his wife. And Charlotte arranges to spend a week helping her brother move into his new apartment without bothering to check it out with her husband. And Lloyd (although he did check it out with his quite indignant wife) leaves her at home and goes away on a trip with his younger sister "because she said she really needed the company."

A sister is also the spur for the fights Jory has with her husband, Mac, who, according to Jory, "is perfectly willing to take all kinds of advice from his sister, but if I try to give him exactly the same advice, he'll either ignore it or say that it's 'irrelevant.' So then I get pissed and ask him how come his goddamn sister's advice is always relevant and mine is not."

I suspect that the answer may be that Mac relies on his sister's advice because she is a member of his first family and therefore can be trusted in a way that his wife, an outsider, cannot. His wife suspects the same thing, which is why she's so angry about it.

Most family loyalty conflicts, however, involve the competing demands of *parents* and spouse. But it needs to be said that sometimes it is a spouse, not a parent, who creates the difficulties, that sometimes a jealous, possessive, I-must-always-come-first spouse wants such exclusive ownership of her husband or his wife that any time or attention allotted to a parent is seen as disloyalty. So even in a snowstorm, when Lucy's mother-in-law could use a little help, Lucy ungraciously grouses to her husband, "You're driving her to the dentist? Why must you offer to drive her to the dentist? She can drive herself to the dentist. Or take the Metro."

Yes, sometimes it is a spouse, not a parent, who is exerting pressure on the marriage by objecting to what she or he views as her husband's or his wife's excessive loyalty. Sometimes a spouse, not a parent, is playing the heavy. But we also need to remember that loyalty conflicts between spouse and parents can, on occasion, arise without any heavies, even when all the people involved are decent and loving and trying to do the right thing.

A friend of mine learned, just after she married and moved very far away from her widowed father, that he was suffering from a fatal cancer. During the twenty-four months of his dying, she found herself constantly crushed by colliding loyalties. "I needed time," she said, "to become a couple with my husband—we'd never lived together and we hadn't known each other all that long." But she also needed time, she said, to be with her sick father, whom she adored. Her husband was understanding about the days at a time she had to spend away from him. And her father was understanding about the days at a time she couldn't be at his side. Loving and loyal to both men, she felt, until her father died, that wherever she was was always the wrong place to be.

There is sometimes no good way, she found, to balance our painfully divided loyalties.

My friend did not have to deal with a resentful husband or a demanding father, but for others, family loyalty conflicts often put huge pressures on a marriage, pressures that make it impossible to emotionally commit to the new family, pressures that explode into bitter battles and sometimes end up in divorce. On occasion, however, loyalty conflicts are "happily" resolved by merging the old and new families into one big undifferentiated blob.

Evan's wife, Millie, for instance, insisted on cutting him off from his parents, twin brother, and friends and absorbing him completely into her family, which meant that he worked for her family's firm, celebrated all holidays with her family, went on every vacation with her family, and as Evan's dad put it, "took on the identity of her family in a really tribal and primitive way." Millie needed Evan to merge because she can't, and will never, leave her family. Evan needed to merge because he can't—at least right now he can't—leave Millie.

Sometimes family mergers involve truly bizarre arrangements, as in the case of the married couples documented in *Invisible Loyalties* who are so profoundly tied to a family of origin "that they not only live next door to one set of parents, but in at least three reported instances have made a tunnel from one house to the other in order to remain one big 'happy' family. . . . Individual assertiveness, attempts to physically or emotionally separate, or critical comments are immediately stifled. That person is considered ungrateful and disloyal."

With or without a tunnel, whenever there's an excessive tie to a family of origin, a marriage is deprived of an adult partner. Instead, the not-yet-grown-up wife or husband takes the role, vis-à-vis the parents, of grateful child, indebted child, obedient child, placating child, dependent child, better-than-all-of-my-brothers-and-sisters child, I-hate-you-but-I-can't-escape-you child, if-I-give-you-my-life-will-you-finally-love-me child, of a child whose marriage will never be the primary relationship, the true "us."

The true "us," as in "If his mother was drowning and I was drowning and he had to choose one of us to save, he says he'd save me."

The true "us," as in the marriage is what takes precedence.

When the marriage is what takes precedence, husband and wife follow certain rules of the game: A wife, no matter what she thinks, won't publicly side with his father when her husband and his father disagree. A husband won't give his mother her own key to their apartment if his wife doesn't want to let her have a key.

Both husband and wife will refrain from complaining to their mother and father about the various shortcomings of their spouse. And when they speak of home, they'll be talking about the place where the two of them are living rather than their mother and father's house. In other words, the marriage is the primary relationship when each of the partners has first claim on the other's love and loyalty, when each of them is, in effect, the other's home.

But sometimes the true "us" is a consuming love relationship between one marriage partner and that partner's parent, a relationship most often seen between a married daughter and her mother. Profoundly attached to each other, they may talk to each other several times a day, with the daughter using her mother as her sounding board, comforter, fan, interior decorator, financial consultant, psychotherapist, and often the repository of her and her husband's most private marital secrets. Ties of such intensity suggest that the wife has remained her mommy's needy, clingy baby girl, unable to give up the gratifications of being taken care of, unable—or unwilling—to grow up. Although a close mother-child connection can certainly be a wonderful thing in adulthood, it can also make for major marital problems. And it surely will make for problems when the intimacy that a mother and daughter share is seen by that daughter's husband as a threat to the special intimacy that he wanted and expected to share with his wife.

Melissa's husband, Leo, has made his dissatisfaction known: "Your mother," he groans, "is around our house a lot." So Melissa, who wants her mother—a lot—has figured out a way of placating Leo. She meets her mother elsewhere—a lot—and takes pains to keep these meetings a secret from Leo, treating her mother almost like a lover. And that's not such a far-fetched comparison, since Melissa's unspoken (to Leo) but deep conviction is that "no one could ever love me as much as my mom."

Haven't the experts taught us that a child deeply loved by her mother will possess a solid foundation, a reliable inner foundation, on which she can build successful adult love relationships? The answer is yes, but only if that child has been helped, by that same loving mother, to leave her mother—to separate without being scared that she's going to lose her mother or herself, to stand alone with that love securely inside her, and to be willing to accept as good and sufficient a husband's highly imperfect non-mommy love.

Clinginess and daily phone calls and other dependencies are only one set of failure-to-separate symptoms. There are also seemingly independent—*insistently* independent—husbands and wives who, although they neither cling nor call, haven't yet managed to separate from their families. These are the folks who feel compelled to resist their mothers and fathers at every turn because they unconsciously fear that if they don't, they will be totally taken over. They frequently resist their in-laws as well. And they often feel anxious or angry if their spouse is too cozy with either of the families. Ever on the lookout for attacks upon their secretly shaky autonomy, they tend to view most parents as attackers. No issue is too small for them to dispute. No turf is too small for them to fiercely defend.

Like the man who went to visit his parents but turned right

around and went home when his father opened the door and said, "It's freezing tonight. You should have worn an overcoat."

Like the woman who, when her mother sent her a recipe for pot roast, mailed it back to her.

Like the man who stopped the car on the way to a family celebration when his mother-in-law started telling him how to get there.

Like the woman who told her father-in-law that he was being presumptuous when the poor man plucked a few dead leaves off her houseplants.

Like the woman who, when her mother bought her a few new outfits for spring, said, "I'll never wear them," and who, when her mother gave her the family silver "for when you have guests," said, "I don't entertain," and who, when her mother offered some suggestions about "window treatments," scornfully replied, "I don't have window treatments," perceiving all such maternal gestures as "threats to my individuality," as "a diminishment of me as a human being."

Overreacting to the real and imagined incursions of their parents and in-laws, these independents maintain a state of don't-tread-on-me contentiousness that produces conflict not only between generations but also between husband and wife. An important question that they will eventually need to ask themselves is "If we're compelled to seize every opportunity to prove to our parents how free of them we are, how free of them are we?"

It's a question I finally had to ask myself.

Early in our marriage, when Milton and I took a trip from Washington to New York, I insisted we tell his parents that we'd be driving through New Jersey but wouldn't have time to stop and pay them a visit. (Why should I have to sneak through the state of New Jersey, I argued, every time we took a trip to New York?) My husband felt that we didn't need to inform his folks of our trip simply to rub their noses in the fact that we didn't have any plans to see them. I, on the other hand, felt a need to explicitly let his folks know that we wouldn't be seeing them as a way of asserting how independent we were. Milton and I had many marital arguments about what independence really meant.

It took some growing up for me to stop acting like a rebellious adolescent, to give up saying, in effect, "I'm not doing this and nyah nyah nyah you can't make me," to accommodate his and my parents' feelings without always having the feeling that I'd sold out. It took some growing up to learn that the place to sustain my separateness was not on the family battlefield but internally.

That's not to say there won't be times when internal isn't enough; when we need to set limits, draw boundaries, go into battle; when we must make it clear to our parents, whether or not it angers or hurts or disappoints them, that we won't be able to do this for them and that we can't allow them to do that to us. How do we decide when such times have come? Psychoanalyst Harvey Rich, in his work with couples, likes to distinguish between what he calls "injuries to your soul" and "injuries to your sensibilities." He believes that "when your soul is injured you need to fight like hell, and when it's just your sensibilities, let it go."

The more secure we are about who we are and the less afraid we are of being a powerless child in the grip of controlling parents, the better able we are to look at actual or seeming parental incursions not as assaults but simply as annoyances, as injuries not to our soul but our sensibilities. And the better able we are to let them go.

This means that we shrug it off when we're told that we should have worn an overcoat or given instructions on how to cook a pot roast. It means that we needn't attack when an in-law dares to remove the dead leaves of a plant. It means that when we visit the folks and they tell us, "Call Aunt Rose—it would make her so happy," we can afford to make Aunt Rose, and them, happy. And it sometimes means using humor to dismiss a less-than-soul-destroying insult like "How can the two of you live in such a pigsty?" by replying, as Jason blithely did to his mother, "I'm a slob. And she's a slob. And you aren't. Isn't it great that I'm married to her and not you?"

Sometimes a husband and wife disagree on whether shrugging or laughing it off is sufficient. She says, "Why don't you tell your mother to mind her own damn business," or he says, "Your dad shouldn't talk to you that way," failing to understand when an apparently outrageous parental transgression isn't an injury to their spouse's soul. But sometimes our spouse's soul or our soul, or what Dr. Rich likes to call "the soul of the marriage," is injured by an outrageous parental transgression. Sometimes we really do need to fight like hell.

But fighting like hell does not have to mean getting ugly or raising our voices or attacking until there is blood (I'm talking metaphorical blood) all over the ground or—when we have won—gleefully jumping up and down on our defeated family's prostrate bodies. Although we may, in desperate circumstances, display downright uncivilized behavior, there are more evolved ways of strongly asserting ourselves. Taking a stand and standing firm in the face of threats, tears, and guilt trips can be an effective defense when our soul is endangered. Learning to be a good winner is helpful too. It's possible to fight like hell when we must and then, when it's over, to get over it. It's possible, and desirable, to fight like hell when we must without wrecking our relationship with our families.

For whether or not our families are composed of our favorite people, it is important—unless they are truly pernicious people—to maintain the connections between the generations, to meet the obligations that the ties of blood and history impose on us, to find respectful and self-respecting and constructive ways to integrate our old and new commitments. In trying to accomplish all this, it helps, it helps a lot, to be a grown-up.

Grown-ups understand that they must meet their obligations, including obligations that are sometimes inconvenient or uncongenial. Grown-ups also appreciate the love and support and sustenance that extended families, including extremely imperfect extended families, can provide. Furthermore, grown-ups know how to politely listen to their parents' advice and then go ahead and make their own decisions. Finally, grown-ups recognize the truth of "as ye sow, so shall ye reap," which means that if they hope that their children will, as adults, remain connected to them, they need to show by example that this is valuable to do and how it is done.

We need to start doing this even before we have children.

We also need to start noticing our parents' and in-laws' virtues and be willing, as the old cliché goes, to give a little credit where credit is due. Candy, for instance, has found that despite the chaos of her mother-in-law's daily life, she will always, when a crisis arises, come through. "She's the best person in the world in an emergency," says Candy. "Tender, resourceful, and able to deal with everything."

Dr. Beavers says that he has been "most impressed at the comparative ease with which healthy couples relate to their own parents, incorporating them in some fashion into their present lives and deriving satisfaction from these parents in a way that seems to add to, rather than diminish, the pleasure in the spouse's company." Indeed, he believes that maintaining generational connection and continuity is "an intrinsic part of marital health." Echoing this view, the authors of *Invisible Loyalties* observe that "even the intrusive in-laws, who are often thought of as great obstacles to the smoothness of the marriage and to the peace of the nuclear family, are actually reinforcers of family solidarity and shared meaning."

After all, being married is tough enough without doing it entirely on our own. It helps to have our families supporting and rooting for our marriage, infusing it with their love and warmth and benevolence, wanting us to be good to and for each other, wanting our marriage to succeed. While most couples who complain about parents and in-laws emphasize their *overinvolvement,* their excessive need to be needed, their failure to maintain a respectful distance, there also are couples who feel deprived because their families are distant and *underinvolved,* couples who feel the lack of emotional sustenance that extended families provide. They envy those of us who are lucky enough to have families to celebrate with in the good times and to offer us aid and comfort in the bad, even though on occasion—and sometimes on plenty of occasions—we may irritate and infuriate each other.

Polly, the troubled wife in Laurie Colwin's *Family Happiness*, looks around her parents' table, where her often irritating and infuriating family has gathered for their traditional Sunday breakfast. "This was her family, her tribe, her flesh. She felt not forced to love them, or condemned to be angry at them, but as if she were merely seeing them. Her place at this table was optional—she did not have to be there if she did not want to. But she did want to."

When we marry and start establishing our special, separate entity—our "us"—we must work, and sometimes struggle, and sometimes struggle very painfully to disentangle ourselves from our first family. The Bible puts it like this: "Therefore a man leaves his father and his mother and clings to his wife, and they become one flesh." But as we become "one flesh," become adults in our own household, we can see our parents as what a friend of mine calls "our emotional country," we can see our parents-in-law as what she gratefully calls "the extra string in our bow." We can see them as the larger context in which our marriage is lived and in which it is nourished, by their stories and traditions, by their recipes for pot roast, by the songs they sing on car trips, by their sometimes wonderful, sometimes weird ways of doing things. We can look at each other, adult to adult, and reach out a beckoning hand across the respectful distance that lies between us, saluting our common history and offering each other our complicated love.

CHAPTER FOUR

How Kids Change the Couple

Last year I had a shampoo and set every week and
Slept an unbroken sleep beneath the Venetian chandelier
of our discerningly eclectic bedroom, but
This year we have a nice baby,
And Gerber's strained bananas in my hair. . . .
　　　　　　　　　　　　　—Judith Viorst, "Nice Baby"

NO SLEEP. No sex. No privacy. No let's-catch-the-9:20-movie
spontaneity. No leisurely Sunday mornings just hanging out. The
arrival of our first baby can bring us a joy that's perhaps unattainable by any other means under the sun. But it's also an astounding
assault on our marriage.

Nothing we've read or heard or observed can prepare us.

A husband may feel shut out or tied down. A wife may feel
overwhelmed. We're filled with delight—and many anxious questions. Will we ever have grown-up time again? Will we ever have
grown-up conversations, conversations free of charming phrases
like "cracked nipples" and "poopy diapers"? How does a daddy or
mommy have room for anything else but parenting? How do a
daddy and mommy also remain a man and woman, a husband
and wife?

And who comes first in our life—our spouse or our child?

We are warned that "parents who become entirely absorbed in child rearing have emotionally abandoned each other and the marriage, leaving two hungry people whose adult needs are not being met." We are warned that "children add to a family but subtract from a marriage." We are warned, but we are very, very tired, and also very edgy from being so tired. And besides, we've got this hungry baby, whose infantile needs must immediately be met— even if meeting those needs subtracts from the marriage.

I remember my first week of motherhood, when I washed my long hair on a Saturday and couldn't find a minute to comb out the knots until the next Wednesday afternoon. I remember cutting my baby boy's nails and accidentally nicking one of his fingers and crying for three hours because this surely proved that I was an unfit mother. I remember trying to nap and hearing him cry and recognizing, to a degree that I hadn't quite comprehended before, that here was a whole other life for which I was totally, nonnegotiably responsible. I also remember thinking that I had room in my heart for only one thing—my child.

Indeed, I was in a state that psychoanalyst D. W. Winnicott has named "primary maternal preoccupation," a profound and consuming attachment to one's baby that he sees as a normal sickness from which most mothers eventually recover. But sometimes a mother takes a long time to recover. And sometimes a mother doesn't want to recover. And sometimes the husband of this preoccupied mother, the father of this intensively mothered child, feels excluded, neglected, and even abandoned.

"My whole life has been transformed," Barry says. "I can't even remember what it was like two months ago. Everything revolves around my son."

"It's hard on Barry," Jane agrees. "He's not number one anymore. The baby is my little man now. He's my everything."

"It's like," Burke says, "the baby owns my wife's body."

"My wife's devotional focus used to be completely on me," Stewart sighs. "Now ninety-five percent of it goes to our daughters."

And Martin says that he sees, when his wife is nursing their three-month-old baby, "mother and daughter cocooned together in a silent physical communion to which I can never be admitted."

While it's more likely to be the husband who feels squeezed out when the baby arrives, there are wives who complain that they feel squeezed out too. Nancy, whose daughter is four months old, says of her husband, "His love for that baby is so intense that sometimes I feel that I'm a baby machine." She sometimes feels, she says, "that is why he married me."

It's mostly the husband, however, who gets excluded.

Gabe, for instance, was stunned by the abandonment he experienced after the birth of the daughter that he and Maya, his wife, had so eagerly awaited. Having been his wife's best-beloved through courtship and living together and two years of marriage, he was suddenly being treated as a hopelessly inept and intrusive outsider. Maya and his little girl had become the primary couple in the house, with Maya so exquisitely attuned to her child's every need that Gabe, by comparison, couldn't do anything right, couldn't seem to hold or dress or diaper or comfort his baby without feeling, or being told, that he had messed up. As another dad put it, "There are times when, no matter how hard I try . . . everything goes wrong, and I feel like a clumsy jerk, like I can't win, no matter what. Then she waltzes in . . . and all of a sudden, it's okay."

Barry also observes that "ever since the baby arrived, there's a whole new bunch of things to argue about." Like what? "Like, for instance, what weather he can go out in. And whether I am dressing him warmly enough. And what kinds of places it's okay to take him. And whether, when I burp him, I'm being too rough. I want to feel I can trust my instincts when I'm with my baby, but Jane's always telling me what to do and how to do it."

Jane makes him feel, he says, "that there's this whole baby lore that she has and I don't."

Some new mothers are tenderly tolerant of a new father's clumsiness, but others may use his failures—and their expertise—to seize more of the power, and sometimes to change the balance of power, in the marriage, asserting, in effect, that "since I know what the baby needs, and since the baby's needs trump everything else, I'll call the shots." For a woman who never before in her life has felt (I hate this word, but I'll use it) empowered, the role of expert parent may be one that she is eager to embrace, a role that she wants to keep for herself and has no wish to share with the baby's father. And so she shuts him out, as Maya shut out Gabe, making him feel not only inept but irrelevant.

Furthermore, a mother may see parenting as a glorious opportunity to rewrite and repair her own unhappy childhood by showering her baby with the unconditional love she never received. This passionate devotion can offer plenty of gratification to mother and child, but carried to extremes, it can transform a woman into a total mommy who has little time or love to spare for her husband. And if, like Gabe, that husband perceives the birth of his child and the loss of his once-doting wife as a replay of the birth of his younger sister and the loss of his once-doting mother, he may—as happened to Gabe—start feeling not only irrelevant but also depressed.

Indeed, while everyone knows that a new mother may suffer from postpartum depression, we may need to be reminded that a new father may have postpartum depression too, or certainly may experience a variety of distressing postpartum emotions. Maybe he's lonely because he misses the closeness that he always enjoyed with his wife. Maybe he's horny because he's deprived of sex. Maybe he's jealous—maybe he's excruciatingly jealous—because of all the attention his wife gives the baby. And maybe he's embarrassed and deeply ashamed about feeling jealous of his own kid.

He may also hate his demotion to the least significant person in the family. ("I'm above the dog," Barry says, "but below the baby.") He may also, as the bills pour in, feel panicked by his financial responsibilities. ("And she's talking," Gabe sighs, "about wanting to work just part-time.") He may also, if his baby cries whenever he picks her up, fear that he is a failure as a father. And he may be competing with his wife for his child's affections and feeling hurt that "our son likes her better than me."

How come he didn't know how hard a baby—a wanted baby, a nice baby—could be on a first-time parent and on a marriage? His wife, of course, is asking the same question.

———

She's asking the same question because she's exhausted and baby obsessed and anxious about the baby's health and well-being. And because, although she keeps turning to books for guidance on raising her child, she is constantly wondering whether she's doing it right. And because, when her child wants to nurse for maybe the fortieth time one night, she finds herself thinking some ugly thoughts and worries that her child knows what she's thinking. And because she resents her husband for having a life outside the house, for wanting some attention from her (the big baby!), for expecting to make love to her (the sex fiend!), and for failing to give her the nurturing and praise she so desperately needs now that she is dependent and trapped and isolated and flabby of brain and body.

She also, while she may grant that her husband is willing to shoulder his fair share of the parenting, resents the fact that, as Carolyn puts it, "He sees his role as assistant, not as co-pilot, so the final responsibility for whether our child lives or dies is on my head."

Many—most—fathers see themselves as assistants.

Even though fathers who father full-time or spend lots of time with their children can be as attuned to their needs as mothers can, most count on their wives to keep track of their children's emotional state and daily schedule and to always be alert to what they need when. One woman, describing the difference between her and her husband's parenting styles, says, "Once I notice a problem and call it to Paul's attention, he's as concerned about it as I am. But I'm most likely the one who notices it first."

So do most mothers.

"The baby wakes up in the middle of the night," writes Nora Ephron in her novel *Heartburn*, "and instead of jumping out of bed, you lie there thinking: Whose turn is it? If it's your turn, you have to get up; if it's his turn, then why is he still lying there asleep while you're awake wondering whose turn it is?"

As a wife may need to remind herself, it probably really isn't her husband's fault that the baby's awake in the middle of the night.

As a husband may need to remind himself, he shouldn't expect to receive a standing ovation for getting up in the middle of the night.

While a wife may be annoyed, she isn't especially surprised at her husband's obliviousness to their baby's needs. But she may be shocked to discover that the arrival of their first child has generated a major marital crisis.

Maybe a husband, feeling neglected, turns to another woman for sex and solace. Maybe he turns off his marriage when it no longer gives him what he got married for. Kerri's marriage ended, she says, "because my husband's mom died when he was little, and he needed—and got—lots of mothering from me, and then our daughter was born and she was the proper vessel for all those maternal feelings and I stopped mothering him."

Sharon says that her husband, "who felt trapped and panicked and overwhelmed" by parenthood with a one-year-old and another on the way, "decided that there were things that he hadn't done when he was nineteen—and started doing them." This included his going through seven jobs within two years and moving for several months to another country, but as Sharon explained to me, she loved her husband and was determined to save the marriage. "He desperately had some growing up to do, and I was willing to step back and let him do it. And then when he came home, I never once said, 'You made a mistake' or 'I told you so.'" Since he's come home, she says, "he's become an extremely responsible father, a respectful and caring husband, and a better son. He has sorted things out and knows what counts in his life. He has grown up."

Robin, who is describing not a crisis but an ongoing complaint, says that the birth of her baby nineteen months ago means that she now has two babies to take care of, the other baby being Greg, her almost thirty-seven-year-old husband. "The big problem for me," says Robin, "is that I always babied Greg, and I liked it, liked being wanted, needed, important. But now that I'm giving to this little person, I don't really have it in me to be giving to this big person anymore."

She is giving anyway.

"A lot of the time I'm still babying Greg," she tells me, "and I try to do it with a smile on my face. But I don't always want to give to him and I never have time for myself, and I sometimes feel kind of resentful of his demands." To feminists who would fault her for being unduly indulgent of her husband, however, Robin would gently offer this reply: "Maybe I'm neglecting myself, but it's my choice, and I know what I have is good. And millions of times a day I think how good it is, and how lucky I am."

Because of her efforts, their marriage, since the baby arrived, "has changed a lot more for me than it has for him." And although becoming parents "has given both of us a more fulfilling life," it is clearly harder on her than it is on her husband.

———

Plenty of couples concede, however, that parenthood is hard on *both* of the parents and drastically changes the marriage for husbands *and* wives.

They are living, at least for a while, in what one husband has called "controlled chaos" and what one wife has amended to "uncontrolled chaos." Most of what they start never seems to get done. The grandparents of their nice baby are driving them nuts with visits and phone calls and helpful suggestions. And they're finding that there is indeed a whole new bunch of things to argue about.

New arguments may arise because becoming parents raises the stakes considerably, making most couples feel that now they really have committed to staying married. Because of this greater commitment, writes psychotherapist Joyce Block, because of this new view that "there is no exit . . . every blemish in the marriage partner may stand out even more than ever." So wives and husbands become less tolerant of, and more determined to stamp out, each other's flaws. And so they fight.

They also fight about issues that didn't arise in their lives until their roles as parents confronted them with their differing views on child-rearing, differences about spoiling him rotten versus crushing his spirit, about caution versus autonomy and freedom, about bathing and bedtime and picking up toys and finishing what's on her plate, about whether he ever ought to be spanked and how early they ought to start readying her for Harvard, differences that were never discussed in their preparental days but are now the subjects of heated, repeated disputes.

They also fight because parenthood can promote in new mothers and fathers the emergence of certain annoying new ways of behaving.

How come she has turned into such a worrier, such a martyr, such a control freak? How come she no longer shows any interest in what's going on in the outside world? When did he get so damn reckless that he is willing to risk our child's life by drinking a cup of hot coffee while he is holding her? What makes him think it's okay to go play softball on Sunday morning and leave me home alone taking care of our child? Why can't she lighten up? Why can't he shape up? Where is the wonderful person that I married? Where indeed?

"It's like the crush we had on each other didn't wear off," Dawn, age thirty-five, tells me, "until we had kids. As a result of having another human being thrown into the mix, our little couple bubble has been shattered. The sleep deprivation kills us. We're more irritable with each other. Both of us often feel that our needs go unmet. We more easily blame each other. And we definitely experience less support from each other. And we—yuck!—keep tit-for-tat tabs on who does how much."

It's unfortunately true that couples who never, before they had children, had arguments about which of them did how much, now find this issue a cause of continuous sniping. If she is a stay-at-home mom, he can't understand why, with all the time she has on her hands, the house isn't neat, dinner made, and the car inspected, or why he is expected, after a long, hard day at the office, to give the kids their baths and put them to bed. And she complains that he hasn't a clue about all she must do to take care of the house and two toddlers and to do it without any help except what help she can extract from him at night. And he snaps back that he always lets her go for a run on the weekend while he is home vacuuming rugs and watching the kids. And she, ever vigilant, wants to know exactly what the hell he means by "lets her"? And on it goes—tit-tat, tit-tat, tit-tat.

With two-career couples there are, of course, different sources of friction: Like which of them leaves their late-afternoon meeting to pick up their child from day care? And who stays home from work when their child gets sick? And why, although both of them work full-time and subscribe to feminist values, does she wind up doing more child care and housework than he does? He doesn't agree that she does more than he, and quickly prepares a case for the defense, submitting to her the lawn that he mows, the bills that he pays, the games of catch that he plays as evidence that he is just as holy as she is. And so the sniping goes on—tit-tat, tit-tat.

While Dawn laments the fact that she and her husband are bickering over who's doing how much, her husband expresses another complaint about parenthood. "I must admit," he tells me, "that I didn't quite appreciate what an antiaphrodisiac having children is."

Faye is in rueful agreement, recalling the warning she gave to her husband on the first night that they spent away from their child. "Before we leave this hotel," she said, "whether we want to or not, you and I are going to have sex."

And Dexter recalls his wife saying, as she removed his hand from her breast, "If I possibly could, you are the one that I'd want making love to me. But I couldn't possibly."

And Barry's wife, Jane, admits to having blissful "fantasies of getting into a big white bed at night with lots of pillows and beautiful comforters, and lying in that bed nude—ALL BY MYSELF. By the end of the day, after holding the baby all day, I don't want to have *anybody* near me."

A new mother observes, in Perri Klass's short story "Intimacy," that she and her husband now jokingly "refer to making love as 'waking the baby.'" They call it that, she explains, because whenever they try to make love, the baby starts screaming frantically in the next room.

Ah yes, the postpartum decline of sex can occur in even the sexiest of marriages, and it doesn't always decline because a hungry husband is being turned away by a wife who is too sleepy, too sore, or too baby fixated. Indeed, both wife and husband may be so exhausted and so stressed by the exhausting, stressful demands of being parents that lovemaking may look as tempting as root canal. And both wife and husband may be so distracted by their baby's needs—"Wait! Stop! Don't! I think I hear him crying!"—that they find they just can't concentrate on doing it. And both wife and husband may be so into their new mommy/daddy identities that behaving like lusty lovers may seem unseemly. And both wife and husband may be so annoyed, or worse, by how their spouse has been acting ever since the day the nice baby arrived that they may be more inclined to make war than love. And even when they finally muster the inclination and energy to have sex, it's often programmed, perfunctory, and . . . boring.

And just try having an evening of marital passion when a wife and husband and baby share the same bed.

―――――――――

When Milton and I were new parents, our baby didn't share our bed, but the "family bed" has become a popular concept, along with other intensely child-centered concepts more popular now than they were then. Although the parents of our generation were less into sleeping with, or "wearing," our babies, less horrified at confining them to a playpen, more willing to put them on some kind of feeding schedule, and even at times prepared to let them cry, and although we also tended to be more protective of our needs both as individuals and as a couple, the impact of kids on our marriages—as in every generation—was huge.

Ginger, a busy photographer who once had assignments all over the world, describes herself, before-baby, as "a clown on a unicycle trying to juggle Limoges china"—her demanding career and her marriage—"when someone from off-stage suddenly throws me a running chainsaw"—her first child. "Being married without a child," she says, "I was keeping the [marriage and work] plates in the air, managing to be romantic and sexy and available. . . . But then comes the chainsaw, and the next two-and-a-half to three years are just a blur of triage—letting the husband bleed to death on the gurney while I resuscitate the photography, then letting the photography fight for its own life while I perform emergency surgery to save the marriage." What doesn't get short shrift in all this is Ginger's mothering of her little girl, the beloved chainsaw that's wrecked her juggling act.

Older parents—couples in their late thirties and early forties and sometimes fathers a good deal older than that—may find the impact of kids especially huge. Having become accustomed to a good deal of freedom, tranquillity, and control, older mothers and fathers have more difficulty than younger mothers and fathers adapting to the disruptions and messes of parenthood, relinquishing what Ned calls "the self-absorbed pleasures of wine and clothes and travel and stuff, of living a life that is only about you."

Then there's adapting to the responsibilities, adds Ned, who wasn't ready for them until age forty-three, when his daughter was born and confronted him, for the first time in his life, with "a responsibility that never goes away." He says, "It has grown me up, including spiritually—I have gone back to the synagogue," hoping to learn enough to teach his girls (he now has two) how to live in this world.

Amy Kass and Leon Kass, introducing a book of readings on marriage, seem to be speaking directly to Ned's experience when they write, "It is fatherhood and motherhood that teach most of us what it took to bring us into our own adulthood. And it is the desire to give not only life but a *good way of life* to our children that opens us to a serious concern for the true, the good, and even the holy."

A man who once didn't want kids, Ned says he recently found himself with tears in his eyes when his younger one asked, "When you die, will you still be my daddy?" and then went on to assure him he could live to be a hundred "if you exercise a real very lot." He observes that being an older dad has made him think about death "a real very lot" because, if "I want to prepare them and protect them, I'll need to be their daddy for a long time." He says that his mortality isn't just about *his* life anymore because, in the most literal of senses, "I want to be there for my kids."

Yes, kids change the couple. The wife is changed. The husband is changed. The marriage is changed. Life never again will be what it was before. But while parenthood makes parents short on sleep and very long on emotional deprivation and gives them new things to bicker and battle about, it is also, or can be, a chance for a husband and wife to develop some admirable new qualities. It can be what Block has called "a jolt into adulthood."

Here's what I hear from husband after husband after husband: "My wife has turned out to be such a great mom." And here's what I hear from wife after wife after wife: "My husband has turned out to be such a great dad."

"To see Erik with our daughter," says Jenny, "moves me in a way that wasn't even on my radar screen before. He's a kind, sweet, patient, gentle, awesome dad."

"I could not have imagined, before we had children," says Ron, "that my wife would be able to give them this much love."

My son Tony says that before they had kids Hyla, his wife, was working "as a competent but uninspired lawyer. After the birth of our daughter, it was clear she adored her new job and had finally found her true calling—full-time motherhood."

And Robin says of Greg, "I always knew he was good with kids. But I didn't know he would be such a wonderful dad. He's become so much more demonstrative since we've had the baby. He's huggy and kissy, and you should see how he looks at him!"

She adds, "He really loves saying 'my family,' and he loves spending time with 'his family.' I think that being a grown-up is becoming more attractive to him. I think he may be starting to grow up."

So is Ezra, who, watching his son sleeping "like an angel . . . quietly breathing at the center of our home, my world," writes in his journal: "I've entered a realm of feeling I never knew existed . . . a brand-new continent within." He then continues: "I commit myself to providing for my family, preserving my family, fighting to govern my own unworthy passions and nourish right actions."

"He makes so many sacrifices to accommodate the baby," says his wife. "I do see fatherhood growing Ezra up."

Parenthood can help to grow us up.

For as we look at our baby, asleep or awake at the center of our home and our world, we may find ourselves reflecting upon our own childhood, perhaps reliving parts of it and trying to understand how we became the person we've so far become. We may promise ourselves that we will do parenting differently, maybe better, than our own parents. We may promise not to repeat the mistakes of the past. We may promise, for the sake of our child, to make our peace with our family, with our history. We may promise that we'll strive to fight and govern our unworthy passions and that whatever changes we make will last. We may promise ourselves that our child will always be safe in our sheltering arms because we will try to be grown-up enough to take care of him.

Most of the couples I spoke with told me that having a baby greatly enriched their lives and brought out some fine new qualities (along with some vexing ones) in their husbands and wives. They said that raising children together has been the most rewarding thing they've done. Also the most challenging. Also, on the good days, the most fun. They told me that the sacrifices of parenthood were certainly outweighed by the delights. They said that they pitied those couples who had forsworn the gratifications of raising children in exchange for freedom and order and untroubled nights. But except for Robin, most of them agreed with the woman who said that "ever since the baby was born, our marriage has been put on the back burner."

Indeed, it's been more than five years since the birth of Ron's first and then his second son, and he is feeling concerned that his marriage continues to be put on the back burner, concerned that—even though "we're a good strong family"—he and Liz, as a couple, are getting shortchanged.

"That's the big thing," says Ron. "I feel we don't spend enough time together. And I feel that spending time together ought to be more important than it is. We need to make an effort to keep our marriage vibrant. We can't take it for granted."

In his late thirties Ron, like many men of his generation, including my sons, is an extremely adept and committed dad, who not only knows his kids' shoe sizes and the names of all their stuffed animals but cooks their meals and drives them to and from the day care center and bathes them and puts them to bed when Liz works late.

His wife, he proudly reports, is a great mother, a "perfect" mother, then adds a "but" that I've heard from several husbands: "But motherhood has made her less of a sexual human being. These days she's more of a mommy and less of a woman." He tells me he sometimes jokingly (maybe not totally jokingly) says to her, "Well, you got the two kids out of me, and you now have no use for me." And although he is quick to acknowledge the difficulties of her wife-mother-lawyer juggling act, and although he understands how hard it is "to be a smiling, loving wife when she's working till nine at night and then she's being with the children the whole weekend," he's always pushing for more just-the-two-of-them time. He wishes that she were pushing for it too.

"Motherhood seems to completely fulfill her," says Ron. "I think that I'm a good father, and I think life is better since we had the kids, but fatherhood doesn't completely fulfill me."

Ron isn't asking that much—he'd like a date alone with his wife two times a month. Liz agrees in principle, but it never seems to happen, and "she's not," Ron says, "as frustrated as I am." Nor is she as worried about the marriage's vulnerability as Ron, who cites his parents' divorce, his sister's divorce, his friends' divorces, and all the other divorces erupting around them.

"I think we've got to work at it, to be careful not to let it drift away. In this day and age, we have to work even harder. When the kids get older, I know we'll have more time for each other. But I don't want us asking, eight years down the road, 'Where did our marriage go?'"

———

Tending the marriage after becoming parents can be an enormous challenge for many couples, especially two-career couples faced with multiple, often competing obligations. A marriage-watching psychiatrist notes, "When they're dealing with their kids, their jobs, and their marriage, they do what they need to do for the job and the kids. It's almost always the marriage that gets neglected."

It gets neglected even though, as Lori explains, "I'm very consciously thinking I need to take care of it. But I work, so it's really hard for me to leave my little girl when I'm not working. I want to be in her face every waking minute."

"I am happier now," says a mother of three, "and my life is fuller with kids, but there's a drastic reduction in the attention my husband and I pay to each other. We have to make an effort, a very conscious effort, to reconnect."

Ron, too, wants to reconnect, but Liz is resisting his suggestion that they make a specific appointment to have sex. "She's says it's unromantic, and maybe it is," he says, then adds with a heartfelt sigh, "but God, how I would love to have an appointment."

Most couples know that when they have kids they must make a special effort to tend their marriage. They know that they should, as Jane puts it, "feed the fire." The marriage experts support this view, warning them that attention must be paid and offering them some suggestions on how to pay it: Make a regular (once a week, once every two weeks, or once a month) date to go out with each other. At home wait until the kids are in bed and enjoy, on a regular basis, a cozy candlelit tableclothed dinner for two. Claim for yourselves the right to be alone with each other while the kids are awake, for ten or fifteen or twenty minutes a day, establishing the rule that they are expected to play by themselves and not disturb you. Teach them ways of comforting or entertaining themselves so that they'll be less likely to disturb you.

Doesn't this all sound sensible and doable? Here's more: Preserve your sex life by getting a baby-sitter on Saturday night and stealing away with your spouse to a local motel. Restore your camaraderie by getting a baby-sitter on Sunday morning and going off for a hike or bike ride or run. Make a deal with another couple to mind their kids while they take a weekend together, then give them your kids and take a weekend for you. And (this is especially addressed to working mothers) try to work through your child-neglect guilt and separation anxiety and understand that you don't owe your children every free waking moment of your existence, that you also have obligations to the marriage.

Oh, and one more thought. When you are having that just-the-two-of-you time together, talk about anything—anything!—but the kids.

In the earliest parenting phase, during those desperate months in the trenches with that first baby, none of the above is even imaginable. And although some of it may be imaginable in the months after that, new fathers and mothers may find that reconnecting as husband and wife can be a lot harder than the experts suggest.

For even when a husband and wife arrange a date to have sex, there's no guarantee that they will reconnect. Elsie, for instance, tells of the night she dropped the baby off at her mother and father's and then went home to fall into bed with her husband, only to find, she laughingly confessed to me, "that both of us were too tired to make love." Meredith describes arranging a candlelit dinner for two after the baby was sleeping, only to find that the moment they lit the candles and put the cloth napkins on their laps, the baby started screaming and kept on screaming and kept on screaming until they finally gave up on the candlelit dinner. Another pair of new parents recalls going out to their favorite restaurant to reignite the spirit of romance, only to discover that they'd spent the entire evening discussing teething, gas pains, croup, and diaper rash. And many a wife has informed me that what with her tear-streaked, heartbroken child wailing, "Mommy, don't go," whenever she's going out on a date with her husband, working through her child-neglect guilt and separation anxiety isn't an option.

Many a wife has also informed me that making time for the marriage is constantly undermined by the conviction that the children have first priority. As Ann puts it, "There is simply no question who comes first. Billy does. He is two years old and Neil is thirty-eight."

These less-than-successful efforts at reconnecting as a couple don't mean that couples with kids shouldn't try to reconnect, don't mean that couples shouldn't keep trying to balance the needs of their children against their needs as a husband and a wife. Parenthood—grown-up parenthood—requires significant sacrifice and the taking on of heavy obligations. It requires, as Nell puts it, "forever giving up the freedom of being center stage in your own life." But it doesn't require martyrdom or sainthood or extreme self-abnegation. And it doesn't and shouldn't require the repudiation of other love relationships.

Indeed, in an ideal world, couples would feel like Barbara and Frank, the parents of a three- and a five-year-old. Says Barbara, "Becoming parents brought a new dimension into our marriage. We both felt that it was a natural extension of our love. We absolutely adore being parents, and we are so supportive of each other. And our children are so adjusted and special because they know that Frank and I love each other."

That's all very nice, but most parents find that, especially in the first years, their needs as a couple conflict with the needs of their child. There is no way around this. Living with these conflicts, trying your best to resolve them, and then dealing with the guilt that your resolutions may bring (no matter which way you resolve them) introduce new tensions into the marriage.

You give up your theater tickets even though it's your anniversary because your son has the flu and wants his mommy and daddy. Or you get a sitter and go to the theater because it's your anniversary and worry all night that he's got something worse than the flu. Psychiatrist Peter Kramer once said, when a father asked for advice about his child, that whatever decision he made would be the wrong one. Parents may have to accept that, when they choose between their kid and themselves as a couple, they will often feel wrong, whatever they choose to do.

They may take some comfort, however, in knowing that many marriage experts believe that happy parents make for a happy child. And they may be relieved to hear that they're not necessarily being selfish if they sometimes put themselves ahead of their kids. It's important too, says Nell, to remember "that having the kids at home full-time is a wonderful but temporary stage. It helps to remember that you are a couple first."

It also helps to notice, if every now and then you can turn your attention away from the nonstop demands and disruptions of parenthood, that having children and raising children together can add both to the family *and* to the marriage. If traveling, taking a walk, having dinner with friends, going to the movies, and the many other things we share as a couple strengthen our marriage by helping to bind us closer, then raising a child together, which binds us emotionally, biologically, and historically, must surely be the ultimate shared experience. For Milton and me, though our children are grown and have children of their own, it still is.

I've heard it said that "adults don't make children; children make adults." Most parents have discovered that this is true. They say that parenthood gives new meaning and purpose to their lives. They say that parenthood teaches them to love far more deeply than they'd dreamed they could do. They say that becoming parents has made them more generous and patient and understanding, and more flexible, caring, selfless, and stable too. They say, in the words of Hyla, my son Tony's wife and the mother of Brandeis and Miranda, that with each new baby "my heart grew." They say that becoming parents has pushed them, pulled them, cajoled them, commanded them to grow up.

It prompts us to grow up as individuals. It prompts us to grow up as a couple as well, and part of that growing up includes enlarging our previous repertoire so that we can be both parent and marriage partner. It's true that, at least at the start, we may not—as a couple—reap any benefits from the caring and patience and selflessness and other virtues in which parenthood instructs us. It's true that, at least at the start, our baby may be the sole beneficiary of the new, improved person each of us becomes. But eventually we may find, if we help it to happen, that these better parts—these more grown-up parts—of ourselves are going to shine upon the marriage too. Eventually we may discover that our heart grew, expanding to make room for our love for our children and for the deepened love we have for each other.

CHAPTER FIVE

Ordinary Everyday Married Life

Love begins as a sonnet, but it eventually turns into a
grocery list. Therefore you need someone with whom you
can go to the supermarket.

—Joel Achenbach, "Homeward Bound"

E V E R Y D A Y married life is prose, not poetry. Everyday married life rarely rhymes or soars. Everyday married life is taking the dog to the vet and the kids to the pediatrician, rushing to work and doing weekend chores, making the beds and going to the market and spraying Endust on the scuffed-up floors, plus family obligations that require our not-always-thrilled-to-be-there presence at holiday visits, birthday parties, weddings, confirmations, anniversaries, and other aggravations.

When did being together become so duty filled? When did our "shoulds" start dominating our days? When did we go from "How do I love thee? Let me count the ways" to "What do you feel like tonight—chicken or fish?"

What we feel like, not always but often, is dimmed and diminished. We've become a little bit boring, a little bit bored. Routine is sinking romance, not all of the time but too much of the time. And what wonderful things will tomorrow bring is not a question we ask ourselves much anymore.

Instead, we may be asking ourselves, and it won't be the first or the last time we raise the question, "Is this as good as it gets, and is that good enough?"

This question is an umbrella under which are huddled a number of complaints—some seemingly trivial, others monumental, but all of them addressed to what being married may feel like day after day after day. This question extends far beyond concerns with obligations and grocery lists and routine. It has to do with how easy it gets not to notice each other or listen to each other. It has to do with sometimes mistaking intrusiveness for intimacy, with sometimes confusing deadened with serene. And it has to do with the trespasses and disparagements and discourtesies and all the other small and large irritations that need to be constantly balanced against the pleasures to be found in ordinary everyday married life.

———

Back when we were falling in love, we delighted in each other, eagerly explored the hidden corners of each other's soul and heart, found each moment together sweeter and shinier than any moment apart, and liked (far more than all our other selves) the self reflected in each other's eyes. But now it's eight or ten or a dozen years later. It's after love has dropped its romantic disguise. It's after the wedding ceremony, the first shocks of married life, the familial negotiations, the advent of kids. And we're trying to figure out how to find some delight, some adventure, some passion, some surprise in a life in which all our sonnets have turned into grocery lists.

"What's hardest for me," says Jimmy, "is knowing what's going to happen tomorrow. And knowing what's going to happen the day after that."

"When I see a young couple in love," says Dolly, "I feel envious of the way they are with each other. My marriage, and it's a good marriage, seems so . . . depleted when I compare it to what they've got."

"And what I hate," says Carla, "are those books that say if your marriage has lost its spark, you and your husband should go have sex on the beach. I mean, you first have to find a sitter, and you next have to find a beach, and then you have to not mind getting all of that sand up you."

I remember, in the eleventh year of our marriage, driving to the beach with my husband and kids, our roof rack laden, our U-Haul stuffed, the back seat vibrating with fratricide and food fights, the front seat snarling with tension because I kept feeling compelled to tell Milton he shouldn't tailgate. At one point a gleaming new sports car stopped beside us for a red light, and because the top was down the scene was clear. The handsome young driver, pointing to our burdened and sordid Chevy, whispered in his lovely companion's ear, after which both of them shook their heads and laughed with what looked to be appalled relief that they weren't in our car, that they weren't us. I had this enraged desire to stick my head out the window and scream, "Just wait, you two! This will happen to you someday!" I also wanted to say that, like them, I hadn't intended to be who I now was.

"I'd planned," I wrote in a poem, "to be Heathcliff's Cathy, . . . Nicole or Dominique or Scarlett O'Hara. I hadn't planned to be folding up the laundry in uncombed hair and last night's smudged mascara." Nor had I planned, as I wrote in another poem, to be visiting the firehouse with the third grade. There are women—and men—completely unsuited for dailiness. But even those of us who are inclined to domesticity may find ourselves resentful and dismayed by the what's-for-dinner, where's-their-sneakers,   why-hasn't-this-bill-been-paid,   who-didn't-flush conundrums of everyday life.

Somewhere, however, between the courtship highs and the lost-sneakers lows it is possible to take note of what is good, or at least good enough, in what we've got now. It is possible to accept, enjoy, and sometimes even transcend ordinary everyday married life.

Here's what acceptance can feel like: "The rain had stopped but it was still a wet, gray day and good to be indoors. The radio was dimly playing Mozart and a gentle, sherry-scented repose set-tled over the kitchen. This was the way he had often wished his marriage could always be—unexcited, companionable, a mutual tenderness touched with romance. . . . He felt himself at peace."

Here's what enjoyment can feel like: "I was thinking of a morning . . . when all three girls had climbed into bed with me and Daniel. I kept trying to get up to make breakfast, and this became the game. . . . They were shrieking, 'No! No breakfast! You must stay in the nest! You must!' . . . It lasted only a minute or so, the shrieking, the laughter, everyone's nightie hiking up, all the bare flesh, the bones and angles, feet big and small, soft parts, damp parts. Our familiar smells.

"Ordinary life. . . . It was my world. . . . I was wrapped in it, held in it."

And here's what transcendence can feel like: Charles and

Betsy's youngest son, Drew, was starting his first day of kindergarten, and Betsy was getting ready to walk him to school. But when Drew's sixth-grader sister and fourth-grader brother insisted that *they* were prepared to escort him, Drew—always eager to be included by the older kids—was beyond thrilled. As Charles and Betsy watched Drew, holding his brother's hand and his sister's hand, head proudly for school under their loving protection, the scene wasn't bathed in a golden glow and no heavenly choir sounded from on high. But that's close to what it felt like to Betsy and Charles, who looked long at their kids and then at each other, in silent agreement that moments like this were exactly what marriage and family were all about.

It may be that, if we start paying closer attention, we'll become more aware of, more sensitized to, the fleeting transcendent moments of everyday life. On the other hand, we may also become more aware of, more sensitized to, how dowdy and boring, how messy and inelegant, how repetitious everydayness can be.

Joel Achenbach, father of three, compares the glory days of romantic love—agreeing on everything, finishing each other's sentences, feeling your minds meld—with his current domestic realities. "We sometimes go out to dinner and talk . . . , trying to remember how and why we got into this mess, and we plan fantastic, improbable trips, usually child-free, where we imagine recapturing the ol' mind meld. . . . But on a typical day, we have no conversations whatsoever, just one or two 'information transfers.'"

"I want to wake up in the morning and feel that there's no other place on earth where I belong," says a woman who has been married eleven years, "but by the time I'm done dealing with my

husband's precoffee snarkiness and the whining, you're-
neglecting-me call from his mother and the children's usual
crimes and misdemeanors, I can't believe I've signed on for this
for life."

We may also find it hard to believe what everydayness can do to a
husband and wife: How the daily grind can assail the marriage
relationship. How inattention can alienate even the most passionate of partners.

"In July 1965," Joanne recalls, "wearing new sandals, blind to
life's possibilities, I met the boy who would immediately become
my husband. . . . In the wedding pictures two months later, we're
staring, falling into each other's faces, telling each other the story
of our supervening, inordinate love." Ten years pass and she real-
izes something is wrong. "It was something ordinary. It was this:
I'm young, my children are young, my husband and I have
become estranged while we were looking the other way."

I think about other couples I know, couples who grew
estranged while—and because—they were looking the other way.
I think how easy it is for us all, caught up in the everyday, to turn
away, to fail to pay attention. I think about what writer Richard
Ford calls "the puzzlements of keeping life interesting and vigorous while maintaining the nuclear unit intact" and about the need
to be careful, "take heed, and live life as if it mattered what we do,
inasmuch as to do less risks it all."

Ford was discussing a marriage that was destroyed by inattention. I'm talking here about less cataclysmic effects, about how

married love can slowly be eroded by carelessness and indiffer-ence and neglect. I'm talking about the fact that if we fail to look and listen and pay attention, if we don't give the everyday enough respect, we may not lose our marriage, but we may make of our marriage a diminished thing.

I'm talking here about the stuff not of tragedy but of comedy, stuff that we laugh at except when it happens to us.

"He didn't even notice that he was now married to a blonde, not a brunette," says Harriet, who waited all day before giving up in disgust and pointing out her new hair color to her husband.

"My wife doesn't ever wait for me to sit down at the table," says Leon, "before she starts eating."

Says Patrick: "I clipped all the hedges and fixed the leg of our dining-room chair. I even got our fax machine working again. But all she could say when she came home was 'You promised to mail that package—and it's still sitting there.'"

Says Linda: "My husband never voluntarily pays me a compli-ment, like you're looking great or this dinner is delicious. If I want to hear anything nice, I have to ask him for it."

Didn't it used to be easier to give to each other and get from each other? How come it seems that we're always having to ask for it?

In a recent *New Yorker* cartoon, a wife is offering her husband one million dollars if he can tell her which subject—her mother, her job, the approaching election, or kitchen makeovers—she has been talking about for the past ten minutes. The husband, who is sitting with her in the living room, is holding a magazine, which I suspect he's been reading throughout her entire discussion with him, maintaining his end of the dialogue with a strategically placed occasional grunt. Perhaps he believes, as my husband believes, as most husbands seem to believe, that he can read and listen to her simultaneously. Or perhaps he thinks that giving a woman his undivided attention isn't required when that woman is his wife.

Standing in a corner at a crowded cocktail party, a husband describes to me how the world-class grouch his wife was through the entire day (because the kids were impossible, because she just had another fight with her mother) became a world-class charmer within seconds of their arrival at the party. She is interesting and interested, amusing and amused. She throws back her head and laughs. She is adorable! Perhaps she has forgotten, as I often forget, as most wives seem to forget, that charm—like charity—ought to begin at home. Or perhaps she thinks that knocking her brains out trying to charm a man isn't required when that man is her husband.

In everyday married life we too often are careless with each other's feelings, not only in private but in public as well, engaging in put-downs, zingers, sarcasms, criticisms, and minor humiliations. A wife rolls her eyes and groans, "Oh, no, not *that* one again," when her husband starts telling a story she's heard before. "Only my wife would be capable . . . ," a husband begins, regaling their friends with some really dumb thing she has done. Tossing off joking insults, making faces, making hostile fun of each other are what a friend of mine calls "Lucy and Ricky-isms," entertaining if you're watching reruns of *I Love Lucy* but not if you happen to be Lucy or Ricky.

A soon-to-be-married woman and man are appalled to hear a husband make an only-my-wife remark about his wife, "a rude, a withering remark" that sarcastically seemed to suggest "that she was the stupidest woman in the world." They confidently assure themselves, as we probably once did, that they will never disparage each other in public. They also intend, as we probably once intended, to be gracious to each other in private too. I don't know what happened to them, but I know that I and probably you, probably most of us, aren't as graciously married as we intended to be. Publicly and privately we find it all too easy to display a casual disrespect for each other.

John Gottman, a psychologist who has studied some two thousand married couples, observes that "one of the first things to go in a marriage is politeness." Indeed, when matched with a stranger, "even newlyweds," he found, "accepted the other person's opinions more readily, disagreed less, and were more polite than they were with their partner." Some of us defend this by saying we're being less phony, more "natural," with our partner, that we don't have to put on airs with a husband or wife. Some of us even defend this by insisting that we can't have true marital intimacy unless we're our natural, genuine, graceless self.

According to this view, marriage is where we are able to let it all hang out. Married means never having to put on an act. It means that we can stop bothering to give our full attention to each other. It means we should not be expected to pour on the charm, say "thank you" and "please" and "excuse me," use tact, or treat each other respectfully in public. It means that we can be the plain, unvarnished person that we really are.

Ava's husband, for instance, although he has manners aplenty for others, frequently fails to greet her when he walks into the house at the end of the day, his habit being, she says, "to shamble past me, head over to where we put the mail, and without a single word start looking through it." Since complaints have failed to move him, she has gone for the playful approach, treating him like a naughty little boy and insisting that he go back out the door, walk into the house again, and give her the kind of nice hello that he'd give to anybody he wasn't married to.

Sometimes marriage means treating a wife or husband worse than anybody we aren't married to.

Sometimes it means, as one husband put it, "coming home and dumping a day's worth of shit and complaints on each other, which doesn't make home a pleasant place to be."

It can also mean feeling free, when we are alone with the person we've married, to maintain an open-door policy in the bathroom, to drastically lower our standards of hygiene and dress, to scratch ourselves wherever it is that we're itching, and no longer to bother suppressing our body's most unbeguiling smells and inelegant noises. It means that we can be the back-to-basics person that we really are.

When we're wondering whatever happened to excitement and romance in marriage, we might start by asking what happened to charm and to manners. We might start by asking exactly how plain and unvarnished and back-to-basics we ought to be. Yes, we want to know that, seen at our worst emotionally or physically, we still will be loved by the person to whom we are married. And we want to come home from the watch-your-back struggles of the outside world to a place where we don't have to edit what we say. We want to feel free to repeat ourselves, to blow off steam, to complain, to be dumb, to be boring. And if at dinner we've eaten too much and our belt is feeling too tight, we want it to be okay to unbuckle it right there at the table, to unbuckle our belt and let it all hang out.

But if we imagine that marriage is where we can let it all hang out day after day while continuing to excite and delight in each other, we are mistaken. If we imagine that marriage is where we can bitch, burp, snicker, and snipe day after day without paying a price, we are wrong. We're indulging in a fantasy of unearned, effortless love, the love that an infant seeks from a perfect mommy. We're indulging in a fantasy that has little to do with love in a grown-up marriage.

———————

Some versions of letting it all hang out also include the view that we should be willing to hear and to tell the truth, that marriage is where we should speak with perfect honesty. But those of us who enter a marriage embracing the virtue of "telling it like it is" very quickly learn how bruising and alienating certain truths can be and how much we still need to know about being married.

"I used to believe," says Kristin, "that being close to each other meant telling each other everything. But some of the things he tells me I don't want to hear. I don't want to hear what he really thinks about my older brother. I don't want to hear I could lose a couple of pounds. And even though I asked him whether the woman he shares an office with turns him on, I didn't want to hear the answer he gave me."

I made him swear he'd always tell me nothing but the truth.
I promised him I never would resent it,
No matter how unbearable, how harsh, how cruel. How come
He thought I meant it?

We speak hurtful truths to each other on the grounds that if we're not honest we aren't communicating. But we can communicate plenty without ever needing to say, "Last night I wished you'd drop dead." There are devastating truths that we should never, no matter how heartfelt, say to each other, because once the words are spoken, they can't be unsaid. Says Joan to her cruelly frank husband, "Now you've said things that I'll always remember," things that she may never get out of her head. And when these things are said, it can sometimes be difficult to tell honest from abusive.

Says Bobbie, age thirty-four, "Some married people I know use honesty as an excuse to be rude and small-minded and mean. They may think they're taking the high road, but it's not the way they ought to treat a relationship." She adds that when there's a negative comment she needs to make to her husband, "I want to make it without making him feel small. So I think very carefully about how to make it," or whether, in fact, she needs to make it at all. "You can't bite your lip all the time," she says, "but even though I might explode in my head, I think before I speak— there's no knee-jerk reaction."

Thinking before we speak, we may discover that it is hard, as Philip Larkin observes in his poem "Talking in Bed," to find words that are both "not untrue and not unkind."

"I'm not one of these people," a wife of eight years tells therapist Lillian Rubin, "who thinks openness or honesty in a relationship means spilling your guts or telling your partner every angry thought that comes into your head. There's plenty I don't talk about—like when I wonder do I really love him sometimes, or do I want to be married. Those things don't have to be said; they're damaging."

"The truths I don't tell my wife," Howie says, "do not have to do with lies but with omissions. I go through times of feeling—doesn't everyone?—despair about life, about the limits of love, about wanting something different from what I've got. But these are *transitory* feelings—real but transitory—and if I say them to her I'm afraid they'll take on a permanence that will cause her pain."

He adds, "You can't control how you feel, but you can control how, and if, you express those feelings." He believes that it is "too punishing" for a husband or a wife, in the name of truth, to express "every passing negative emotion."

But sometimes we do. One husband recalls a bad night when his wife, upset that he had quit yet another job, called him a "loser." Although she apologized, took it back, swore that she didn't mean it, begged for forgiveness, and although a lot of time has passed since she said it, the word still stabs him in the heart and he cannot shake the conviction that a "loser" is what she truly believes him to be.

And maybe she truly believed him to be—not always but during those difficult months—a loser. But is this the kind of truth that she ever needed to speak, that he ever needed to hear?

A husband or wife may also not need to hear about the many, many fine qualities possessed by a former love-of-their-spouse's life, like Tim's iconic Tamara, a paragon of wild passion and eager-to-please submissiveness, the woman he didn't marry but maybe (his wife has sometimes hissed) he wishes he had. In fact, all that Tim really wishes is that he had never mentioned Tamara to his wife.

We sometimes tell truths to our husbands and wives that make them feel unhappy about themselves. We sometimes tell truths that are tough on ourselves as well, truths about our present failings and flaws and ugly thoughts and ignoble actions, truths about our past when "I used to do a lot of drugs" or "I didn't visit my dad when he was dying" or "I slept with my best friend's husband" or "I slept with your best friend" or "I never paid back that money my cousin lent me." We offer these truths in the hope that we can be totally known and still be loved by our partner. Actually, what we want is not just to be totally known and still loved, but forgiven too. Such confessions, however, are sometimes too hard for a husband or wife to hear, to handle, to live with. Confession, I suspect, is often better for the soul than it is for the marriage.

In everyday married life we must figure out how honest we can and can't be with each other. But what to reveal is part of a much larger question about how united and how separate we wish to be. How much—not just of our feelings and thoughts but also of our time and our space and our stuff—do we want to share with each other? How much do we want to label "Private—keep out"? Finding a way of being together while holding on to some distance, some zone of privacy, may be one of the more difficult accomplishments of ordinary everyday married life.

On the one hand, as Peter Kramer points out, "Too many are eaten alive in the name of relationship." She swallows him up, or he swallows her up, or they swallow up each other by incessant communication, by insisting on doing everything together, by refusing to acknowledge the legitimacy of closed doors or private thoughts. On the other hand, Kramer also points out, "Awareness of trespass can be overlearned," with a wife freaking out because her husband walks in on her while she's tweezing, or a husband freaking out because she threw away his tie with the catsup stain. A person, says Kramer, can be "unnecessarily concerned about incursions."

For those of us concerned about incursions, for those of us who insist upon a lot of separate space, a lot of privacy, it may seem that being married has given our spouse the right to trespass and encroach. Personal matters that once were nobody's business but our own—and that's everything from how often we take a shower to how often we see a doctor—may become after marriage, like it or not, the business of the person to whom we're married. Personal freedoms—like separate nights out or unpooled bank accounts—may not survive the marital insistence on increased sharing and joint decision making. Personal opinions—on a play, a book, a restaurant—may dissolve after marriage into a glob called "we," with a husband, for instance, telling their friends, "We really loved that movie," when in fact he loved the movie but she only liked it.

"But even if we both *did* love the movie," Carla says, "maybe we loved it for very different reasons. Let him say what *he* thought and then I'll say what *I* thought. I don't want the two of us turning into one person."

As for our personal stuff, consider the husband who—while his wife was away on a business trip—rearranged her closet (not *their* closet but *her* closet) "for greater efficiency." And then consider the wife who—when her husband got certain handwritten notes in the mail—accidentally (she *swears* accidentally) opened them.

Everyday married life involves the intricate intertwining of two lives, but must it erode all distinctions between "yours" and "mine"? And must it always involve forsaking the pleasures, the very real pleasures, of being alone?

> Alone I could own both sides of the double bed . . .
> Alone a hard-boiled egg could be a meal . . .
> Alone I could give Goodwill my boots and my skis
> And switch to beaches.

The longing to be by ourselves, to do as we please without any consultations or compromises, can certainly, as most of us know, coexist with wanting to stay married. So can the wish to reconnect to the person we were before we were part of a pair. Sometimes we need to know who we are when our husband or wife isn't there. Sometimes we have to retrieve, from the tangled adaptations of marriage, our separate, autonomous, individual self.

This self may be best retrieved and renewed not with another person but in emotional or geographical solitude.

The poet Rilke wrote that "*togetherness* between two people . . . robs either one party or both of his fullest freedom and development." He believed that "once the realization is accepted that even between the *closest* human beings infinite distances continue to exist, a wonderful living side by side can grow up," and that this distance between them "makes it possible for each to see the other whole and against a wide sky!" And so, in his unconventional view, "a good marriage is that in which each appoints the other guardian of his solitude."

In solitude we can shut out the world and come face to face

with our deepest needs and feelings. We can think things out, think things through, regroup, recover from disappointments, heal our wounds. Solitude can serve as a private refuge where we live inside our head or engage in pursuits that allow us room to discover and develop new parts of ourselves. And since, as Anthony Storr points out in his thoughtful book *Solitude,* even the best relationships are flawed, we might make fewer demands on our marriage (and thus be less dissatisfied with our marriage) if we sought—through the creative uses of solitude—supplementary sources of fulfillment.

Solitude allows us to live some portion of our life apart from our partner. So do other kinds of separateness, occasions when we choose to use our free time (such as it is when the children are young) working out, volunteering, seeing a friend, or attending a lecture series on art. We might even leave the kids with our folks while one of us (speaking of beaches) heads for Bermuda and the other (speaking of skis) heads for the slopes. But we can't go our separate ways or pursue our individual interests without some husband-wife negotiations. We cannot ignore the fact that marriage sets limits on our freedom to act unilaterally.

"I make a plan to do something outside my family, away from my family," says Penny, whose children are nine and seven and two, "and I clear it with my husband in advance. I need some freedom from all of them—it keeps the marriage healthy. It lets me come back a better person, refreshed."

Her husband isn't happy, she says, with her wish for separate experiences and relationships, though he doesn't doubt her love or fidelity. He accepts it, she says, "because he knows how important this is to me. He knows that this is what I need to do."

Not every husband is as accepting as Penny's. In discussing her divorce from the man who's been called the last tycoon, the flamboyant Ted Turner, Jane Fonda told a reporter, "He needs someone to be there one hundred per cent of the time. He thinks that's love. It is not love. It's babysitting."

Unlike Penny and Jane, a good many wives (and a good many husbands) complain that they have more separateness than they want, that—what with their jobs and their chores and their kids—he and she live mostly in parallel universes. She comes home and makes dinner; he comes home and feeds the kids while she goes to the store; one does dishes while the other does baths; and on Saturdays he runs errands with the six-year-old while she takes the three-year-old to Creative Play. Most of the time that remains belongs to the family as a family. A little of it may be claimed by the husband and wife. A good many couples with children, especially two-career couples with children, say they want more, not less, of a life with each other.

But sometimes they don't. And sometimes one of them does, and one of them doesn't. And sometimes it happens that husband and wife both actively choose to live in parallel universes, enjoying separate interests, friends, vacations, leisure activities, even residences. Sometimes a husband and wife (and I know a couple of such couples) are both uncomfortable with too much intimacy and are happily married only because they maintain a good deal of distance between each other. But most of us get married because we want to be with, not apart from, the person we've married, even though we may need some separateness too. Most of us have to figure out how to be an "us" as well as a "me" and a "you" as we keep living day after day with each other.

Living together day after day with some modicum of grace requires, among many other things, balancing togetherness with separateness. And being honest without overdoing the truth. And being relaxed and comfortable and genuine while not allowing *all* of it to hang out. It also requires accepting the sometimes relentless routineness of everyday married life while noticing, when it's sweet, how very sweet, how unbelievably sweet, it is.

It may also require accepting some new definitions of what we call sweet, as well as some new definitions of what we call romance.

An image sticks in my mind of my at-the-time-unmarried son (I won't name which one) having lunch with his lady love at our kitchen table. He has set a romantic scene: There are crystal candlesticks and a pair of bright red candles. There is, in a bucket, a bottle of chilling champagne. And across his lady love's plate he has placed a single, perfect American Beauty rose. I adore the poetic soul in him, but when he started thinking about getting married, I had this urge to point out that lunch after marriage rarely comes with roses and candlesticks. I wanted to point out (but now I think I'll just hand him this book) the realities of everyday married life.

Like dealing with bills and chores and stopped-up toilets and his-and-her-and-the-children's stomach flu.

Like wanting to watch the basketball game instead of having to entertain the relatives.

Like engaging in discussions that go, "Do you know how

much you spent on long-distance phone calls this month?" And "I can't believe you forgot to make reservations." And "Didn't we visit your parents only two weeks ago?" And "Who lets a broiler pan soak for seven days?"

Like engaging in these discussions in a very unromantic tone of voice.

I had this urge to point out that there'll be, in even the liveliest marriages, some dreary, dull, emotionally deadened phases. That marriage—in the words of John Updike—oscillates between "apathy and renewal." That sex will sometimes be boring, sometimes nonexistent, and sometimes just sex instead of making love. And that simply because you have talked things over and come up with a perfect solution to a problem, it doesn't mean that you won't be having to solve that same damn problem again—and again.

Marriage, I wanted to tell him, is a problem we have to solve again and again.

But I certainly didn't, and certainly don't, want to denigrate romance. I would never knock ecstatic, inordinate love. I do, however, agree with psychologist Michael Vincent Miller, who asserts in *Intimate Terrorism* that romantic passion "is both too fierce and too fragile" for couples to rely on and who believes that romantic passion alone cannot help them surmount the "domestic messiness" of everyday life.

His answer to this—a fine answer, I think—is to advocate what he calls "a romance of the ordinary." This involves the recognition that love is not only what we possess at the beginning but something that we create, a choice that we consciously, actively make, a "willed performance." A romance of the ordinary allows us to look upon married love as a grand accomplishment, the outcome of the pleasing and strenuous process of being together over time, the outcome of making the effort—as the poet Paul Muldoon puts it—to

> rouse ourselves each dawn . . .
> with such force and fervor as spouses may yet espouse,
> and then some.

It also allows us to understand that the ordinary in everyday married life does not always have to be boring or repetitive, that everydayness, if we're attentive and grown-up enough to work with it, can include the virtues of gracefulness and surprise. A romance of the ordinary might even enable us, if we open up our eyes, to discover a few sonnets at the supermarket.

Paul Muldoon, who seems well attuned to the romance of the ordinary, celebrates—in his lovely poem "Long Finish"—the wonder of having withstood "the soars and slumps in the Dow of ten years of marriage and parenthood," taking tender note of his wife's breast, waist, bare shoulder, and—it's part of the package— her "all-but-cleared-up patch of eczema." Writing of the "bitter rapture" and "blissful rows" of everyday married life, he has discovered the poetry in the prosaic.

My friend Tommy, who has had his share of prosaic everydays in his twelve years of marriage, also believes in the romance of the ordinary.

"Because sometimes," he says, "when the four of us are out ice-skating together, or snuggled in bed together reading a book, or I'm on the commuter train and I've had a really rough day at work and there's nothing but violence and misery in the newspapers but I'm going home to my quiet street and my house and to people who love me, my heart floods with feeling. And I know that everything else in the world is meaningless compared to having this family. I know that I'm the luckiest man alive."

CHAPTER SIX

Marital Sibling Rivalry

What is a troubled marriage, after all, but a grotesque
version of sibling rivalry . . . ?

—Michael Vincent Miller,
Intimate Terrorism

We have a healthy competition. I am trying to write
poems that will still be read after all her buildings have
fallen down.

—U.S. poet laureate Billy Collins
talking about his wife, an architect

LIVING EVERYDAY LIFE as a marriage partner and parent and member of a family, we may sooner or later discover that a husband and wife can be competitors too. Nor does such competition necessarily happen only in troubled marriages. Just as brothers and sisters vie with each other to be their parents' best-loved child, so may husbands and wives—in their wish to be best or first or most—engage in a marital version of sibling rivalry.

I can speak with some personal knowledge of such rivalry:

My husband has been at the party for an hour before I arrive. I can see right away that he's having a wonderful time. There's a drink in his hand and a blonde at his side, and a circle of people are laughing at what he is saying. "Your husband," the blonde confides to me when I join the merry throng, "really ought to be a stand-up comic. He's keeping us all in stitches with these adorably funny stories about your kids."

Somewhere deep inside me resentment stirs. What is it? I ask myself. What's going on? Am I jealous of the blonde? Angry that he went to the party before me? No on both counts. Up close, the blonde is decidedly not his type, and he went to the party before me because I insisted. What's bothering me is the fact that he's being funny about the kids when funny about the kids is *my* department. What's bothering me, I'm ashamed to say, is a matrimonial version of sibling rivalry.

Am I crazier or more contentious than most? Again I say no. It's been my observation that sibling rivalry lives in many a married heart and sometimes flares up in even the hardiest marriage, setting spouses competing (although they often don't acknowledge that they're competing) with each other.

They compete over which of them the children love best. They compete over which of their friends are basically *his* friends rather than *her* friends, or vice versa. They may, if they both have careers, compete professionally. And they compete when—innocently or not so innocently—they start encroaching on each other's turf.

By turf I mean those qualities, talents, interests, achievements, and realms of expertise that we claim as ours and that set us apart from our mate—or from our brothers and our sisters. Indeed, many brothers and sisters avoid competing with each other as they grow up by deidentification, a both conscious and unconscious divvying up of the turf. This useful tactic allows us to distinguish ourselves from our siblings by allotting one set of characteristics to them and another, often opposite, set to ourselves. She is the emotional one; her sister is the rational one. She is scientific; her brother is literary. He is psychological; his brother is athletic. You get the idea. Living together under one roof, brothers and sisters need to have their own thing—and the love or recognition or admiration or gratification that thing may provide—without having to fight over it. Like siblings, husbands and wives may try to mitigate marital rivalry by staking out some turf as theirs alone.

Looking at several marriages, mine among them, I see that we all have indeed staked out our own turf. Seth, the husband of Lynn, is the movie expert. Jean, Todd's wife, is the person people confide in. Grace's Dick is the fixer. Peg, who is married to Max, is the world-class beauty. Milton, my husband, knows everything about the Middle East. And I am the one who is funny about the kids.

So is Joanne—at least, she aspires to be.

Joanne to her husband, William: "When we ate dinner with the Rosemans, why didn't you let me tell my funny story about the kids? I'm with the kids all the time, at least you could let me talk about it. Deenie Roseman told *her* story about *her* kids and everybody listened. It makes me feel better to be witty and entertaining, and I don't have that many chances—"

William to Joanne: "Frame a question."

Joanne: "As an only child you have never experienced sibling rivalry. Can you be experiencing it for the first time, now, with me?"

Could be.

Dividing up the turf can modify marital sibling rivalry, allowing each partner to feel, You've got yours, I've got mine, allowing each partner a certain amount of unchallenged satisfaction, allowing each partner to hear their friends admiringly say: That Seth can tell you the name of every Robert Altman movie! And Jean, she has such insight, such understanding! And only Dick could have gotten that garbage disposal working again! And doesn't Peg look marvelous! And aren't Joanne's stories entertaining!

Yes, dividing up the turf works very well, as long as each spouse gives the other a chance to shine. It works very well until one of the partners—deliberately or more or less inadvertently—begins moving in upon the other's turf.

Take Peg, for instance, the world-class beauty whose husband, Max, when they married, was a skinny, gawky guy with a rather weak chin. Max had plenty of highly commendable qualities, but sexy good looks was clearly not among them. That was—or always had been—Peg's department. Then things changed.

Lean and bearded, Max—as he has grown older—has turned into a very attractive man, while Peg's lush beauty has ripened into matronly. In recent years, whenever people run into Peg and Max, they tend to comment on how great *Max* is looking. Peg hardly can bear it.

She doesn't, of course, say anything crude, like "Naked, he's bony," or "Behind that beard there lurks a receding chin." But the pain that she feels is very much like the pain a little girl feels when her parents start fussing over her baby brother. It is, in fact, the pain of sibling rivalry.

In their book *American Couples,* an intensive examination of couples' relationships, Dr. Philip Blumstein and Dr. Pepper Schwartz found "that beautiful people become accustomed to the power that derives from their looks, and do not want to lose it. This can generate competitiveness between partners. Our study shows that the more attractive heterosexuals are, the more they compete with their partners and resent the attention paid their partners by others."

They resent their partners' encroachment on their turf.

Jean and Todd have—or had until very recently—a quite successful division of the turf. Todd was brilliant and witty and successful. And Jean knew how to really relate to people. Todd always understood about places like Cuba. And Jean always understood the human heart. Todd was one of Westchester County's leading tennis players. And Jean was Westchester's leading confidante.

Then, about five months ago, Todd's brother called to discuss some personal problems with him. A month after that, Todd's law partner called, also to discuss some personal problems with him. And in the past two months or so, three other people called, all to discuss their personal problems with *Todd*. Suddenly it was Todd, not Jean, who was Westchester's Dear Abby. Jean hates it a lot.

She finds herself harping at Todd, "Don't talk with your mouth full." She finds herself poking fun at his Georgia drawl. She finds herself listing all the chores that he has been neglecting because he is on the phone with call after call. She finds herself saying mean things to him because what she wants to say is "Stay off my turf."

But she doesn't feel she can say this because her husband isn't upsetting her on purpose. He certainly doesn't intend to do her harm. And besides, what kind of wife begrudges the fact that her husband is learning to really relate to people? How can she resent the fact that he's starting to understand the human heart?

The rivalrous feelings Max and Todd stirred up in their wives were stirred up inadvertently. But there also are times when a husband or wife quite purposefully moves in on the other's turf. Like Lynn, the wife of Seth, the movie expert, who decided to be a movie expert too, perhaps because she envied and wanted what Seth had, perhaps because he'd acquired too much power and Lynn was trying to level the playing field, or perhaps because she'd lost, or he'd taken, some of the turf that was hers—and she wished to get even.

All she said to Seth was that she was trying to share his interests more completely. Maybe she said that to herself as well. And then she enrolled in some courses in film, and now, whenever they're out with friends for the evening, she is the one who talks about jump cuts and freeze-frames and tracking shots and can name every single movie by Ingmar Bergman.

Some wives and husbands complain that they've taught their spouses everything they know about a subject—about modern art or what's going on in Russia—and soon thereafter their spouses are sounding off about Pollock or Putin as if *they're* the experts. "I hear him repeating my ideas as if he'd thought of them all by himself," one woman told me, "and he doesn't give me the slightest bit of credit. If he's going to steal my ideas, I at least want some credit."

Jo, in Sue Miller's novel *While I Was Gone*, makes the same complaint, saying of her husband, "I overheard him on the phone passing judgment on a movie we'd seen in exactly my words, without crediting me."

She admits that it is petty to feel aggrieved. Nonetheless, she's aggrieved.

I would be too, even though I'm aware that it would be far

more generous if I'd just enjoy the fact that my spouse is learning from me. I wish I could be like the husband who says, and truly seems to believe, "Whatever I can do to help enhance my wife's self-esteem is in my best interest." But it's hard to enjoy or feel generous or help enhance our spouse's self-esteem when they fail to give us the byline we deserve. Instead, we feel rivalrous.

Rivalrous behavior can become, in the course of a marriage, appallingly juvenile, with husbands and wives interrupting each other or taking over a story because their partner "is telling it all wrong" or sometimes rushing in to deliver the punch line—and thus be the one to garner the laughs. I actually know a man who is so determined that he, not his wife, will hold center stage that he stamps his foot, and keeps stamping it, until she is silenced and everyone has turned to him. Before he gets going, however, his wife strikes back at him by icily announcing, "I'll now defer to my well-informed husband. I'm going to sit here quietly while he tells you everything you want to know."

Is this nice? Is this right? Is this grown up? No, it is not. But marital sibling rivalry, though usually more subtle than what I've just described, is probably far more common than we might think, even if most wives and husbands may not recognize it or be willing to discuss it. But when they do start to talk about feeling excluded, preempted, supplanted, squeezed out by their spouse, they offer emotional evidence of the wife's or husband's or couple's sibling rivalry.

Particularly when the children are involved.

"Rivalry over the kids?" says Denise. "It totally exists. I see it with my husband. I also see it with some of my women friends. Competitive people compete for their children the way they compete in every other area. They aren't satisfied until they win, until they become the favorite parent."

She tells about her friend Trudy, "who's always saying with fake regret, 'My husband just doesn't know how to handle the kids or talk to the kids. It's such a shame they can't make a better connection.'" According to Denise, "That is absolute bullshit. She wants it that way. She contributes to it. No, 'contributes' is too weak a word. She sets it up."

She sets it up, says Denise, by always aligning herself with her daughters against their dad, by strategic sighs, by rolling her eyes, by shrugging and saying to them with bemused contempt, "You know how your dad is."

Trudy's husband, says Denise, doesn't stand a chance.

If Denise sounds agitated about her friend's victory in the who-do-the-kids-love-best sweepstakes, it's because she has lost that contest in her own life, with not only her sons but her daughter having been wooed and won by her irresistible husband. Like Trudy, he encourages a subtle there-goes-your-mom-again disrespect, and when they mouth off at her, "he never, ever," she says, "tells them, 'Don't talk to your mother that way.' He's the fun person in this house, he knows how to make them laugh, he's heartwarmingly marvelous with them. I don't want to take that away from them. I just want to be included. But when they confide in him, not me, and tell him big news before they tell it to me, and direct all their questions to him, never to me, I feel so left out. And the truth is, though he'd never admit it, he likes it like that."

Psychotherapist Block discusses the pain and envy one mother felt when her three-year-old repeatedly declared his love for his daddy without saying a word about his love for her. At the same time this mother realized that her husband's far more lenient parenting style most likely had a great deal to do with her little boy's intense devotion to him. And so she came to regard her son's so-called rejection of her as not just "an issue between her and her son, but also an issue between her and her husband, a competition about who was to be the good guy in the family and who was to get all the love."

Although every wife will tell you that she wants her husband to be involved with the children, although many wives complain that their husbands work so much that they don't have time for the children, although most wives wish their husbands were more attentive and attuned to the needs of the children, they may find themselves in a state of acute ambivalence if their husbands become too deeply involved, available, attentive, and attuned.

Indeed, some women, while grateful that their husbands are willing to share a good deal of the child care, are concerned about being displaced as the primary parent. As one mother put it to therapist Lillian Rubin, "I want him to be important in their lives, but . . . if I could only be sure I was just a little more important."

Afraid of not being her children's number one, this woman becomes quite competitive with her husband, which makes him, he says, feel excluded and hurt and mad. And so *he* starts competing with *her*, though he adds that he's "not looking to beat her out. . . . I'd be content just to be a little more equal."

Competing for the children can begin as soon as they're born or at any other stage. A father, holding his screaming, squirming two-month-old, refuses to hand her back to his pleading wife, saying, "*I'm* taking care of this. You're not the only one who can settle her down." The mother of a four-year-old who is very close to her dad both likes and resents their closeness and tells Dr. Rubin, "I get into a crazy kind of competition with him. . . . How can a mother feel okay unless she can believe she's the most important person in a child's life?" The mother of school-age children admits that although she complains that her husband's an unengaged dad, "I love being the more involved and active parent and I think I may have pushed him to the periphery." A husband takes his teenage son on a just-us-guys canoe trip, leaving his wife home scheming how she'll even things up by taking her son to New York. A husband and wife, each of them on an extension phone, start bickering whenever their kid calls from college, accusing each other of "nonstop interrupting" or "never letting me get a chance to talk" or "always having to be the first to answer her questions and give out all the advice." And I've seen this kind of rivalry continue unchecked unto the next generation, with husbands and wives competing over who is going to be the favorite grandparent.

Sometimes just one of the spouses is aware that a competition is under way. "It's nothing he's doing on purpose," Dale says of her husband and their young sons, "but he's got all this male bonding stuff going on with the kids. So it bothers me that after they finish playing ball or wrestling or whatever, he offers to read them a book instead of stepping aside and letting me read them the book. And I'm *really* bothered when *they* want *him* to read it."

Dale concedes that her husband, unlike Denise's husband, isn't trying to be the best-loved parent. But she is determined to get not a single crumb less than her full share and therefore fights for what she feels entitled to.

Which means, she confesses to me with some embarrassment, that "even if I'm not in the mood to read to them, I do it because I don't want to let him get in there."

"Where there is sibling rivalry," writes Michael Vincent Miller, "anything one brother or sister gets leaves the others feeling deprived. If one child wants something and gets it, the others raise a fuss whether they want it or not because they feel in danger of being cheated." This sometimes can be just as true, Dr. Miller suggests, and Dale confirms, when that brother is a husband, that sister a wife.

———

Some wives and husbands seem to be especially alert to the danger of being cheated of their kids' love. Some feel the same concern about their friends. Sally puts it like this: "I'm not intending to get divorced, but I've already figured out—because I think that way—which of our friends, if we did get divorced, he'd win custody of, and which of them I would."

She adds that her husband would probably wind up with most of their friends because, she notes somewhat bitterly, "in this marriage I make the friends and then he steals them." She also says that "those he can't steal, which doesn't happen too often, he wants to drop."

Would a different kind of woman, one who doesn't "think that way," be scanning the horizon with such vigilance? Would a different wife be pleased that her husband likes her friends and wants to make them his? But that's the problem, says Sally. Her husband wants to make her friends *his*. He wants to squeeze her out in order to be the favorite friend, in order to be the best-loved child in the family.

Let me quickly acknowledge that *not* liking, rather than stealing, each other's friends is the more typical problem between wives and husbands. There's Louise with the giggle, Jerome with the complex, his unevolved buddy from high school, her spendthrift ex-roommate, and various other odd types that our spouse brings into the marriage or subsequently meets at the office or health club. We are bored with them, annoyed with them, have nothing whatsoever in common with them. We don't really want them to like us; what we really want them to do is go away. And if we can't get rid of them, we want our husband or wife to find a way to be with them without us.

"You know why God invented lunch?" Martha asks her husband. "So you can spend time with Ralph and I don't have to." Stealing her line, I have said to my husband, "You know why God invented meeting for drinks? So you can see the Bronsons and I don't have to."

But sometimes such friends can't be shunted off to lunch or meeting for drinks. Sometimes, for the sake of our husband or wife, we have to see them together and try to be nice about it. All of us have certain friends whom, should we wind up divorced, we'd be happy to let our spouse win custody of. But most of the friends in most marriages are people we meet as a couple and share as a couple. And sometimes, instead of sharing them, we compete for them.

One husband has the habit of engaging in lengthy chats with

the women or men who call and ask for his wife. He sometimes remains on the line while she is talking to them. She thinks he should say, "Hello, I'll go and get her," after which he should get the hell off the phone. He thinks she has serious problems with sharing friendships. She thinks that he can't accept the fact that they're calling to talk to *her*. He thinks she can't accept that they're *his* friends too. She thinks that they love her the most, but she also thinks that her sibling rival of a husband won't rest until they love him as much or more. He thinks that she is being the sibling rival.

Our wish to be loved as much as or more than our sibling—or our spouse—is sometimes expressed as our wish to be the best, which in turn is sometimes expressed by our engaging in open or covert career competition. Siblings may vie with each other to be the featured star of the family, to be their parents' most successful child. Some people carry this rivalrous wish to be the most successful into their marriage, pressing to be the one who makes the most money or achieves the most recognition.

Because my husband and I both write for a living, I'm often asked whether we compete professionally. My answer is no, not because we wouldn't be capable of such competition but because we have, in the subjects we choose to write about, never trespassed on each other's turf. (At cocktail parties, yes, but not in our writing.) There's no question in my mind that if Milton decided to write a children's book or suddenly began composing poems, I wouldn't be rooting for a big success. And he would feel less than thrilled, he admits, if I produced a political best-seller. We're safe from rivalry only because I do domestic affairs and he does foreign affairs. And we don't have to share the spotlight—he has his and I have mine—because we have different audiences for our work. We've never had to and never wished to and certainly never intend to go head-to-head with each other professionally. When couples do, their marriage can take a beating.

This happened to the Corrigans, a two-lawyer family bringing up two little girls. Both of them were capable and ambitious, but only her career, and salary, soared. The more well known and well paid she became, the harder it was for her husband, who eventually ended the marriage on the grounds—he was quite frank about this—that he could no longer live with her success.

In a similar situation, a lawyer husband—who simply couldn't be frank about it—responded to his lawyer wife's huge success with icy silences and no sex. A minister they both trusted brought the rivalry into the open and helped them not to get rid of it but to manage it.

Husbands and wives needn't necessarily work in the same field to become embroiled in professional competition. One woman, married to the brilliant head of a famous think tank, held a teaching job at a private school. She always became enraged when people treated his opinions on, say, public policy as weightier or more informed than hers. In recent years she has garnered one, then another, advanced degree, more—she likes to point out—than her husband possesses. We who are watching bet she won't rest until she is the head of her own famous think tank.

More typical than this fiercely competitive woman, however, is the man who is troubled because his wife is clearly the star of the family professionally. Although views on working wives are rapidly changing, most women and men in two-career marriages still expect and prefer the husband to be more successful. Blumstein and Schwartz established, and later researchers agree, that "most modern-day egalitarian husbands do not want to play a secondary role to their wives, either in their own eyes, their wives' eyes, or the eyes of the world." They say that while a husband may encourage his wife to achieve, "he is likely to become competitive if she begins to surpass what he has done."

A man who has helped and guided his wife to the point where she surpasses him professionally may be especially troubled by her success. Although rivalry wasn't an issue during those years when he was her wise, benevolent mentor and she was his adoring and grateful mentee, he may start feeling competitive if she not only no longer needs him but outshines him. He may express his competitiveness by turning on his wife for what he tells himself was exploitation, for using his encouragement, his tutelage, his financial support, and his contacts to (as one husband, mixing his metaphors, angrily complained) "drain me dry and leave me in the dust." Or he may express his competitiveness by pointing out her inadequacies as a woman, a mother, a lover, a nice human being, or by denigrating—privately and sometimes publicly too—what she has achieved. He may express his competitiveness by attacking her emotionally and verbally or even by having a not-too-secret affair.

Of course many husbands, perhaps most husbands, of women with booming careers are proud of their accomplishments and glad for—and often in need of—the money they earn. But in their book *The Good Marriage*, psychologist Judith Wallerstein and Sandra Blakeslee conclude, "Even when couples have egalitarian ideas, a wife's successful career can pose a major threat if the husband's career does not match hers in status and income." Her success can pose a major threat because, even in our liberated times, some husbands have trouble living with this role reversal.

And so do some wives who, even though they think of themselves as feminists, are embarrassed to admit that they also think that the men they married ought to provide for them, allowing them the luxury of working out of choice, not out of necessity. Whether or not these women actually want to quit their jobs, they need to know that their husbands can support them, for as one young married professional confessed to Dr. Rubin—and I've heard other working wives express this view—"I feel terrible about it, but I know that if [my husband] can't get his act together this marriage is in jeopardy. . . . I just don't think I can respect him if he isn't capable of taking care of his own family, even if he doesn't have to because I can."

She doesn't want to win this competition.

Are women less inclined than men—less socialized, let's say—to want to beat out their spouse professionally? The evidence seems to suggest that this is so. They tend to be pleased, not threatened, by their husband's greater success and heftier salary. They're not as undone as men by reflected glory, by being introduced as "spouse of . . . ," or even—as the wife of a much-admired celebrity put it—by "sometimes feeling as if I am invisible." They're more willing than men to sacrifice a chance to advance their career for what they regard as the greater good of the family. And they also, if they earn a higher salary or if they've achieved some measure of fame in their field, tend to make more of an effort, when they're out with friends or acquaintances, to showcase their husband's talents and accomplishments.

Indeed, when the star of *A Star Is Born*—whose actor husband has killed himself in the wake of his ruined career and her huge success—stands on the stage before her adoring audience, she doesn't introduce herself by her own name, Vicki Lester, the name with which she has won her fame and her Oscar. She chooses, instead, to present herself as Mrs. Norman Maine, using the name of the husband who, back when he was big and she was small, helped her get started, helped her become a star. Although this thrice-filmed movie made its first appearance back in 1937, I suspect that most women today would still applaud Vicki Lester for honoring her husband.

Wives also seem, if forced to choose, more willing than men to choose kids over career. Libby, for instance, says that she and her husband, Ira, actively competed "over which of us was going to get the time to be more successful in our work." They were, she explains, "professionally pretty even, and I had the chance to be where he is now." But raising two children and wanting to raise them responsibly, they had to decide "which one of us would make the bigger splash and the higher salary, and which of us would be the one who would take off from work whenever the kids got sick." She says that the choice was hers, that the high-pressure, high-scoring job was hers, "but when I stopped and looked it in the face, I decided that it was not for me—that the children were more important to me than the job." Libby still works full-time, but, she says, "we both have more invested in Ira's success." And she is the one who takes off when the children get sick.

None of what I've just said is true of *all* women.

There is, of course, the woman who wants her husband to

take off from work just as often as she does. Or prefers to talk about her—not her husband's—accomplishments. Or is quick to let it be known that she is the éminence grise, the power behind the throne, the person without whom her husband would still be in sales. Or makes it very clear that while her husband is earning big money from bad corporations, she is engaged in work of far more importance to the world, although underpaid.

There's the woman who takes legitimate pride in what she does professionally and wants family, friends, and acquaintances to hear about and credit her for her accomplishments. And there's also the woman who wishes to triumph over any and all professional rivals, even when those rivals include her own husband.

———————

Do all married couples suffer from sibling rivalry? Maybe not. Some people may always have felt securely superior. Some may have learned to settle for what they've got. Others may have succeeded in maintaining a fair division of the turf. Or perhaps they possess such a sturdy and substantial sense of self that they're able to let another cross their borders and walk on their turf without fearing that something of value is being taken from them.

An artist friend of mine swears she has never competed with other artists, including her husband, though he is the more successful of the two. "I do what I do," she says, "and because it's mine, my perception, my style, my sensibility, I'm never in a contest with my husband or anyone else. My only sibling rival, if I had a sibling rival, would be me."

Would that we all could be so self-defined, so self-possessed, so unassailable.

I suspect, however, that most wives and husbands are not fully free of rivalry toward each other. Most of us married couples sometimes feel, as most siblings do, that there isn't enough of the good stuff to go around. And sometimes we are correct. Sometimes there isn't enough to go around, and we simply need to be grown-up enough to figure out how to live with that riling reality.

We also need to recognize when we are, in fact, competing or being competed with. We'll be better able to deal with such competition when we are ready to call it by its true name—better able to live with it or modify it or even try to transform it from competition to collaboration.

Consider this:

When Archie and Megan's son, Sean—their only child, their much-competed-over child—was applying to college and writing his personal essay, he asked his mother and father to critique what he had written, relying on them both for their skills as published writers and clinical psychologists. Archie made two copies of Sean's college essay, one for him and one for Megan, intending that each of them—separately—would examine it and edit it and then go over it—separately—with Sean. This is how they had always dealt with their work and with helping their son, separately but equally and, although not quite acknowledging it, competitively.

But this time Sean had a different idea. It's late, he said, and I'm beat, and I want to get this application done. So couldn't you save me some time, he asked, by reading it together, figuring out your best suggestions together, and then—together—discussing them with me?

What a wild idea!

Archie and Megan gave it a try and found, as they—

together—studied Sean's essay, that they were working together amazingly well, agreeing on most of the points that they raised and finding solutions where they disagreed. And when they discussed Sean's essay with him, neither of them felt the need to be seen as the wiser parent or the shrewder psychologist or the better writer.

"After eighteen years," says Megan, "of never actually admitting to our rivalries, we were helped by Sean to see them and, at least in this one instance, to overcome them." She isn't sure, she says, that this is the start of a new, more grown-up way of being together. But, she adds, "I'm feeling that maybe it could be."

CHAPTER SEVEN

Married Sex

Her: "Why is it like this?"
Him: "What do you mean?"
Her: "Sex. It's gone for so long, not happening much, or
just routine. And then it comes thundering back."
Him: "What's the alternative? . . . Always fantastic?
Always hot?"

—Sue Miller,
While I Was Gone

ALWAYS FANTASTIC, always hot is not how most married couples describe their sex life, at least not after the early stage of marriage. Indeed, for some married couples their sex life isn't, perhaps never was, that big a deal. But for many other couples, an ongoing sexual connection, even when it's less than hot and fantastic, is both a very fine thing in itself and the juice, the glue, the music of the relationship. Shakespeare tells us that sleep knits up the raveled sleeve of care. A lot of wives and husbands say that sex does.

The sexual connection, whatever its place in a marriage, is almost always about much more than sex.

She says, "It's the only time he tells me he loves me and that I'm beautiful. It's also the only time I see him vulnerable."

He says, "When things are bad between us, making love can usually make them better."

She says, "When we're done, we have these really cozy conversations, and I like the talking almost as much as the orgasms." She smiles and corrects herself: "More than the orgasms."

He says, "We get preoccupied and busy with other stuff, and sex gets us back into each other's souls again."

She says, "In sex the partnership of our daily life is communicated to my body."

He says, "She's more successful and she makes more money than I do, but the pleasure I can give her evens things up."

She says, "Sex lets me experience, momentarily, that I'm not alone in this world."

He says, "Sex takes all the pieces of our marriage and ties them together, makes them whole."

She says, "He doesn't snuggle and hug unless we're having sex, so sex is the way I get my snuggles and hugs."

He says, "Having sex with my chosen partner is a spiritual experience—not just physical or emotional but sublime."

She says, "We get along beautifully, but if we don't have sex for two or three days, my husband"—who, by the way, is seventy-six—"starts feeling disconnected from me, starts to feel emotionally deprived."

He says, "It's by far my favorite way to have fun."

She says, "There's a real reconnecting every time we are together. The physical intimacy is irreplaceable. There are no adequate substitutes."

He says, "One might consider our sex life routine but it's very enjoyable. Who tires of hitting a good golf shot?"

"Routine" is a word that is often heard when married-a-while wives and husbands discuss their sex lives, even when their sex lives are as enjoyable as hitting a good golf shot. "There is no way around routine sex," says thirty-something Betty Jane. "It's reliable but predictable and routine," says Kim, after fourteen years of marriage. And Albert, eleven years married, observes, "We do it well. We've got the routine down pat. But there are no surprises." On the other hand, notes Mary, married fifteen years longer than Albert, "Routine has a safe, reassuring, and very comfortable side." And Lainie, whose sexual history has allowed her, she says, to "make plenty of comparisons," happily observes that "no more intense sex ever existed for me than this familiar everyday married sex."

What's good—what can be good—about routine, familiar, everyday married sex is being able to please and feel at ease with each other. "We know what turns the other on," says Nan, "and we each can say what we want during sex." Adds Sascha, "So even though there isn't the newness and the discovery—and the frequency—that we had at the beginning, what my husband and I have instead is more freedom and honesty."

While everyone seems to agree that sexual frequency decreases the longer a married couple is together, some husbands and wives insist that their familiar married sex offers more satisfaction than the sexual fireworks of their early days together. Because, says Stan, "It's less hungry and more loving." And because, says Irene, "The 'Ooh, can I actually say this? Ooh, can I

try this?' fear-of-embarrassment factor is gone from our bed."
There's a "closeness, a trust, an openness that comes with familiarity," says Rhoda, "and that makes us feel safe to completely
relinquish ourselves, for a little while, to another person."

There's also a certain confidence, a growing and a grown-up
recognition, that good sex is simply what good sex is for *us*,
although it may in no way resemble what was good for Lady
Chatterley and her lover or what Julie Christie and Donald
Sutherland did with one another in *Don't Look Now,* an otherwise
grim movie with the sexiest married sex scenes you'll ever see.
Good sex is what satisfies a couple's exquisitely specific physical,
spiritual, and emotional needs—and if both partners like it more
tender than lustful, more playful than earnest, more kinky than
straight, more straight than kinky, more cool than hot, or even
more "wham bam thank you ma'am" than slow and sweet, then
that is exactly what good sex is for that couple.

Time and familiarity can help us figure out what's good for
us. Familiarity need not breed contempt. "I have grown accustomed to your face, and other sections" ends my poem "Familiarity Breeds Content," which affectionately suggests that longtime
married sex indeed has certain benefits.

One woman, married fifty-one years, cheerily informs me, "I
don't understand what people mean when they talk about having
bad sex. The only kind of sex I've had"—and it's all been with her
husband—"has been good." When I ask her what keeps it good,
she even more cheerily replies, "Enthusiasm and imagination."

As another long-married woman, I could elaborate on the
benefits of enthusiasm and imagination. I could, but I won't.

A friend of mine, married twenty-three years to a man she

met when both of them were teenagers, also sings the praises of longtime sex. "One of the real benefits of marrying your high-school boyfriend is that he is always your high-school boyfriend," she says. "Kissing him, I connect to hot summer nights and teenage lust. Inside that three-piece suit is the guy who made me"—and continues to make her—"melt."

As most married people know, there are—from fairly early on—peaks and valleys in sexual desire and in sexual pleasure. Some of this has to do with our stage of life. Some of it has to do with the emotional weather between a husband and a wife. And some of it has to do with unconscious aspects of our past which have—uninvited, unwanted, and unrecognized—climbed into bed with us.

If our stage of life is new parenthood, there may be a serious slump in sexual interest, especially (husbands complain) on the part of the wife. If our stage of life is building a career, time once spent making love may be spent making partner. (As one outraged wife complained to her working-late-every-evening husband, "I'm fed up with being your Saturday-night lay.") If our stage of life is later life, husbands may begin having problems with potency or wives may experience diminished desire. And at many stages of life, if we are doing—as couples often do—far too much and are chronically trying to manage on minimal sleep, we may be too exhausted to think about sex, make time to have sex, or give ourselves over wholeheartedly when we have it.

Reviewing a book that recommends making "tantric" love—making love with our whole mind and body—Erica Jong observes that, although we may know the value of this, it's hard to achieve, what with the in-laws calling, the dog throwing up, and the kid high on drugs in Atlantic City. "You want to be tantric lovers transported to nirvana—but for that you'll have to go on vacation to Uttar Pradesh and meditate on the Taj Mahal."

As a matter of fact, most married couples agree that, at any stage when sex is waning, a vacation—to Uttar Pradesh or maybe even Atlantic City, but without the kids—can be Viagra. Among the other ways to what's called "rekindle the passion," many how-to books suggest trying new positions and new sex toys, and (for the wives) wearing lust-inspiring nighties, and (for the husbands) engaging in longer and more inventive foreplay, and (for both) doing some daily touching of, and thinking about, each other erotically. In addition, the couples therapists I spoke with recommend that women agree to have sex even if they're not interested (surely men could do this too), on the grounds that (a) it's an act of love, like making your husband a sandwich when he's hungry instead of telling him to make it himself; (b) the less you do it, the less you want to do it, also often known as "use it or lose it"; and (c) you might surprise yourself and discover that you *are* in the mood after all.

What do women think of this advice? I talk to a woman, married thirty-one years, who says to me, "When I agree to have sex with my husband even though I really don't want it, I think of it as an investment in our future. I'm keeping the machinery oiled for when I'm in the mood to want it again." (When I ask her if she feels, as some wives do, that she is "servicing" her husband, her answer is "Not at all. I'm priming the pump.") I talk to a mother of two young children, married seven years, who says, "I wouldn't let myself be used and I wouldn't let myself be violated. But we do things for each other—like I'll go eat Chinese food with him even though I don't love Chinese food—so sometimes I'll have sex when I'm not in the mood."

The emotional weather of a married couple's life together can also affect what happens to them in bed. (Or on the kitchen table or in the shower or on the floor or in one of those back-breaking places where the experts keep advising us to have sex.) "Our sex life is an exact reflection," says Gwen, "of what's going on in the rest of our life." Which means, she explains, that when things are going well, their sex is loving or playful or "as intimate as he will ever be." And which also means, she explains, that when things are going badly, they sometimes wind up sleeping in separate rooms. On the other hand, they also sometimes have angry sex, or heartless or disconnected sex, or sex that feels an awful lot like warfare. Bad feelings, it turns out, don't necessarily dampen passion or keep a husband and wife from having sex. But under the circumstances, the sex that they're having may be very far from loving.

A couple's emotional climate is also negatively affected by issues outside their personal relationship—concerns about money, pressures at work, problems with teenage kids or aging parents—issues that may require so much time and attention and emotional energy that there seems to be nothing left to give to each other. Yet I know of a long-married couple who dealt—generously and competently—with death, drugs, and mental illness in their family while insisting upon protecting and sustaining their treasured sexual connection. Indeed, this connection helped give them the strength to do what they needed to do as the disasters and tragedies accumulated. Their loving sexual bond helped keep them strong.

How could they want to have sex with such awful things

going on in their life? "Maybe I didn't, right away," the wife tells me, "but if we started making love, something often happened that gradually let me lose myself in the experience. I then could put everything else away, and when the lovemaking was over, I felt renewed and was able to sleep at night. I even was able to cope a little better."

Sex clearly knit up her raveled sleeve of care.

Our desire for sex, our ease with sex, and the way we want to have sex may also reflect the influences of our past, conscious and unconscious influences that can always/sometimes/occasionally intrude on our sexual interest or sexual pleasure. "I'm not one woman sexually," a wife explains to me. "One night I'm wide open for it and the next time I'm ice. I know it has to do with whether or not I feel that he's trying to control me, and I know the control thing has something to do with my mother, but I can't—so far— figure out what he does (and it's nothing to do with technique) that sometimes makes me love it and sometimes makes me lie there thinking, 'Let's get this over with.'"

A man who overcame his terror of closeness only long enough to get a "yes" from the woman he asked to marry him can rarely make love to her now because (so his psychotherapist tells me) he unconsciously feels she will eat him up alive sexually. Their marriage, which is about to die, has had—from the wife's point of view—far more sexual valleys than she can live with.

It needs to be said that some couples enjoy a warm and loving marriage or an otherwise friendly and highly compatible marriage without having sex, or with having it only occasionally. If both partners find this arrangement okay, if both partners say that sex isn't high on their list, who are we to tell them that they are wrong? Minimal sexual interest needn't *always* be the result of pressures or problems or unconscious anxieties; sometimes both husband and wife have a low-key libido. But if one of them wants it and one of them doesn't, or one of them wants it much more than the other one does, the one who wants may feel hurt, unloved, resentful, rejected, or furious, while the one who doesn't want may feel inadequate, guilty, pressured, or put upon.

So what do you do if you yearn for a twice-a-week (rather than twice-a-month) sexual partner? Or a more enthusiastic (rather than merely grin-and-bear-it) sexual partner? Or a more experimental (rather than how-can-you-ask-such-a-thing-of-me) sexual partner? And what do you do if *you* are the twice-a-month or grin-and-bear-it or how-can-you-ask-such-a-thing-of-me sexual partner? The experts say: Communicate. Accommodate. And masturbate. Try therapy. Try fantasy. Watch porno flicks and sex-education videos. And if the sex isn't what you want but you otherwise cherish your marriage, learn to tolerate.

They also say that husbands and wives need to stop blaming each other for their sexual disappointments and discontents and recognize that they're in this together, that troubles with sex are troubles for both of them, and that they might try addressing these troubles not as adversaries but as friends. Who don't call each other names like "frigid," "emasculating," "a fucking machine," and "insensitive." Who understand that he may need sex to get close and that she may need closeness to want sex. Who see their sexual difficulties as problems to be solved, not faults to be found. Addressing these troubles together may not result in a fabulous sex life, just as dancing lessons will not make them Ginger and Fred. But it can probably help them get better, maybe even a whole lot better, at moving with some pleasure and grace to the music.

———————

And if, despite our best efforts, we are sexually (although not otherwise) bored or unhappy, can we go out and look for good sex somewhere else?

In John Updike's novel *Too Far to Go,* a straying husband arrives at the home of his lover. She awaits him, "naked at the head of the stairs . . . , her shoulders caped in morning sun coming through the window, the very filaments of her flesh on fire." This, we would all acknowledge, is one hell of a hello, and it shows what a woman can do if she really tries. But it may be a rather impractical way for married-with-children couples to enliven their sex life with romance and surprise. Like weaving daisies in and out of each other's pubic hair or sipping French champagne from each other's navels, this is the kind of effort that is often—far more often—made extramaritally.

So it's time to talk about extramarital sex, also called infidelity or adultery or cheating or playing around, all of which involve a married person having sex with a person to whom he or she isn't married.

Extramarital sex can be secret or open, once or repeated, casual or serious. It can be paid sex with a hooker, a brief encounter with a colleague on a business trip, a series of recreational relationships, or an enduring body-and-soul affair. It can sometimes be done with a spouse's consent or tacit understanding, but more usually the spouse is unaware. For with the exception of couples who agree in advance to have an "open marriage" with no expectation of fidelity, most married couples commit to sexual exclusivity, to forsaking all others.

Nevertheless, some surveys find that almost 50 percent of husbands and 30 to 40 percent of wives are unfaithful at some point in their married life. Other surveys find that "ten years of monogamy does not mean the eleventh is safe. Sex outside the relationship can occur at any point, and both new and well-established relationships are at risk."

Although the wish for new or more or more exciting sex may propel some wives and husbands into adultery, there are plenty of other reasons, including those having little to do with the sex act itself: Like wanting emotional intimacy and warmth. Like wanting to feel desired or young or free. Like wanting to conquer, rebel, or prove you've still got it. Like wanting, just for a little while, to be somebody totally different from what one woman calls "boring old married me." Like wanting to celebrate when you're feeling up. Like wanting some solace when you're feeling down. Like wanting to alleviate your loneliness when one of you has been, too long, out of town. Like wanting . . .

There also are people who have an affair as a way of denying the coming of middle age. And those who have an affair to serve as a buffer against too much intimacy in their marriage. Some have an affair to punish, humiliate, hurt, or take revenge on their spouse. And others have an affair for the excitement of discovery, for the thrill of not knowing what will happen next.

Here's what some people say about their adultery:

"I never felt I had any right to give in to temptation, though I've been tempted," says a woman who has been married for fifteen years. "But once I found out that my husband had had an affair, I felt under no obligation to stay faithful. As a matter of fact, I actively went out looking for a man to have an affair with. I needed it, not to get even exactly, but to help myself feel less like a victim."

"During our eighteen years I've been unfaithful many times, but only with call girls," says a man who is very clear on his reasons why. "There are these interesting things they do with ice cubes and stuff, but the best thing of all is that I never have to get personally involved."

"My wife was constantly critical," says a man who had an affair after twelve years of marriage. "She never let anything go. She bitched and she carped. The other woman wasn't any sexier or prettier, but she seemed to approve of most everything about me."

"I wanted to know what sex would be like with a man who wasn't my husband," says a woman who has been married for thirty-eight years, discussing a brief affair she had twenty years ago. "I also wanted to know what I would be like in bed with a man who wasn't my husband."

"I wasn't that attractive when I was young," says a man who started being unfaithful in the last ten years of his forty years of marriage. "But as I got older and very successful, women who'd never have looked at me before started kind of throwing themselves at my feet."

"I fell in love," several men and women told me.

In a series of conversations with Hope, a strictly brought-up Catholic from New England, I've been listening to her complicated and varied explanations for engaging in seven affairs (the seventh is going on as I write this) while remaining deeply committed to her husband and her thirty-nine-year marriage.

A virgin when she married Craig, Hope was "hot to trot," eager for sexual pleasure and for the intimacy of the sexual connection. What she got was a man whose sexual habits were, and have remained, "four thrusts, he comes, and then he falls asleep" and whose separation of sex and love, of sex and intimacy, has yielded neither to Hope nor to psychotherapists. Can a man be so constrained sexually and still be a devoted and decent husband, a wonderful father, and a terrific grandpa? Hope says that Craig is all of these and more. But beginning after eight years of marriage and extending in time from young wife and mother to grandma, she has sought from a series of lovers "the loving and passionate intimacy" that Craig cannot give her, along with the excitement and romance and admiration and playfulness that adulterous relationships so often provide.

"I met this painter," Hope explains, describing her first affair. "He talked to me. He listened without interrupting. We made love for hours and hours. And he made me feel so cherished. That's what started me down the path of sin."

And on she went down that path with a rock musician, an army colonel, a lawyer, a dot-com whiz, an actor, a shrink, taking time between lovers to reproach herself with "You slut! How can you keep doing this to your husband!"

She discovered, she says, that each time "I stopped being Emma Bovary, longing for romance, and went back to doing my duty, one foot in front of the other, the laundry folding and all, martyred at every step, it would gradually begin to dawn on me that I was content and that I had a very good man that I lived with."

This serene and sensible mode never lasted too long because,

Hope says, "I am a love junkie." So although she sometimes feels "horrible" about what she's doing to Craig, she says that "the child in me stamps and dances and wants what it wants." She also says that although "I have come to believe that infidelity is caused by restless, spoiled children who believe there is more and better and different out there, I'll never say I'm sorry about these lovers."

Using junkie jargon, Hope says, "I was clean for the last seven years. I directed my passionate, sensual side to my grand-babies." But then she encountered a man she had known when he and she were kids, when both of them wanted but couldn't have each other, a man with whom she is now engaged in what she calls a "geriatric" love affair. She says she is aware that grown-ups can be deeply stirred by former boyfriends and girl-friends without ever actually acting on their feelings, seeing and treasuring instead what they have in their marriage. "The grown-up in me is often there," she says. "But then the child in me wants a lover telling me how beautiful I am at sixty-four, when the mirror laughs back at me." The child in her wants pas-sion, not just contentment.

Although there is love on both sides in this current love affair, she says, and although "I feel grateful to be given this gift," she also says that her marriage to Craig continues to be—as it always has been—unthreatened.

I wonder why. "Because," she tells me, "our marriage is com-panionable and comfortable. We're a good team. And the long-range pleasure of sharing a life together, sharing children and grandsons together, outweighs my longings for a different life."

Besides, she adds, "Can you imagine my telling my children and grandchildren, 'Listen, Grandmother has found someone she wants to live with more and is going to leave Grandfather alone now'? What an example! I am trying to show them the power of family. Am I such a hypocrite? Shit!"

I don't intend to sit in judgment on Hope. She sits in plenty of judgment on herself, torn between her stamping, clapping child who wants what she wants and her reportedly more "grown-up" perspective. Although it seems fair to say—and Hope would be the first to say it—that her behavior is childish, compulsive, and extreme, it seems to be serving the purpose for her (as affairs will sometimes do) of stabilizing the marriage by providing what the marriage cannot provide. Indeed, some unfaithful husbands and wives insist that their affair has *saved* their marriage, though if they're discovered there may be hell to pay. Still others serenely say that discovery wouldn't rattle the marriage because, at some level, their spouse already knows about their affair and has—more or less, sometimes more, sometimes less—come to terms with it.

Hope, who believes that Craig, at some level, knows and has come to terms with her affairs, is not concerned that he will walk away, perhaps because her lovers are meeting important needs of his as well as hers. They enable Craig to live within the context of a marriage that he values while continuing to hold his wife at bay, while continuing to maintain his emotional distance. They relieve Craig of Hope's demands for sex with love, for sex with romance, for sex with intimacy.

In her impressive examination of the subject in a book entitled *Adultery*, sociologist Annette Lawson reports on the pleasures and the pains of adulterers.

FROM A WOMAN: "I cannot convey to you how marvelous

I felt. . . . I felt I had been made whole. That I had been made complete in some way."

FROM A MAN: "I felt ten feet tall. I came out of there and knew I was alive. . . . I felt as if, suddenly, I was dealt a new set of cards as far as life was concerned."

FROM A WOMAN: "I have learned to live without fierce sexual passion though I'm glad I had that brief experience to see what it was like."

The pleasures of infidelity can include, along with fierce sexual passion, the joy of loving and being loved and needed; "novel and uncomplicated sex"; a friendship between the two lovers; the opportunity to expand the boundaries of self; "pleasure in conquest . . . a boost to be thought attractive"; and the excitement, the drama, the giddy fun of having a risky sexual adventure. "Marriage tames adventure to a journey involving hard work but little play, . . ." writes Professor Lawson, "with little opportunity for heroism or rebellion, excitement or danger. Indeed, the only heroism may be in overcoming obstacles in making the marriage work and endure." She notes that adultery offers husbands and wives "the chance to play—the chance to escape from marriage as the emotional and everyday workplace."

Adultery also offers pain, however, often in conjunction with the pleasure but sometimes drastically overwhelming the pleasure.

FROM A MAN: "I felt sick—really sick. I mean I had to stop the car and get out to vomit. I felt so awful."

FROM A WOMAN: "The whole affair made me . . . ill. I just couldn't cope. All the lies and everything. Horrible."

FROM A MAN: "By everything I'd been taught and knew, it was wrong."

The pains of committing adultery include living a life of

falsehood and deception, of alibis and excuses and sneaking around. Dubin, the unfaithful husband in Bernard Malamud's *Dubin's Lives*, "worried about the spreading dishonesty he was into. Awful, if you thought of yourself as an honest man." And Laura, married to Fred but in love with Alec in the movie *Brief Encounter*, observes that "it's awfully easy to lie when you know you are trusted implicitly—and so very degrading." There is also the guilt of doing harm (even if it's not known) to an innocent party, the guilt of breaking a vow, of committing a sin. And because, as one wife told me, "I'm not just a bad human being; I'm also a very bad liar," there's the constant anxiety about getting caught.

Some wives and husbands, of course, never get caught and never tell—on the grounds that "the truth would kill him" or "what my wife doesn't know won't hurt her" or "it's over and done with so why should I make us both miserable?" They never tell because the relief that confession would offer them would be outweighed by the damage it would do. In a treacly novel and movie called *The Bridges of Madison County*, which had hundreds of thousands of women dissolving in tears, dutiful housewife Francesca bids a final farewell to sensitive, manly Robert after a brief but beautiful affair, choosing her obligations to her children and unknowing husband over the man she will love (and who, presumably, will love her) forever after. In the heartrending *Brief Encounter*, which also had hundreds of thousands of women dissolving in tears, two decent married people—two perfect soul mates—deny themselves the love of a lifetime, turning away from "the overwhelming feeling we have for each other" and returning to their families without his wife or her husband being any the wiser. And in everyday real life there are plenty of undisclosed and undiscovered adulteries that begin and end or continue on for years because some wives and husbands can live with their guilt and deception—and also are very good liars.

Some unfaithful spouses, however, feel impelled to confess—usually out of guilt, but sometimes out of a wish to cause pain or stir up jealousy, and sometimes because they believe that keeping such a secret from their spouse is more harmful to the marriage than the adultery. Still other cheating husbands and wives leave telephone bills or love letters to be found, unconsciously arranging (for the reasons that the confessors need to confess) to be discovered.

They will be discovered.

> He is playing around, my husband Henry.
> And that is against all my principles.
> He says he's working late.
> He works on weekends, too.
> He makes excuses
> Instead of making love to me.
> He thinks I don't know that he's got another lady.
> He thinks that I can't smell her rose perfume on his body.
> He actually thinks he has made me believe those
>   careless lies he tells me.
> He doesn't lie well.

> Yes, he is playing around.
> How can this be?

Cheated-on husbands and wives are assailed by a multitude of feelings when they learn about a past or current affair—jealousy, hurt, humiliation, suicidal feelings, anxiety and anger and despair. They now have to deal with the shock of being deliberately and repeatedly lied to, of being betrayed, rejected, and deceived. And they have to deal with the fact that what they believed they had with their spouse is no longer, and may never have been, true. This appalling new information—this infidelity—may completely undo their perception of their marriage and may have the power, as one woman puts it, "to completely destroy the ground upon which I stand."

Then there are the questions: How can I possibly continue in this marriage? How can I ever trust her—trust him—again? Am I that inadequate and unlovable? Was it my fault that he wanted other women? Was it my fault that she wanted other men?

The closeness, or seeming closeness, of the marital relationship can add to the anguish.

"My husband was my best friend," Dorrie says, "and I needed my best friend to hold me while I wept in his arms about having been betrayed. Except that my husband was also the one who betrayed me."

"Every affair," writes Professor Lawson, "even the one-night stand, is a relationship of some sort." Even the one-night stand is adultery, though most married people say they would make a distinction between a "meaningless" brief encounter and a serious affair in which the lover is loved more than the husband or wife. But despite what they say, infidelity, including a "casual" fling, is usually deeply disturbing to the cheated-upon because it means that something important is lost and gone, perhaps forever, from the marriage. What is lost and gone, Lawson says, is "a deep knowledge of the other and a profound trust that what one knows is reliable." It's a big loss.

This loss can end the marriage. It can permanently debase and diminish the marriage. But it can sometimes—painful as it may feel and obnoxious as these words are sure to sound—serve as a spur to creative growth in the marriage.

Indeed, psychoanalyst Henry Dicks dares to use the phrase "*benign* infidelity" to describe a "self-healing, even a necessary crisis in the growth process" of a couple. Dicks says there are some situations in which a spouse's infidelity is "a last desperate attempt to get blood out of a stone," a desperate attempt by the "erring" partner to provoke the "injured" partner into seeing him or her in a new light. This wish to revive the relationship via adultery, says Dicks, may explain "why the unfaithful spouse . . . so often succeeds in letting the partner into the secret." Although Dicks is well aware that such "searing experiences . . . are always potentially tragic," there are also happy endings, he notes, with some husbands and wives eventually able to say: "We have been much closer since that awful time."

But first there has to be a decision to stay. On the part of the wife or the husband who has strayed. And on the part of the partner who's been betrayed, who may be struggling with some tormenting images.

> Yes, I am going to stay.
> And we will see
> If I can stop picturing Henry
> Holding a rose-scented woman.
> Kissing a rose-scented woman.
> Touching a rose-scented woman.
> Doing all those things with her he once did just with me.

Maybe she can't stop picturing Henry holding a rose-scented woman, but she *can* stop reproaching him for having done it. As one therapist notes, "She can't take him back like a bad child or a pariah or a whipped dog," because sooner rather than later he will start to feel he has paid in full for his sins. And then he will start to wonder why he's living with an unforgiving wife when he could be making love to a rose-scented woman.

A question this therapist asks the husbands and wives who come for counseling after one of them has had an affair is "Where do you feel most like yourself?" Some say they feel most like themselves in the marriage. She also asks them, "What is your primary goal—what do you want more than anything else?" Some say their primary goal is to save the marriage. But saving the marriage, when it means welcoming back an adulterous spouse to one's heart and one's bed, may also mean having

> ... to choose between
> Keeping my pride, and Henry.
> Between making him pay
> And making my peace with Henry. . . .
> Between trying to live without him for the rest of my life—
> For the rest of my life—
> And Henry.

It may often mean having to say what we once believed we could never say:

> I am going to stay
> With my husband Henry.
> And that is against all my principles.

If the partner who has had an affair wants to remain in the marriage, he or she must make some choices too, picking the marriage partner and the marriage itself—that third thing—over what may be, or may seem to be, something far more romantic, stirring, and passionate. Fidelity may mean that sex will never again be so hot. It certainly puts an end to the fulfillment, in the flesh, of illicit yearnings. It requires the recognition that being faithful isn't in the lap of the gods but a decision that is always ours to make. And it often requires making that decision not just once but over and over again.

Some married people, some husbands and wives who have never been unfaithful, have had to decide to stay faithful over and over again, have had to remind themselves—in the face of powerful temptation—why it is important to resist it.

Says a woman married for twenty-four years, "What's tempting is being seen with fresh eyes by a man who's never seen you in ratty underwear, who's never seen you holding a barfing child. But whenever I ask, 'Could this possibly be worth it?' the answer is 'No.'" It's no, she says, because "I still believe in one true love, a love to keep forever, a lifetime commitment. And if I were to be unfaithful, the way I define myself would be shattered. I'd be giving up the core notion of myself."

In contrast to this highly romantic antiadultery argument is another woman's highly pragmatic view of the downside of extramarital dalliances. "Either I'd fall in love and then it would be a big drama and torment because I'd never leave my husband and my kids, or I wouldn't be in love and I'd be risking my marriage, my family, my whole life, for some sexual thrills, some adventure, some admiration." And if, despite her intentions, she fell so passionately in love that she'd leave her husband and children for a lover, "I know that the sex would simmer down, and so would the excitement, and then we'd be stuck with all those annoying quirks people have—his and mine—that we'd have to get used to."

Having played out these various scenarios in her head, she concludes that, for her, "unfaithful isn't worth it."

Newly married Maryanne says this: "There is a guy at work who is devastatingly attractive . . . and I know the feeling is mutual. Once there, for a moment, I was really tempted and then decided, no. If I did succumb, there would be that loss of innocence. Once it's done, it's like you put your finger in the cake, and it's not going to look the same anymore, or feel the same either."

A man married seven years offers his reasons for refraining from adultery: "It's the deal. It's the commitment. Once you step out of that commitment, once you direct your energy somewhere else, the marriage is over."

A man married sixteen years, who says that he's still "profoundly ashamed" of a one-night stand he engaged in more than a decade ago, is committed to fidelity because being together sexually, he believes, "is the most intimate relationship a person can have with another human being. It so belongs to the two of you that if you betray it, what do you have left?"

And a man married thirty-nine years sent an e-mail explaining to me why he has remained faithful throughout his marriage. "My own experience demonstrates that Jimmy Carter was right about the ubiquitous presence of lust in the heart. But my experience also demonstrates that lust is only one aspect, and a necessary but far from exclusive aspect, of sex, of love, of a surpassing reach for intimacy. For all of these qualities, fidelity is the condition, the instrument, the means of access. Fidelity enables each partner to come before the other and offer as well as expect a full, voluntary surrender. Fidelity is the sweetest thing."

And a difficult thing.

"The man who resides in a large urban area and who never once, during thirty or more years of married life, is sorely tempted to engage in adultery," writes psychologist Havelock Ellis, " . . . is to be suspected of being indeed biologically and/or psychologically abnormal." Monogamy "is not natural" and "not easy" for either men *or* women, say psychology professor David Barash and psychiatrist Judith Lipton in *The Myth of Monogamy*. And the authors of *The Good Marriage* maintain that "the desire to have an affair is part of the human condition. . . . At one time or another, everyone imagines having sex with a stranger, covets the lusty neighbor down the street, or daydreams about going to bed with . . ." (pick your favorite sex object).

While most of us married people have indulged in some adulterous yearnings and fantasies, have had lust in our heart and some porno flicks in our head, we also believe that infidelity injures the marriage—and may also injure the self. As Adam Phillips notes in his book *Monogamy*, "The opposite of monogamy is not just promiscuity, but the absence or the impossibility of relationship itself. Indeed, one reason monogamy is so important to us is that . . . we fear . . . if we don't choose monogamy, our fate will be isolation or the chaos of impersonality." Or, as Barash and Lipton suggest, "perhaps monogamy is like Winston Churchill's description of democracy: the worst possible system, except when you consider the alternatives."

The alternatives—with their promise of passion, intimacy, romance, joy, the love of a lifetime—may seem, at times, impossible to resist. But the alternatives—with their burden of betrayal and their capacity to inflict enormous pain—may also carry the risk of dismantling something that is precious and irreplaceable.

What's a grown-up to do?

The grown-up solution might be to enjoy our fantasies, stay out of other beds, and invest ourselves in the person we have married, that very same person with whom we discuss the children, the Visa bill, and roof repairs. A grown-up solution might be to put our best into our marriage, a best that might even include weaving daisies in and out of each other's pubic hair. With rue our hearts may be laden and our eyes may burn with tears as we turn away from a possibly perfect love while Rachmaninoff's music swells in the background. But in making these difficult choices, we are betting that we will gain more than we lose when we choose, and choose, and choose to forsake all others.

CHAPTER EIGHT

Making War, Making Up, Making Do

The law says you and I belong to each other, George.
The law says you are mine and I am yours, George.
And there are a million miles of white snow-storms, a
*   million furnaces of hell,*
Between the chair where you sit and the chair where I sit.

—Carl Sandburg,
"Two Strangers Breakfast"

IT'S HARD TO BELIEVE:

That the very same two bodies that only recently were passionately intertwined are holding themselves apart from each other as if there were a million miles between them.

Poor Georgie-Porgie, put-upon pie . . . what are you doing? Are you sulking? . . . Is that what you're doing?

That the very same two souls that only recently were in accord have turned into strangers with irreconcilable differences.

It's your smugness that is really intolerable. Your stupidity I don't mind. Your sexlessness I've learned to live with. But that wonderfully smug . . . it really does gall.

That the very same two people who only recently traded endearments are speaking to each other in monosyllables or between clenched teeth, or hurling words intended to humiliate or flagellate or annihilate.

> MARTHA: I can't even see you. . . . I mean, you're a blank,
>   a cipher . . . a zero . . .
> GEORGE: *Monstre!*
> MARTHA: *Cochon!*
> GEORGE: *Bête!*
> MARTHA: *Canaille!*
> GEORGE: *Putain!*

(And it's hard to believe that George and Martha are calling each other, in French, "monster" and "pig" and "beast" and "trash" and "whore.")

Yet hard as it is to believe, it seems painfully clear that we married couples can make war every bit as fiercely as we make love, that we can *hate* as fiercely as we can love, and that we can, nonetheless—unless, of course, we decide to divorce—manage to work out a way of living together.

"He who is not arguing," according to St. Jerome, "is not married." "Quarrels are the dowry," Ovid tells us, "which married folk bring one another." And Nietzsche says, "If married couples did not live together, happy marriages would be more frequent."

Most married couples, of course, tend to live together. And in living together we press our views and needs and demands and wills upon each other. We limit and intrude upon each other. We encounter, day in and day out, each other's weaknesses and failings and inadequacies. Although we may try to endure or ignore some of the things we don't like about each other, we often resent putting up with, don't want to put up with, refuse to put up with all that we have to put up with from each other.

And so we fight. About money, sex, the relatives, the division of chores, the kids, and whether the painting over our couch should or shouldn't be two-and-a-half inches lower. About when to eat and where to live, about what movie to see and whether to sleep with the window open or closed. We fight about you don't listen to me, you don't treat me with respect, you're a slob, you forgot my birthday, you're too controlling. We fight because— despite the love that we had, and still have, for each other—there is so much to fight about.

The Applemans fight because "he lies down on our dreamy, expensive white bedspread with his shoes on, and then when I beg him to take off his shoes, he says I care more about things than I do about him."

The Phillipses fight because "he goes over every penny I spend and thinks he's entitled to scold me, like a parent scolding a child, for buying a plant that cost $19.95."

The Conroys fight when he wants to make love and she turns him down, adding sweetly, "Why don't you call up that editor with the big boobs you spent the entire evening salivating over?"

The Glicks fight because "she asks me—no, she tells me—to do these chores, and after I do them, she tells me I've done them wrong."

The Kaminskys fight because "we're both oversensitive, immature, and dramatic, and he feels I put my friends first at times, and he's probably right. Then he uses the silent treatment and sleeps in another room, and I go nuts and get mean and tell him everything I've always hated about him and that this marriage is over, and he says okay, he's out of here, and after a while something shifts and we bond again."

The Emersons fight when her mother is being intrusive, "which," he says, "her mother has been for the past twenty-six years."

The Zimmermans fight when "I don't give him enough 'I'm happy to see you!' and 'Aren't you smart!' and 'Don't you look cute today!'"

The Meyers fight when she's worried about the children or her job or "maybe some health thing" and she tries to discuss it with him and instead of listening sympathetically and offering her comfort, which she really doesn't think is a lot to ask, he tells her she worries too much and should just stop panicking and calm down, which always makes her, she says, want to kill him.

"Most loving couples begin their relationship with a stern resolution to honor and respect," writes psychiatrist Leston Havens. "And yet they have hardly left the church before the slowness of one or the haste of the other, the disappointment of one expectation or the unwanted fulfillment of another, reveals the snarling beast."

Our fights may be as brutal as the blood sport Martha and Georgie-Porgie engage in, in Edward Albee's *Who's Afraid of Virginia Woolf?* Or we may eschew raised voices and vicious invective and rely on icy prosecutorial skills. Those of us who are more repressed or more tactful or maybe more civilized may, instead of hollering, point out, and point out, and helpfully keep pointing out, the error of our wife's—or husband's—ways. And some of us may opt for tears or guilt-inducing reproaches or

My mother's technique,

Which is silence for a week,

A brooding stare into the ruined future,

And no rouge for that look of

You are making me so miserable you are giving me

A fatal illness.

There are husbands and wives who hate confrontation, who brood instead of fight. There are couples, "avoidant couples" in psychologist Gottman's language, who prefer to sweep disagreement under the rug. There are couples who won't fight because he can't stand her tears or because she fears his rages. There also are couples who say and do the most terrible things to each other while insisting that they've never had a fight. The rest of us fight.

Indeed, some wives and husbands fight all the time and everywhere and over everything, counting on the excitement of warfare to keep them connected, to keep their marriage vibrant, or perhaps to keep them from noticing the yawning emptiness that lies beneath. Or they fight when they get too close, because closeness scares them. Or they fight because, like George and Martha, when he cries out to her, "I CANNOT STAND IT!" she replies, "YOU CAN STAND IT! YOU MARRIED ME FOR IT!" Or they fight, if they are the couples that Gottman labels "volatile couples," because their constant "volcanic arguments are just a small part of an otherwise warm and loving marriage. The passion and relish with which they fight," says Gottman, "seem to fuel their positive interactions even more."

Even those of us who have less need or relish for fighting may still have plenty of fights. And we don't only fight over issues that directly affect our personal sense of well-being. We fight over issues that, even though they don't affect us directly, we deplore. We deplore the fact that he's such a stingy tipper and that she always votes Republican. That she often speaks brusquely to salesclerks and that his belt invariably fails to match his shoes. That she can't meet anyone new without letting them know she volunteers once a week at a soup kitchen. That he can't meet anyone new without letting them know he is a graduate of Harvard. We deplore his or her insufficiencies of character, manners, or taste, and unless we are willing to do our deploring in silence, we criticize, we complain, and we engage in provocative, end-of-the-evening postmortems:

> On the way home with my husband from the dinner party,
> I thought I'd very tactfully point out
> That he shouldn't interrupt, and that
> He shouldn't talk with his hands, and that
> He shouldn't, when discussing politics, shout.
> And that he shouldn't tell that story while people are eating,
>   and that
> He shouldn't tell that joke for the rest of of his life, and that
> He shouldn't have said what he said about that terrible lady in
>   red because
> She happens to be the-person-he-said-it-to's wife.
> And that he didn't need that second helping of mousse cake,
>   and that
> He didn't need to finish the Chardonnay....

All the above, we'd all agree, are reasonable grounds for criticism and complaint, which in turn will often bestir the criticized and complained-to person to counterattack, which in turn, more often than not, is going to lead to escalation and conflagration. Even though the poem concludes that after many years of marriage

> I finally understand what not to say
> On my way home with my husband from a dinner party,

too many of us—wives and husbands—say it anyway. And then we fight.

———————

We find ourselves fighting the same old fights as decade follows decade because he won't give up and she won't give up and neither one will give in and each still hopes the other will eventually be persuaded to see the light. And we find ourselves fighting some brand-new fights as decade follows decade because time brings changes, life brings changes, he changes and she changes, the marriage changes, and the former compromises and adaptations and arrangements just don't work anymore.

Some marital fights are urgently important. Other fights are utterly absurd. Some serve a purpose. Others are a waste. Although there are probably fights that cannot and should not be avoided, it might be useful to ask ourselves, before we launch an attack—or before we respond to one—"Is this fight necessary?" By "necessary" I mean: Will this fight resolve a current problem, prevent a future one, or serve as a badly needed emotional outlet? Or will we both just wind up feeling bruised? Sometimes—not always, but sometimes—having decided a fight can't do anything but damage, we might persuade ourselves to desist or abstain.

On the other hand, when we fight (whether or not the fight is necessary), we might want to hew to certain rules of engagement, rules that my married friends and I have figured out over the years, rules that we practice less often than we preach, rules that— when we practice them—seem to help us fight in cleaner, more constructive, more grown-up ways. Here are the basics:

- We shouldn't ever irretrievably lose it. In addition to refraining from physical violence, intimidation, or coercion, we need to forget that old nursery rhyme, because words *can* be as harmful as sticks and stones, battering the heart and soul, inflicting damage that may never heal. No matter how brutal the battle, how snarling the beast, how right we are, how wrong our spouse is, how impelled and entitled we feel to smash and destroy, all of us have the capacity to choose to exert some restraint, to choose to control ourselves. Or as a woman I know once very crudely and colorfully put it, "No matter how badly you have to go, you wouldn't defecate on the living-room rug."

- We should keep in mind that we probably won't always feel the way we currently are feeling. One of the reasons we shouldn't say things like "I hate you, you disgust me, I don't love you, I never loved you, I wish you were dead"—yes, some of the nicest people say such things—is because these negative feelings are often fleeting. Although we can't, in the midst of a fight, imagine why we married such a rejecting, demanding, selfish, insensitive, critical, domineering, withholding person, chances are that we'll think of a reason later.

- Much as we'd love to evade it, we need to accept responsibility when we're responsible. This isn't what Wally was doing when he blamed his tension and subsequent defeat in the Shadybrook Tennis and Swimming Club tennis finals on Jennifer's refusal to make love that morning.

- We shouldn't practice psychiatry without a license. This is what Shari was doing when she informed her husband, Paul, who had promised to show up at three and showed up at four, that he was unconsciously seeing her as the feared and hated mother of his childhood and making her pay for his mother's rejection of him. (On second thought, we shouldn't practice psychiatry on our spouse even if we do, in fact, have a license.)

- If possible, we should try to laugh about it. While it's outrageous and irresponsible that he drove straight home from work, completely forgetting to pick up our daughter at day care, maybe we could also find it funny. Well, maybe not.

- We shouldn't wait too long before saying what's bothering us. We need to consider the story of the genie in the bottle who, during his first thousand years of incarceration, thinks, "Whoever lets me out will get three wishes," and who, during his second thousand years of incarceration, thinks, "Whoever lets me out I'm gonna kill." Many of us, like that genie, seem to get meaner and more dangerous the longer our grievances are bottled up.

- We ought to know in advance what we want from the fight. Rebecca says that her idea of a clean and constructive fight is delivery of the following crystal-clear message: "I'm upset; here's why I'm upset; here's what I want"—though it may take her time to figure out what she wants. Recently, for instance, while she was fighting with her husband about his working late at the office again, it suddenly occurred to her that she didn't want him to say, "Okay, I'll stop working late—to hell with my deadline." All she really wanted was for him to say to her, "I miss you. I miss the baby. I feel terrible about not being home at night. And you're such a fabulous person for being able to handle everything while I'm gone." She got what she wanted.

• We need to beware of reproaching our spouse with "If you really loved me . . ." She could love him and still forget to mail the tax return he stayed up all night preparing. He could love her and still not figure out exactly what she wanted for her birthday. There are many battles that escalate because what we're really fighting about, what's really getting us so angry and hurt, is the conviction that if our wife really loved us she'd surely have remembered to mail the tax return, that if our husband really loved us he'd surely have been able to read our mind.

• It's best to stick to the point. If we're having a fight because he criticized us in front of our friends at the party last night, it will not advance our argument if we mention, at the same time, that he's overdrawn at the bank and talks with his mouth full.

• It's best to stick to the present. A sense of history is a wonderful thing. Total recall is certainly impressive. Memory and the long, long view surely contribute to the richness of life. But reaching back in time for marital crimes committed many years ago, when we're fighting about a crime committed two minutes ago, contributes—I speak from experience—only trouble.

Before I became a more mature marital fighter, I displayed, in my fights with my husband, an astounding capacity for total recall, providing him with what I rather smugly liked to call "a sense of perspective" as I cited the nature and date of every one of his former transgressions, going all the way back to our engagement party. After a couple of decades of this, however, it slowly began to dawn on me that my husband's reply to these historical references was never "Hey, thanks for pointing out that destructive pattern of mine; I sure do appreciate it." Instead, he replied with "Bookkeeper! Scorekeeper!" and other far less charming epithets, and the fighting always deteriorated from there. I now follow, and strongly recommend, the statute of limitations that Candy and Mort have successfully established: "No matter how perfectly something proves your point, you can't dredge it up if it's more than six months old."

· We're never allowed to attack an Achilles' heel. If our husband has confessed to us that, during his high-school years, his cruel classmates nicknamed him The Hairy Ape, and if, in adulthood, he still has fears about being furrier than most, we can—when we are furious—call him many names but we can't call him that one. I talked to a woman who (excuse the mixed metaphor) locates her Achilles' heel "in my fat butt, which I always worry about and which my husband has always assured me he loves." She says that if, in the course of a fight, he told her that he'd never liked her butt, she might never forgive him.

- It's counterproductive to overstate our injuries. While it's tempting to score a few points in the middle of a fight by moaning, "Get me my pills—the pain is blinding," it isn't a good idea to claim that he's giving us a migraine unless he is. And while it may also be tempting to show him how beastly he's being by bursting into tears, we should try to stay dry. Overstating our injuries is not just dirty fighting; it is, sooner than can be imagined, ineffective. If we want to make him believe that he's gone too far when he's gone to far, we've got to try to maintain our credibility.

- It's counterproductive to overstate our threats. Many wives and husbands, during the course of a fight, make threats they don't mean. Like, "If you don't slow down, I'm getting out and walking." Or "If you keep doing that, I'm getting divorced." Like overstatements of injury, these threats—if we're called on them and we don't follow through—will significantly damage our credibility. And if to save face, we do follow through, we might wind up walking down a lonely highway or ending a marriage that maybe could have been saved.

- Tempting though it may be, we should not cite authority. Telling a husband that every single human being we know agrees he is wrong will not persuade him that he is wrong. Citing a dozen articles that demonstrate the correctness of our view will not persuade a wife of our view's correctness. I don't know why husbands and wives keep on doing or saying what they're doing or saying in the face of overwhelming proof that they shouldn't. But I do know that citing authority will probably prompt them to do it or say it more stubbornly.

- We can't just talk; we also have to listen. We needn't go along with a single word that our husband says, but we need to keep our mouth shut and let him say it. We may have already grasped and rejected the point that our wife is making, but we must hear her out. As a husband (and lawyer) once announced to his wife in the midst of a fight: "You can disagree with what I say as long as you can repeat my views to *my* satisfaction."

- We must respect the feelings as well as the facts. We're not allowed to say, when our husband tells us he's feeling ignored, "You can't possibly feel that way." We're not allowed to say, when our wife complains that she's feeling put down, "That's absurd." We may argue that perhaps he is oversensitive or perhaps she is misinterpreting, but we always have to acknowledge how he or she feels.

- We can sometimes simply agree to disagree. Although it took us a while, my husband and I finally figured out that we no longer have to agree on all matters of taste. He is entitled to hate a movie I love. I am allowed to be bored by a book he calls "spellbinding." We each can have our own point of view without a scornful "You *liked* that? How can any intelligent person *like* that?" We each can express that point of view without needing to beat the other over the head, trying to get agreement that our view is right.

- When we've finished fighting, we shouldn't continue sniping. Having agreed, after much dispute, to attend the dinner party, we shouldn't sulkily add, "Okay, I said I'd go but I didn't say I'd enjoy it." Nor should we be gazing bleakly into the middle distance because, as we explain when asked what's

wrong, "I guess my wounds don't heal as quickly as yours do."
- There needn't be a winner and a loser. We both could agree to compromise. We both could agree to try harder. We both could agree that both of us were at fault. It's possible to lose without regarding it as a devastating defeat. And it's possible to win—this takes a lot of class, however—without rubbing it in and treating it as a huge victory.

While it's all very nice to agree that there doesn't need to be a winner and a loser, it's nonetheless difficult not to wish to win. Winning means getting through to our spouse and having our needs respected and acknowledged. Winning means getting our partner to do what we want. Winning can also mean—lots of luck!—getting our partner to change, which means that he or she *wants* to do what we want. And winning often means, when we are clearly correct or when we're the injured party, that our wife or husband owes us an apology.

Losing, on the other hand, may mean that we owe our husband or wife an apology.

An apology is often required before we can stop making war and start making up. The apologizers need to admit that they have inflicted injury; those apologized to need to hear that they have been wronged. The giving and receiving of an apology, however, can create as many problems as the problem that caused the war that the apology is intended to put an end to.

Apology problems often begin with a harsh and heated discussion about whether an apology is called for and, if one is called for, who owes one to whom. In other words, did he or didn't he speak very curtly to you at the Beckers' last evening? And was this or wasn't this due to the fact that you kept interrupting him the entire evening? There are at least six different ways to think about this matter; half put him in the wrong, half put you in the wrong, and none is a draw.

"You're out of your mind—I didn't speak to you curtly."

"You're imagining things—I didn't interrupt you."

"I only spoke curtly because you interrupted."

"I only interrupted because you were curt."

"Just because I spoke to you once in a way that, believe me, no one but you would call curt, doesn't give you the right to interrupt me."

"Just because I once interrupted—and tell me how else I could get a word in edgewise—doesn't give you the right to speak to me curtly."

This isn't the ideal way to pursue an apology.

We're most likely to get an apology if we're willing to concede that what we're fighting about may be partly our fault. It's rare that a marital argument involves one total sinner, one perfect saint. But even when there is an absolutely-no-doubt-about-it injured party and an injurer no judge in the land would acquit, it doesn't always follow that the injurer will own up to the crime. In fact, there are many people (their spouses tell me) who have never, not once, in their married life apologized, not because they don't believe in apologies but because it just so happens they're never wrong.

"How did I get so lucky?" the wife of one of these paragons gloomily inquired. "What did I do to deserve being married to someone who's always been right for seventeen years?"

In other marriages, husbands and wives may be willing to say they're sorry, but it may take them time to notice that "sorry" is called for. There's Lou, for instance, a man who is often oblivious to his surroundings, a man who can totally tune out family life. So even though his wife, Aileen, may stomp around the house, even though she may stop speaking to him entirely, it could be forty-eight hours or more before he begins to suspect that she is at war with him. Once, Aileen says, after days of acting hostile and sullen and cold, she glared at him and declaimed, "You have now lost a friend." Lou, completely confused by her words and utterly missing the point, looked wildly around the room and asked her, "Who?"

But most of us, at least some of the time, are aware when we've done wrong and when we ought to offer an apology. So why do we, a great deal of the time, find it so hard to freely admit we've been wrong, find it so hard to simply say, "I'm sorry"?

Perhaps we fear that saying "I'm wrong" will set, as one husband put it, "a dangerous precedent." (As in "If I apologize, she'll expect an apology *every time* I'm wrong.")

Perhaps we fear it will lead to a loss of authority from which we'll never recover. (As in "You admitted to being wrong about that. Why should I assume you're right about this?")

Perhaps we're convinced that our spouse will see our apology as a weakness to be exploited. (As in "Since you're apologizing, I think you should let me get the kitchen painted and cancel our trip to your sister's place next weekend.")

Or perhaps we're tired of being the only person in the marriage who ever apologizes.

We might find it hard to apologize if we're going through a phase when it seems to us that we cannot get anything right. We arrive too late at the movies. We misplace an important file. We overcook the roast. We bang up the car. So when, quite accidentally, we use up the last of the milk in our morning coffee, forcing our husband to drink his coffee black, we can't face admitting we've screwed up yet again.

Instead, we take a very defensive position: "Now how am I supposed to know that you object to drinking your coffee black?"

And he comes back with a very offensive reply: "I figure that even a dimwit like you should know after twenty-two years how I drink my coffee."

Sometimes an apology on one specific issue will encourage a spouse to generalize from the particular. When Doug, for instance, says he's sorry for not taking time to go to the doctor with Myra, Myra says she'll be grateful if he manages to find time to go to her funeral. This tends to quash future impulses to apologize.

In addition to the above, we will certainly hesitate to apologize if we fear that the apology we're offering will be anything less than wholeheartedly received.

All of us, when we apologize, want a full and loving forgiveness, and we also want to get it right away. But sometimes we must settle for less, and sometimes we have to be patient while the wife we've called "smug" and "sexless" or the husband we've called "a zero," "a cipher," "a blank" decides if and when she or he will let us retract it. "Come over here and give me a kiss and show me I'm forgiven," we may lovingly say to our wounded, dumped-upon mate. "I'll come over there and give you a kiss and show you you're forgiven," that mate may answer, "tomorrow."

Sometimes, in an effort to let it be known that we're really sorry without losing face, we'll offer an apology nonverbally, by bringing home an unexpected present, by being uncharacteristically nice to our in-laws, by becoming—like one grumpy husband I know—so unnervingly attentive and solicitous that he almost drove his wife out of her mind.

A lot of nonverbal apologies take place in the double bed, and I'm not talking now about sex, although that's nice too. I'm talking about those subtle, low-key gestures of contrition, like her sliding over and bumping his hip with her bottom, like him stretching out his foot and brushing her ankle, like me throwing my arm across Milton's back to straighten out the blankets and then just leaving it there. (King-size beds, I would like to note, aren't as good to make up in because there is far too much space. We could easily sleep there all night, stretching and sliding and twisting and turning, and never make contact.)

Most of us, both husbands and wives, accept a fair number of these wordless apologies. But we do need a verbal "I'm sorry" now and then, sometimes only a little one, sometimes a somewhat bigger one, sometimes nothing less than total abasement. And when the "I'm sorry" we give or receive is smaller than the "I'm sorry" that is desired, we are probably going to have apology problems.

We certainly can agree that the small apologies have to do with arriving late and that the large apologies have to do with adultery and that the medium apologies are going to lie somewhere between. This tends to be truer in theory than in practice, however, because one person's minor offense is another's all-out assault on human dignity, turning an unmade phone call into a crime that demands an "I'm sorry" on bended knee.

And sometimes "I'm sorry" on bended knee is what we ought to have, and anything less quite justly leaves us unsatisfied. Take the example of the suitcase on top of the car.

Donna told Randy to tie it onto the roof rack.

Randy said it was safe and wouldn't fall off.

Donna said that her favorite clothes were packed inside that suitcase.

Don't worry, Randy said. It won't fall off.

Donna said that even though he was swearing it wouldn't fall off, could he please just be a darling and tie on the suitcase?

Randy said he wouldn't.

The suitcase fell off.

Now let it be understood that Randy apologized. He urged her to go to a store and replace what she'd lost. Then he said that further discussion would serve no useful purpose. The discussion, he announced to Donna, was closed.

Not for Donna it wasn't. She wanted . . . what did she want? She wanted some groveling. Some suicidal remorse. Some tearing of hair. She wanted some time to reproach him while he writhed with shame and guilt and regret and embarrassment. She wanted a bigger, a much much bigger, apology.

Sometimes what's wanted is a *slower* apology. "I don't want to hear so quickly that you're sorry," one young husband told his wife, who'd apparently failed to sufficiently ponder the wrong she had done. "I don't want to hear so quickly you're sorry that you did it. I want to hear that you understand why you did it."

In addition to too small or too fast, there are various other unsatisfying apologies, mostly variations on "I'm sorry, but . . ." Like "I don't take back what I said but I'm sorry I said it." Or "I'm sorry I said it in such an unpleasant tone." Or "I'm not really sorry for anything, and it's actually all your fault, but being a very big person, I'll apologize." Or "I'm going to say I'm sorry because you want me to say I'm sorry but I think you should see a psychiatrist about your neurotic need to be right all the time."

As a friend of mine says, "There's admitting, and then there's *admitting.*"

And then there's the time I told Milton, at the end of a long self-justifying speech, "I didn't just want to apologize. I wanted to make myself clear." To which my husband briskly and briefly replied, "You're A-plus on clear. You just flunked apologize."

It's important to keep in mind that a lot of the time, when it's time to apologize, it's better not to try to make ourselves clear. Instead, we could end some fights by simply deciding to call a truce—and to hell with who's right. We could also do what Milton and I have been doing more and more as we get older: Reach out a hand and say to each other, "Life is short. We have no days to spare. Let's make up."

Some of our fights and apologies strike us as amusing—but mostly in retrospect. We're rarely entertained when we're making war or making up, no matter how dopey our battles may seem later on. And as for those life-and-death fights that sometimes jeopardize a marriage, they can be, as all of us know, no laughing matter, especially if we've forgotten—as, alas, we will sometimes forget—that we shouldn't ever irretrievably lose it, that we're never allowed to attack an Achilles' heel, and all those other civilized rules of engagement.

Some of the fights we engage in will never be a laughing matter. And sometimes we'll feel, while we're fighting over whatever we're fighting over, an encompassing alienation from all things marital, resenting the shit we must take and the massive effort we have to make to keep our marriage afloat. Sometimes, while we're at each other so bitterly, so brutally, with tones of such coldness, such harshness, such contempt, we'll be grimly aware that when it comes to inflicting heavy damage, nobody does it better than one's own spouse. And sometimes, if the damage inflicted is especially heavy, an apology will be just a bunch of words, empty words and gestures that can't even begin to repair the harm that's been done. Sometimes we cannot move from the dark, awful place where our battle has left us unless there is an offer of reparation.

Reparation is not a piece of jewelry a straying husband presents to his wife after she has discovered his infidelity. It is not a conciliatory back rub a woman provides to her husband after she has trashed him in front of his friends. It's a bone-deep recognition and a sorrowful admission of having caused pain, accompanied by a promise—to our spouse or maybe only to ourselves—that we will do better, that we'll at least *try* to do better. It's saying, or conveying, "I love you. I don't ever want to hurt you again. Please forgive me."

Most of the time we'll forgive each other, hurt each other again, and again forgive each other, sometimes with and sometimes without reparation. Most of the time, even after we've done the worst we can do to each other, we'll somehow survive.

"We would rage at each other late into the night, on a battlefield littered with smashed crystal and swirling with cigarette smoke and the fumes of alcohol," says Lydia's husband, Alexander Cleave, "and wake in the ashen light of morning, a salt bitterness in our mouths and our throats raw from drink and shouting, and reach out a hand to each other, tremblingly, under the sheets, not daring to move our heads, and one would make a shaky enquiry and the other would croak some hoarse word of reassurance, and then we would lie there, counting our wounds, surprised that the war was done for another day and we were still breathing."

After the war is over (for now) and after (for now) we've made up, we are left with the reality that not all of our disputes have a resolution. After the talking, the screaming, the weeping, the verbal knife to the heart, the sulks, the big chill, after apologies grudging or sincere, we are left with the reality that some of our troubling differences cannot be fixed.

Indeed, we could thoroughly document all that we don't and will never, ever, agree on, bitching and moaning and sighing and groaning about how he won't, she can't, he insists, she refuses. We could make a compelling case for how much better our marriage would be if only he, if only she, would change. We could count the scars and betrayals, the failures of loyalty and love, that conspire to make our spouse our adversary. We could keep meticulous score and prove that we're almost always right and often wronged.

We could look, with a heavy sigh, at all our irreconcilable differences and hate that we're stuck with them for the rest of our lives. We could look at them and resignedly, resentfully, say to ourselves, "That's how it is."

And sometimes, resigned and resentful, that's what we say.

But at other times—maybe more and more as we gradually grow up and into our marriage—we might focus on our shared pleasures and common connections. We might let the emphasis fall on what is right, not what is wrong, about our relationship, remembering what we find so hard to remember while we are fighting—why we married each other. We might look, with a rueful sigh, at all the differences between us and know we must figure out how we're going to live with them. We might look at them and say to ourselves, indulgently, bemusedly, even tenderly, "That's how it is."

CHAPTER NINE

The Divorce Option

"Every Day a Little Death"

—Stephen Sondheim,
A Little Night Music

*"You're such a nice woman. . . . I can't understand why
I'm so miserable with you."*

—John Updike, *Too Far to Go*

*"You could kill him or . . . there's always the divorce
option."*

—advice from a friend

IT'S SO HARD TO BE MARRIED. It's so damn much
work. There's so much—choose one or more or all of the following—pain, rage, disillusionment, betrayal, bitterness, sacrifice,
loneliness, boredom, contempt, despair, disconnection. This isn't
the person I married, or this isn't the person I want to be married
to now, or I can't be who I want to be in this relationship. Could I
leave you? Should I leave you? How do we decide how much
blood and sweat and tears we owe to our marriage?

At many stages of married life, and for many different reasons, we may find ourselves considering divorce. That time may

be in the early years, when getting to know each other has started us wondering whether we've made the wrong choice. Or it may be after the children are born, when the pressures of work and demands of family life leave us with too little left to give to each other. Or it may be middle age, when we begin to feel a yearning to feel something we're not feeling in our marriage. Or it may be late in life, when aging, illness, the looming prospect of our own death prompt us to start asking ourselves, Do I want to spend my last precious years with this person?

That time may be when we recognize that we hate each other, or love somebody else, or are two nice people who make each other miserable.

That time may be when we can't face another day of large-scale battles—or little deaths.

Although "that's how it is" can be the way some husbands and wives make peace with their marriage, others recoil, resist, and consider divorce. And although married people consider divorce more often—far more often—than they do it, the "divorce option" pushes many of us to the brink. What brings us there is the feeling, on the part of one or both partners, that continuing together is intolerable. What brings us there, and what catapults some of us over, may be a single defining event or that last little death that is one little death too many.

Some of the women and men who divorce, or are thinking about divorce, do so because they've been hit with a marital bombshell: Adultery. Violence. Drugs. He's gay. She's become a religious fanatic. He's Tony Soprano. Some contemplate leaving because they have discovered their one true love, and it isn't their spouse. But most of the husbands and wives who come early or late to the brink of divorce are there because what is broken now feels irreparable, because living apart seems better than trying to live any longer with what they've been living with.

One woman who constantly thinks of divorce speaks of her husband's eviscerating rages, of his "anything can set him off" verbal abuse, of his "talking to me, not just privately but sometimes publicly too, in ways that most people wouldn't talk to an *animal.*" Another speaks of a physical coldness and absence of intimacy that increasingly makes alone look less lonely than married. Still another speaks of a husband "who's nice to me only when we do what he wants, and who's very unpleasant when things aren't going his way." And others speak of husbands who are rigid, perfectionistic, or so controlling that "he insists on knowing exactly where I'm going and exactly when I'll be back. And I can't say 'I'm going on errands' and 'I'll be back in the late afternoon'—I have to say 'Bloomingdale's,' 'Safeway,' and 'four-fifteen.'"

She adds, "I don't think I can do this anymore."

There are, of course, plenty of husbands who also believe they cannot do this anymore. Because "My wife doesn't need a husband. She needs someone to pay the bills while she raises the kids, sees her girlfriends, and works out." Because "No one is ever going to measure up to her perfect dad, and I'm fed up with trying." Because "I know there are women who think I'm funny and want to have sex with me, but my wife isn't one of them." Because "She's resentful of my success, of the attention I give to my work instead of to her, and that's making her angry at me almost all of the time." Because "She thinks she's too good for me" or is "witheringly disapproving" or "treats me like shit." Because "I'm sick and tired of being unhappy."

Most of these husbands and wives will grant that they've made some contribution to the terminal unhappiness of their marriage, although a few of them—convinced of their virtue and of their spouse's villainy—honestly believe that they bear no blame. Several of them are willing to own up to a failure or two, and some, not a lot, take equal responsibility. All of them, however, feel desperate enough, despairing enough, unhappy enough to consider putting their marriage out of its misery.

Some of the women and men who give serious thought to ending their marriage will confess that they would much prefer death to divorce, but they aren't talking suicide (though this sometimes crosses their mind) and they aren't talking murder (though this sometimes, even often, crosses their mind). Instead, what they are talking about is the premature death of a husband or a wife by means of a fatal accident or illness.

"A nice little plane crash," Sarah says, "would be the perfect solution. No fights over money or custody of the kids. Instead of being a failure at marriage, I would be a valiantly coping widow. And I'd never again have to torture myself about whether I should or shouldn't get divorced."

Many of us have tortured ourselves, plenty, over whether we should or shouldn't get divorced.

On the one hand, it is comforting, in the midst of marital misery, to cheer ourselves with the thought that we can get out. On the other hand, being out of the marriage can sometimes seem even harder than staying in.

So we try to make the case for staying in.

We tell ourselves nobody's perfect, that every marriage has its terrible moments, that only a fool would insist upon some unrealizable dream of marital bliss. We tell ourselves that, despite insufficient love or trust or respect or support or kindness, plenty of couples stay married and make do. We tell ourselves that nothing we want could ever be worth the risk of having to live alone for the rest of our days. We tell ourselves that we can stay married and still have a good life, even if we do not have a good marriage.

Bad as our marriage is, or so we tell ourselves, divorce is even worse.

Meredith, for example, has been putting off her decision to ditch a husband "who sleeps with every woman who walks through our door" because, "when I look out our window and see a homeless person lying in the gutter, I think to myself that that will be me if I leave him."

Jonas dreams of escaping his scolding, hypercritical wife, but he finds himself unable to divorce her because he would rather live in a marriage emptied of all love than live, even part of the time, apart from his children. "I couldn't stand doing that to them," he says. Then he adds, "I couldn't stand doing that to myself."

Lola, whose husband of thirty-five years has been screwing around for half their married life, says she has "very often thought of divorce. But what stops me is that, when I look around, I don't see my divorced friends being very happy. What stops me is the insecurity and the 'dating.' There's nothing especially positive about my spouse," she says, "but"—affairs aside—"nothing negative either. I've got a comfortable lifestyle with my family and my friends, and for the most part he just doesn't bother me anymore."

Then there's Conrad, age eighty-seven, married for sixty-two years and thinking about divorce for the last fifty-two of them. Married to a woman who has bored and annoyed him for most of their life together, he has never been able to leave her because he's a pillar of his community and church and he's always been afraid, he says, "that if I walk out they'll think I'm a terrible person." (I suspect he has also always been afraid of being alone, but he doesn't quite say that.) I cannot use his real name, but he somehow would like the world to know that although he has hung in there he has been miserable. And until his dying day he will doubtless dream of getting divorced—or at least separated.

In contrast, John Updike's Richard and Joan, who've been making each other so miserable, finally do separate. But he wonders, "Can even dying be worse than this? His wife sat crouched on what had been their bed, telling him, between sobs, her state of mind, which was suicidal, depressive, beaten. They had been living apart for a year and a half, and that time had achieved nothing, no scar tissue had formed, her body was a great unhealed wound crying, *Come back.*"

Perhaps it isn't so wrong to decide to come back to or remain in an unhappy marriage because we're causing the person we're leaving such pain, or because we're too scared to be out there on our own, or because divorce is so damaging to the children, or because we like our comfortable lifestyle. Perhaps an unhappy marriage couldn't be worse than "suicidal, depressive, beaten." Perhaps it makes sense just to settle, or to redefine "settle" as "mature acceptance." Perhaps we should grin and bear it: "How do you bear it?" Sally asks Ben in a wrenching moment in Stephen Sondheim's *Follies.* "Me—I read a lot."

We may even start thinking it isn't necessarily delusional to continue to hope that our marriage could get better.

"So I told my husband," says Gail, "that he doesn't listen to me, doesn't know me, doesn't know what I need, doesn't care about what I need, and his answer was 'You got a problem with that?'"

Well, maybe it *is* delusional to continue to hope that our marriage could get better. Maybe it's time to make the case for divorce.

Bruce, who doesn't intend to wait for his marriage to get better, argues this point: "Baseball players don't stay on the same team. Companies don't keep people on forever. So why expect a marriage to be permanent?"

The writer Jane Smiley offers up this turns-the-blood-cold, they-should-have-divorced example: "When the grandfather of a friend of mine died . . . his last words to his wife of fifty years were 'I'm sorry I married you.'"

And the disillusioned Cynthia Heimel—we met her in chapter 1—wants everyone warned: "Marriage is a bloodbath!"

But must our marriage turn into a bloodbath before we're ready to climb out and divorce? How bad must being together become before we know we need to break apart? How many times must we fight and forgive before we no longer can seek or offer forgiveness? How often must we hurt each other before we decide it's too painful and too dangerous to open our heart to our wife or husband again?

Should we, for instance, divorce if the marriage was a mistake from the start, and—fifteen years and two teenagers later—it's still a mistake, a much, much bigger mistake?

"I married," says Meg, "because I didn't have faith in my own ability to be in the world, and because my best friend got married, and because my husband had Yale and other credentials, and because I was afraid that if I didn't marry him I'd miss the boat. But we never should have been married—there were such differences between us, and they just kept getting greater and greater and greater. He wanted me home for him and the kids, not working or going to school. I wanted to go for a doctorate. He forbade it. I was resentful, he was resentful, and our marriage became so cold and so oppressive to me that I gave up eating and started drinking too much. He didn't want a divorce, and I didn't want to hurt my sons, but I saw I was going to get very sick, very sick emotionally and physically, unless I got out."

Should we divorce if, although we married for better or for worse, the worse turned out to be worse than we ever expected?

"My wife was a psychological mess," says Abe, who was married three years, "and at first I tried to help her but I couldn't. She was needy and dependent, and I found that I didn't respect what she did or was. When counseling didn't help either, I decided I had to leave—even though she said if I left she would kill herself. We didn't have any children, and at that point I felt it was either her or me."

Should we divorce if all our children are grown and out of the house and our marriage is not awful but juiceless and joyless?

Says Mel, married twenty-eight years, "I saw couples married longer than us who still talked to each other in restaurants and had fun together, and I thought with a different wife I could have that too."

Honor, married forty years, has a grimmer variation on Mel's theme. "My husband never talked to me. He hardly talked at all. And he certainly never talked about his feelings. As a matter of fact, though it's terrible to say this, I honestly don't think he *had* any feelings." So after the children left home and after twenty fruitless years of therapy and after an especially awful vacation, "where he treated me as if I didn't exist," Honor announced that she wanted a divorce. "I felt," she explains, "that my husband was dead and was trying to drag me into the grave with him." So although "the divorce cost me very dearly financially, I decided I'd rather live with some joy in my life and eat beans every day than continue living with this man any longer."

Meg, Abe, Mel, and Honor ended their marriages. Meredith, Jonas, Lola, and Conrad did not, although they and others still torture themselves as they hover at the brink, wondering whether they should or shouldn't divorce.

—————

I've talked with husbands and wives who deeply believe in staying married, no matter what, but nevertheless decided to divorce. I've talked with husbands and wives who swear they can't live another minute with their spouse's infidelity, insensitivity, coldness, craziness, or criticism, but still remain married. I've talked with husbands and wives who did enough work, when their marriage was threatened, to save the marriage. And I've talked with husbands and wives who, even though they gave it their all, simply could not keep the marriage going.

I'm thinking in particular of the mother of three little girls who said she was fiercely determined to rescue her marriage in spite of some serious difficulties with intimacy and respect, as well as her husband's affair with her best friend. "I promised myself," she told me, "that I would put my two feet in my marriage, that I'd make a deep inner commitment to my marriage, that I'd do whatever hard work I had to do in order to make my marriage good."

For a while, she says, her work worked. "It was okay. The sex was okay. And we were great as parents and as a family. I was immersed in my kids and career. I had my close girlfriends for intimacy. I was finding ways to feel alive." Then one night "I had this awful dream in which an anonymous man was raping me, and to save myself I took a knife and killed him." Forced to confront the reality "that trying to hang in there was making me feel oppressed and caught and raped"—and homicidal?—she understood that she needed to stop trying. "After I had that dream," she said, "something in me closed off, and I knew I was done."

On the other hand, Ruth Caplin, a Maryland therapist, has found that "if one member of a couple very much wants to save the marriage, the chance of its survival increases enormously. One dedicated mate can change the climate." She also says that "focusing on what divorce will do to the children has prompted quite a number of angry, restless, dissatisfied couples to make some changes in interactions and attitudes." A strong religious background, she finds, can enable a wife whose husband has been unfaithful "to try again without losing self-respect." And a woman who enjoys a lifestyle "where there is lots of money, position, and travel, may decide"—as Lola decided—"that she likes her life sufficiently to balance its disappointments against its pleasures."

But Caplin also observes, as does Los Angeles psychotherapist Joan Willens, that as women increasingly earn their own money and make their own social lives, they become less willing to stay in a significantly unsatisfying marriage. "The more financially independent the woman," says Dr. Willens, "and the greater her belief in her capacity to function alone in the world, the less inclined she may be to work it out."

Not everyone is inclined to work it out. Where is it written we have to work it out? If there aren't any children around—and sometimes, maybe, even if there are—why shouldn't a woman or man walk away from their marriage if their marriage isn't significantly satisfying?

The risk, of course, is that, walking away, we take our unhappy self with us, that significantly unsatisfied self that imagines the grass is greener everywhere else. The risk is that we perceive the banalities, battles, and banked fires of everyday life as the consequence of our having picked the wrong mate. The risk is that we persuade ourselves that if we two were truly meant for each other, we wouldn't be feeling so desperately discontented. The risk is that we fail to understand how much real misery there can be in even the very best of marriages.

"Marriages," as one husband observes in Donald Margulies's play *Dinner with Friends,* "all go through a baseline wretchedness. We do what we can to ride these patches out."

But sometimes we cannot ride these patches out.

In *Scenes from a Marriage,* Ingmar Bergman's compellingly intimate look at Johan and Marianne's marriage, divorce, and beyond, it is hard not to feel that if only they'd been able to grow up *within* their marriage, they might have stayed married. Instead, their divorce, which takes place over time and goes through many complicated phases, begins with Johan informing the unsuspecting Marianne that he loves another woman and is leaving her; after which there's a period of relative calm and civility, tentative overtures and bitter tears; after which they move on to her berating him for having "wiped your feet on me" and his berating her for sexual coldness and withholding—"You cashed in your sex organs. They became a commodity. If I behaved well,

I was rewarded with a lay"; after which they go after each other with violence and vicious epithets—"you fucking bitch," "you goddamn shit," "I could kill you"; after which they finally sign the divorce papers.

Good-bye and good riddance? Actually, no. Not at all.

Several years after these papers are signed, Marianne and Johan slip away from their current spouses to spend a night together, connecting with each other with the physical passion, emotional tenderness, mutual generosity, and mutual openness that had always eluded them during their married life. Johan, having confronted and accepted his limits, his "smallness," is kinder and sadder, less arrogant and less defensive. Marianne is sexual, strong, self-possessed. And both of them, much more conscious of their own failings and much more forgiving of each other's, are finally able—Johan in his "imperfect and selfish way," Marianne in her "fussy and pestering way"—to truly love each other.

As they savor a few stolen hours, his arms embracing her "in the middle of the night, in a dark house, somewhere in the world," she wonders, "Have we missed something important . . . you and I?" Or—and those of us who are watching their story must ponder this question—can they offer each other their acceptance and comfort and love only because of what they've become (and perhaps can continue to be) by living apart?

Now there are, of course, happy stories of husbands and wives who divorce and then remarry each other. Sometimes they marry each other several times. In the magazine *More,* I read about Pattie, who "promised" herself to her high-school sweetheart, Monte, when she was a small-town Texas girl of fifteen, married him at twenty in June of 1978 without ever having dated anyone else, got the marriage annulled a year later because she had started wanting to "see what was out there," and remarried him three months later, having decided that "dating . . . sure isn't much fun."

Neither, it turned out, was their second marriage.

After they had a daughter, Pattie launched what turned out to be a successful business, and soon she was making plenty of money, traveling to new places, seeing new things, and becoming estranged from Monte, who went off hunting on the weekends when she came home. "Basically," she says, "we were never together," either physically or emotionally. Basically, they were living two different lives. So in 1992, Pattie and Monte ended their marriage again, and Pattie moved with her child to another town.

Oddly enough, the divorce and the move brought them closer. Whenever they had good news, they called on the phone. And when their daughter came down with a near-fatal illness, Pattie didn't have to stand vigil alone. She and Monte "were with her all the time," and "seeing more and more of each other until one day we realized, 'Hey, we can fight this thing, or see where it goes.'"

It went back to the altar, where, in October of 1998, with their daughter, now sixteen, serving as bridesmaid, Pattie and Monte married for the third time.

Like Johan and Marianne, Pattie and Monte were entangled for more than two decades. Unlike Johan and Marianne, they were willing to try being married yet again, perhaps having learned enough when they were living apart from each other to be able, this time, to finally live together.

———————

Some couples—apart or together—eventually learn enough to be able to love and to live with each other. But some marriages are hopelessly irretrievable. Some husbands and wives are so non-negotiably wrong for, bad for, and bad to each other that remaining together is, or should be, inconceivable. The novelist and essayist C. S. Lewis describes such couples, who are chained together "mercilessly . . . two mutual tormentors, each raw all over with the poison of hate-in-love, each ravenous to receive and implacably refusing to give, jealous, suspicious, resentful, struggling for the upper hand, determined to be free and to allow no freedom, living on 'scenes.'" And a therapist tells of a couple who spent their whole marriage—fifteen years!—going from one kind of therapy to another kind of therapy to yet another before being able to recognize that they needed to end the hell they'd created together.

In addition, for husbands and wives who don't have children and who, although they may not be living in hell, want and believe they could love better, be better, give more, get more, have a more meaningful marriage, it may make sense—having first done their best to try to fix the marriage they are in—to choose to get out of it.

In her book *The Starter Marriage,* social demographer Pamela Paul applies that troubling name to childless first marriages that last five years or less and often end around the age of thirty. She notes that the average divorce occurs after 6.3 years of marriage, that most marriages end between years two and five, and that the chance of divorcing reaches its highest point during the third year of marriage, statistics that suggest, so some have argued, that these young divorcés are "spoiled, impatient, selfish, and lazy." And yet, says Paul, she has found that the women and men in starter marriages "truly believe they are getting married forever," although she grants that "we're less willing to tolerate unhappy lives and are more optimistic about our rights and obligations to attain personal happiness." So when things go wrong, these unhappily-married-without-any-children couples make the decision, as one divorced twenty-nine-year-old man told Paul, that "if it's not meant to be, better to get out sooner rather than later."

"It's not meant to be" may mean that marriage didn't fix him or change her or make things better between them, or that it changed him or changed her in ways they deplore. Or that the constraints and responsibilities overwhelmed them because he or she or both were too self-centered or too unstable or too immature. It may mean that they didn't know how to solve their problems when they had problems, or that they weren't feeling happy or happy enough, or that they had two different visions of marriage because she wanted Zen simplicity and he wanted stuff, or that self-fulfillment and personal satisfaction always took precedence over couplehood. It may mean that the couples in starter marriages were "unwilling or unable to either succeed with their marriages or to make themselves miserable by sticking to an unhappy one."

This is not to suggest that divorce from a starter marriage is as easy as tossing a tissue into a trash can. Even when it's a relief, it can also be agonizing. "Even though *every single person* interviewed," says Paul, "believed that divorce was ultimately the best thing for them," none of the people interviewed "would wish a starter marriage on anyone." Or as Kent, now married to the woman he calls his "soul mate," said to me, "Ending my first marriage was the hardest thing I ever did in my life."

Even though ending a marriage may be the hardest thing we've ever done in our life, sometimes we ought to—before we have children, before we've spent too many years in a rotten relationship—be strong enough, be brave enough, to divorce.

Or should we? Whatever happened to perseverance, sticking it out, for better or for worse? What happened to the fond dream of "one marriage per lifetime"? It seems reasonable to ask, and people are asking, whether couples are giving up on marriage too easily.

A recent article in *The New York Times* presented a staggering statistic: The divorce rate in several parts of the Bible Belt is now above the national average by a hard-to-believe-it's-possible 50 percent. Cathryn Hinderliter, whose first marriage was a victim of Oklahoma's "tidal wave of divorce," resolved, the article tells us, that she wouldn't repeat her mistakes in her second marriage. Choosing a man who had, in advance, committed to putting in "an incredible amount of work" on the marriage, she now goes with him to counseling whenever problems arise, convinced that the way for a woman and man to keep a marriage together is to "communicate until your knuckles bleed."

Both inside and outside the Bible Belt, I hear from marital therapists and divorce attorneys that many spouses who choose to end their marriages undoubtedly could, with some effort and sacrifice—maybe a great deal of effort, a great deal of sacrifice—preserve them. (Let's assume they're excluding marriage problems like wife beating, repeated adulteries, and drug addiction.) Indeed,

Indianapolis marriage and family counselor Susan Cahn has concluded, after twenty-two years of practice, "that 70 percent of couples who divorced didn't need to divorce, that they could have made it," if instead of leaving the marriage, "they'd understood that conflict is normal, that conflict is growth trying to happen." She says that she always respects and honors a spouse's wish to divorce but that she is quite openly "biased toward marriage." And she says she thinks that most seemingly doomed marriages could survive if couples "would get a grip and work with the conflict."

Other therapists might be less optimistic about the number of salvageable marriages, but they *are* optimistic. There's no question, they tell me, that many of these couples could manage to live with each other acceptably, if not blissfully, ever after.

There are, however, some questions that these husbands and wives should consider as they contemplate backing away from the divorce option: Is "acceptably" acceptable? And can they live, if they must, without buzz or bliss? And if they decide to stay and do the hard work they need to do to preserve the marriage, is it going to offer them sufficient, if not significant, satisfaction?

These wives and husbands must ask themselves if they are prepared to settle for a marriage that may only be good enough. Keeping in mind that their definition of "good enough" may change at every different stage of married life. Keeping in mind that—as Maryland therapist Sheila Rogovin points out—"what you're willing to put up with for the first twenty or twenty-five years, you might not be willing to settle for after that."

The work of making a marriage acceptable, better, or good enough requires, says Dr. Rogovin, that "the wife and the husband didn't do so much scarring of each other that there's no going back." Barring such permanent damage, she and other couples therapists I spoke with seem to agree that by simply behaving better—whether they feel like behaving better or not—husbands and wives can often interrupt the vicious cycle of mutual mangling and maybe get an "unvicious" cycle going.

"You *can* teach an old dog new tricks," says Dr. Rogovin, who encourages troubled couples "to be together in more civilized ways." She says, "I don't wait for feelings to change before I ask them to start to change their behavior. And once the wife stops being a witch, maybe the husband can then stop being a bastard."

Analyst Harvey Rich will sometimes ask a husband and wife in couples therapy to say what his or her partner is afraid of, after which he'll inquire whether they think that what they are doing with each other is making their partner less or more afraid. Dr. Rich finds that this knowing and naming of each other's fears can be deeply comforting—"like turning on a light in a dark room." And unless the husband and wife "are out to scare the hell out of each other," he says, they often are willing to think about ways of enabling each other to feel safer.

Dr. Willens adds that "not every couple needs a lot—just a little fixing around the edges." And she always tries in her work, she says, to help couples find the pluses in their marriage. Like the optimist of the old joke, who is convinced that the evidence shows that there has to be a pony lurking somewhere, she tries to help troubled couples "find the pony buried under all the shit."

While behaving in more civilized ways may help to put an end to the vicious cycles that devastate married life, and while helping each other feel less afraid may turn a marriage into a safer place, and while finding the pony under the shit may hold a couple together by persuading them that the pluses outweigh the minuses, many therapists feel that it's sometimes essential for husbands and wives to dig deep down into their family history to understand why they're doing what they're doing. They believe that it's sometimes essential for couples to try to understand how the shadow of the past falls on the marriage.

It seems to be widely recognized that the habits of being and doing acquired in childhood can become a part of our repertoire and—for good and for ill—repeat themselves in later love relationships. Indeed, the unconscious replaying of the same old pernicious dramas again and again may underlie most of the reasons why couples divorce. As Fern Miller, a Boston therapist, notes, "Some of this early stuff is so ingrained, so embedded in people, that it's almost at the level of DNA. In my practice I'm seeing wife after wife and husband after husband dumping transgenerational issues having to do with their family of origin into the marriage."

The dumping of unresolved issues from the past onto the present can create distressing and destructive tensions: A husband, for instance, reacts to his wife's request to run an errand as if she were his suffocating mother. A wife treats her husband's wish to go off with his pals for a weekend fishing trip as if her father were yet again abandoning her. A wife who makes a suggestion is seen as the autocratic father who insists on trying to dominate his son's life. A husband who mildly observes that maybe the soup is a little salty is seen as the faultfinding mother whose daughter can never, ever, ever do anything right.

Then there's the man who hates and wants to kill his sadistic father but instead treats his father politely and "kills" his wife, pounding on her without letup until, she says, "I'm crying. I'm crushed. He needs to crush me."

And then there's the woman who, having been disdained and disrespected as a child, shreds her husband the way she once was shredded.

Sometimes we are able to disentangle our present from our past relationships. Sometimes we can't. Sometimes the damaged attachments of early childhood impel us to do to a spouse what we couldn't and still can't do to a parent, impel us to do to a spouse what was once done to us. And sometimes these damaged attachments leave us feeling unworthy of love (prompting us to demand constant reassurance) or fearful of abandonment (prompting us to frantically clutch and cling) or determined to never again depend on another human being (prompting us to pull away from intimacy). What goes on between husbands and wives—the demands, the clinging, the pulling away, the pounding, the shredding—may already have gone on before with our mothers and fathers. Except that our spouses are not our mothers and fathers, nor are we theirs, and our marriage may not make it if, over and over again, we respond to each other as if we were endangered, helpless children and they were the flawed, feared parents of our childhood.

Our marriage may also not survive the unconscious expectations that we bring to it, expectations outside our realm of awareness, unmet expectations that can leave us feeling profoundly disappointed but unable to understand how we have helped to bring our disappointment about. "The more monumental the hopes from love," writes Michael Vincent Miller in *Intimate Terrorism*, "the more devastating the fall into disappointment." Many of us unknowingly crush our marriage with our unconscious, monumental hopes.

Some of us hope that marriage will give us a father or a mother exactly like, or nothing like, our own. Some of us hope that marriage will fill that hungry hole in our heart with the unconditional love we've never known. Some of us hope that marriage will allow us to merge so completely with another that we'll never again feel helpless or alone. Some of us hope that marriage will at long, long last provide us with the longed-for missing pieces of our self.

Father me, mother me, love me boundlessly, merge with me, give me shelter, make me complete. Redress the sorrows of childhood. Redeem my suffering. These extravagant hopes, the insistent legacy of our tenacious past, will certainly collide with the inevitable limitations of married life. And as long as we're unaware of them, they'll compel us to make impossible demands, demands that can't be met by our beleaguered, baffled, hurt, or outraged partner, a partner who eventually may decide that he or she can't be in this marriage any longer.

Now, I'm not denying that marriage can sometimes make up for our past deprivations. It sometimes can heal us, come to our rescue too. Indeed, in *The Good Marriage,* authors Wallerstein and Blakeslee describe in glowing terms "the rescue marriage," a marriage in which two people with wretched childhoods succeed in fashioning a relationship that "fulfills the child's fantasy that early miseries will be canceled by the happiness of adult life." Others have spoken to me about the saving grace of a marriage in which, leaning on each other, a husband and wife repair each other's former griefs. But for many, maybe most of us, the expectation that marriage will heal us, rescue us, wash away our old miseries is likely to remain an unfulfilled fantasy, one that sooner or later could shatter the marriage.

When Sybil, for instance, got married at age seventeen to a man who was "charismatic and strong," she thought she'd been rescued from her abusive father. But Miles turned out to be abusive too—"so controlling," Sybil says, "that a therapist once told him, 'You have your foot on her neck, and if she tries to move you press down even harder.'" Ten years and one daughter later, she finally left him, "afraid," she said, "if I didn't I would die." And when, three years after that, she married Guy, "who really seemed to love my daughter and me," she again believed that she had found her rescuer. Instead, she found "that my second marriage repeated the unhappy pattern of the first," that she had married another "charismatic, dynamic man bent on dominance," a man who saw "any kind of marital accommodation as a defeat."

Eight years later, getting up "enough gumption to light out," she ended her marriage. She says she "expected that I'd be spending the rest of my life alone," which, she added, "seemed like an improvement."

But Sybil married again. This marriage has passed the eighteen-year mark, and they are living together contentedly. Why is this marriage succeeding? I ask her. Is her third husband the rescuer of her fantasies? Has she, after all her travails, been saved? Her answer is no, she has not been saved. Instead, she has saved herself, becoming, in the course of dealing with her difficult husbands, "tougher and tougher." When she no longer needed to find another aggressive man to protect her from the aggressive man she had left, when she was able to find in herself the strength that she had always been seeking outside, "I finally was free," she says, "to pick someone I loved—not someone I needed to protect me."

Figuring out how the shadow of our past falls on our marriage can help us to distinguish the past from the present. Becoming aware of the unattainable hopes we have for our marriage can help us temper what we're hoping for. Recognizing our needs—for strength, for rescue, for whatever—can help us try to meet some of those needs ourselves. And making the unconscious conscious can help us move from child to adult, with more freedom to choose and to change, to grow up and grow.

But "the assumption that change and growth will develop in the direction of reconfirming the couple," notes psychoanalyst Otto Kernberg, "is sometimes wishful thinking . . ." because "individual growth and the couple's growth do not necessarily coincide." Indeed, Dr. Kernberg finds himself "forced to conclude that emotional maturity is no guarantee for a couple's nonconflictual stability." Instead, he says, "The resolution of pathological dependency, for example, may dissolve the marriage."

The marriage, for example, may dissolve with the collapse of collusive arrangements that a husband and wife made together unconsciously, an arrangement of complementary roles that satisfied his and her needs and that both of them—at least for a while—agreed to: That one would be the teacher, the other the student. That one would be the mommy, the other the baby. That one would be in charge while the other obeyed. Or that one would be the bully, the other the victim. That one would be the strong one, the other the weak one. That one would be admired while the other provided the admiration and praise.

So when Brenda, at age nineteen, married Stan, who was nine

years older, they were pleased to sign on for the roles of student and teacher, with Stan introducing Brenda to wine and travel and music and poetry and painting and Brenda paying back Stan by worshipfully seeing him as a "Renaissance man, a genius." Then Brenda began growing up. She developed opinions of her own and wasn't inclined to defer to Stan anymore. In fact, she began to abhor what she now perceived as her husband's "need to completely control me." Soon she was fighting and challenging Stan on everything. And Stan, bewildered and furious at the disappearance of his worshipful student, began fighting back.

A lot of divorces follow the unraveling of these central, though silent, conspiracies. When the collusion collapses, the marriage does too. When the baby stops needing the mommy, when the victim stops needing the bully, when the weak one stops needing the strong one—or vice versa—the marriage all too frequently is through, as it was when Ed left Leah because she continued to need to be the nurtured child long after he stopped being willing to be "the mother she never had, her caretaker mother."

His awareness of what they were doing and his refusal to keep doing it ended their marriage.

But awareness can sometimes help, and it helped in Stan and Brenda's marriage, which both of them were committed to save and to heal. Talking to each other (with the aid of a couples therapist), they became aware of their tacit marital deal. They also began to see that it was possible to live together without it.

I, too, embraced the student role when I married, the first time around, a law professor sixteen years older than I, a man who was happy to further my education in philosophy, politics, literature, and life. The marriage began to fail when I, like Brenda, started to want a more equal relationship and he preferred the adoring young girl I had been. Although I once told a therapist that "my marriage is not on the table; it's permanent—like the color of my eyes," I eventually came to recognize that I had to divorce in order to keep growing up.

Psychiatrist Peter Kramer writes: "As a therapist I lean in the direction of reconciliation. I lean that way in part because of my experience that simple interventions sometimes suffice to hold together couples who seem on the verge of separation, and that those repaired relationships proceed ordinarily well. And because second marriages do not seem gloriously better than first marriages; or, if they do, it is often because the second marriage benefits from efforts or compromises that might as readily have been applied to the first." He adds these words of warning: "*There are limits to how different things will be if you exchange this partner for another.*"

Kramer's words apply to my current, but not to my earlier, marriage, in which efforts and compromises could not suffice and in which many, many, so many things were different. Getting divorced was the right decision to make the first time around, but although, on a few occasions, as angry and hurt as two people could be, we marched to the brink, it was never the right decision for Milton and me. As I look back now on the forty-plus years of very hard work, his and mine, that have allowed our intense, demanding, difficult, sometimes quite wonderful marriage to survive, I believe I can say that both of us finally learned to do what Kramer says we must do: "Change enough. Change yourself. Use the relationship as a place in which to grow. Expect discomfort."

CHAPTER TEN

Marrying Again

Almost everyone who divorces eventually remarries,
which is a testimony to (a) the validity and desirability
of matrimony or (b) the stunning stupidity of the
human race.

—Karen Karbo, *Generation Ex*

There ought to be training courses for stepmothers.
Motherhood comes after nine months' preparation . . .
but stepmotherhood is more like an unexploded bomb in
the briefcase of the man you marry.

—Joanna Trollope, *Other People's Children*

DIVORCED OR WIDOWED, with young or grown children or no children at all, we marry again, and sometimes again
and again. An astonishing number of us, the young and the
middle-aged and the old, are confronting the complexities of
remarriage. In my own immediate family, composed of Milton
and me, our three married sons, and their wives, five out of eight
of us have been divorced. And in the wider world, a significant
portion of those who are married are women and men who were
married at least once before. Losing a husband or wife to death or
divorce, most wives and most husbands will seek the comfort of

couplehood again, and if they want children together, or even if they don't, most will remarry. Since second marriages have a shocking 60 percent chance of failing—it was 45 percent the first time around—it seems that we who remarry will need to be luckier, or work harder, than ever before.

It's been said that widows and widowers are better bets for remarriage than divorcés, perhaps because they're less battle-scarred and less bitter. It's also been said that having to live with other people's children burdens remarried couples in ways that those with adult children—or none—are spared. But as I've talked to husbands and wives in their second, their third, and in one case their fourth marriage, I've discovered a lot of exceptions to what's "been said." I've found that even the most idyllic or seemingly simple remarriage is likely to come with plenty of complications.

We who had starter marriages, which Lynn Darling calls "ephemeral as spring," certainly didn't expect them to be ephemeral, but one of the early clues to our less-than-100-percent commitment to staying married may have been our unwillingness to have kids. Indeed, throughout my first marriage, I thought of myself as a woman who wouldn't ever want kids, but in fact what I didn't want was kids with that husband, not because he wasn't a good person—I think he was—but because, alas, we were not good together.

In Karen Karbo's very funny—and telling—book on exes, she notes that studies show that ex-spouses who don't have children together get along much better than those who do, citing a man

who bears his former wife no rancor at all, even though she slept with, left him for, and eventually married his best friend. According to Karbo, this man can maintain kindly feelings toward his ex-wife because "she's not in his face day in, day out," as she very well could have been "if they had a passel of underage children they were trying to parent." She says that he can feel kind, and even generous, because his former wife is out of his life.

Not everyone is so ready to forgive an ex-wife or ex-husband for adultery with his or her best friend. Even without a passel of children to parent, there might very well be some abiding feelings of bitterness. Still, it's certainly far easier to be gone from each other's life if a former husband and wife aren't sharing kids (or even a dog) they acquired together. On the other hand, the absence of kids can sometimes make it easier to remain in each other's lives as postmarital friends.

My ex-husband and I, for instance, having no children (or dogs or money) to squabble over, maintained a loving friendship until his death, in addition to which his sisters and brothers-in-law and nephews and nieces continued—and continue to this day—to treat me, and to treat Milton, as their relatives. Indeed, the stalwart Libby, who hasn't been my sister-in-law for forty-plus years, has on occasion been heard to proudly say, "Our family has three writers: There's Jimmy [her son]. And then there's Judy. And there's Milton," making me think that along with grown-up marriage, there is also such a thing as grown-up divorce.

Still, I wouldn't want to suggest that a former marriage, although childless, although friendly, will not cause marital problems when

we remarry. If we were the ones who were dumped, we may succumb to insecurity and self-doubt, wondering whether we're losers and unlovable. But even if we've done the dumping, or even if the divorce decision was more or less mutual, we still may feel shaken, question our judgment, worry about our capacity for commitment, think of ourselves as damaged goods, and fear that we will fail at marriage again. These wounds from our prior marriage sometimes prompt us, when we remarry, to try to protect ourselves by hedging our bets, by holding back on the openness, trust, goodwill, and, yes, money we offer our new partner, who might (like our ex) deceive, disappoint, or discard us.

Sebastian complains: "My wife's first husband concealed a lot of things from her, and she always treats me as if I'm concealing things too." Her distrust and his resentment at being "guilty till proven innocent" are sources of serious second-marriage strains.

Some second marriages suffer by comparison with the first, especially if the first spouse is seen as a saint, which is far more likely to happen if the marriage has ended in death instead of divorce. In Malamud's novel *Dubin's Lives,* Dubin's wife, Kitty, has the annoying habit of bringing her former husband into their life, noting, for instance, that "Nathanael thought I was pretty good in bed. He thought me a passionate woman. I *am* passionate," and causing Dubin to say that he "didn't need Nathanael for company or comparison." Later, when Kitty tells Dubin that "we aren't sufficiently suited to each other," he bitterly replies to her, "Who I am is not Nathanael . . . Nate the saint."

Even when exes aren't saints, even when they are seriously flawed, they may have some positive quality that the current mate, no matter how great, is lacking. And sometimes—although

husbands and wives really ought to know better—she'll mention, in passing, her ex's stupendous IQ, or he'll mention, in passing, his ex's stupendous breasts. Such mentions don't contribute to marital harmony.

On the other hand, a troubled first marriage and massively flawed former spouse can make the second marriage and spouse look good.

Gretchen tells me her second husband is all that her arrogant, critical, cold ex wasn't, adding that while her first "was always insidiously putting me down," her second "is warm and supportive, and still thinks, after twenty years, that I'm hot stuff."

In that yummy old movie *Rebecca*, the inept and shy second wife of the rich, aloof, and elegant Maxim de Winter believes she is painfully lacking in comparison with Maxim's dazzling dead wife, but ultimately discovers that Maxim loves her precisely *because* she is nothing like the flamboyant—and faithless—Rebecca.

Malcolm says that while his first wife turned out to be "a woman of narrow horizons," overinvolved with her parents and unwilling to move from the small Vermont town that they lived in, his second wife is open to new people and new places and new experiences, which allows him to feel that marriage (marriage, that is, to his current wife) "is something that makes you grow instead of shrink."

And Josie, in Trollope's *Other People's Children*, admits to "the hope—a very real hope—that Nadine [her second husband's former wife] would not be a hard act to follow [because] . . . she was clearly a rotten mother, a lousy housekeeper, [and] she'd never earned a contributory penny."

Josie also compares the lackluster love she felt for her first with the "excited, triumphant love" that she feels for her second, a happy contrast in loving I heard again and again from couples who have remarried, along with other satisfied comparisons: She's smarter, she has more time for me, she's nicer to my folks. He's funnier, gentler, more helpful around the house. The sex is better. The meals are better. Even the *fights,* according to Wade, are better. "We fight, flare up, get it out in the open, and then it's over," he says. "What a difference from my first marriage, where the grudges and the guilt went on forever!"

In view of all these glowing testimonials, it seems reasonable to ask why second marriages fail much more often than firsts. It just doesn't make sense. Aren't we, when we remarry, older, more grounded, more experienced, clearer on who we are and what we need? Aren't we more careful and more practical? Haven't we figured out that compatible lasts a lot longer than cute, that reliable is as lovable as romantic? Sometimes yes, sometimes no.

Not all of us learn from experience, grow wiser along with older, or are willing to examine who we are. Too many of us look for happiness by picking new partners and entering into new marriages while remaining the same old people we've always been. In addition, too many of us wind up unconsciously repeating our marital history by choosing a spouse like the one we chose before, though if asked we would surely swear that this new husband or new wife bears zero resemblance to our former partner. Furthermore, if we don't, in fact, remarry a first-marriage duplicate, we may, again unconsciously, start pressing our second spouse to behave like our first. We may even, in response to a compulsion to replay our marital history, take on the troublesome traits of our former partner.

Just look, for instance, at lighthearted, fun-loving Rhonda and at Colin, a rigid, stern, and taciturn man, an unhappily married couple who engaged in a power struggle that went on for years over her—in his view—loosey-goosey, indulgent child-rearing practices versus his—in her view—tight-sphinctered inflexibility. Eventually, unable to resolve their conflicting approaches to children, and life, Rhonda and Colin decided to divorce. Eventually each of them married again.

Rhonda picked as her second husband an easygoing, stay-up-late musician, and Colin married a tough-minded mathematician with a rule about virtually everything. Last seen, the once-playful Rhonda was working much too hard to party and nagging her laid-back husband to be more responsible, while Colin, wearing jeans and a beard and showing other signs of hanging looser, was complaining that his new wife was way too uptight.

Psychoanalyst Stephen Mitchell in his provocative book *Can Love Last?* writes, "We all have a tendency to reproduce our miseries with extraordinary consistency. In love relations, we approach each new relationship as the antidote to the problems of the last one, and, with daunting regularity, each new relationship turns out to be a new version of the old." These various ways of creating new versions of our old mistakes can help explain why second marriages falter.

———

Add to the above the special pressures on second marriages when a husband leaves his wife, or a wife leaves her husband, for the lover with whom he or she has been carrying on. Building a second marriage upon the wreckage of the first, they may put excessive demands on their new marriage in order to justify—by its perfection—the vows they betrayed, the price they paid, the pain they inflicted. The quarrels and doldrums of ordinary everyday married life may be harder to take the second time around precisely because this marriage was expected to walk the high romantic road, was expected to be all the good things the first marriage wasn't. But no matter how committed illicit lovers may be to keeping the thrill alive, they tend, when they marry, to turn into married people, with the inevitable frustrations and disappointments that such a relationship implies. Sometimes the thrill fades even before they marry.

Consider Tolstoy's Count Vronsky, out of his head with love for the married Anna Karenina, obsessed by her, pursuing her, entreating her: "Surely you know that for me you are all of life. . . . I'm incapable of thinking of you and of myself separately. For myself you and I are one. And . . . I see a possibility of happiness, and of what happiness!"

Now consider Vronsky after Anna leaves her husband and her son to be with this passionate man who adores her so: "Vronsky . . . was not entirely happy. He soon came to feel that the fulfillment of his desires had given him only one grain of the mountain of joy he had been expecting. This fulfillment showed him the eternal mistake people make when they imagine that happiness is the fulfillment of their wishes. At first . . . he was satisfied. But not for long. He soon came to feel that a desire for desires was rising in his soul—boredom."

An interesting statistic: Some 70 percent of those involved in a divorce have a lover at the time of their breakup, but only 15 percent of them marry that lover.

Marrying the lover can, as I've said, put pressure on a second marriage to make it worth destroying the earlier marriage. In addition, the now-married lovers may encounter some social opprobrium, even exclusion, although committing adultery isn't deplored as much today as it was in the past. Furthermore, the children of lovers who've married may outright hate the "home-wrecking" spouse, who may or may not have actually been a home wrecker. There are even some situations in which the in-laws strongly insist on regarding only the former spouse as "legitimate."

That is what happened to Moira with Jed's widowed mother, sister, and brother-in-law when Jed left his wife and children to marry her.

Indeed, Jed's former wife, Bev, is always invited to Jed's mother's house—along with Moira and Jed and everyone's children—and Bev has yet to decline an invitation. She is there, Moira says with a sigh, for Mother's Day, New Year's Day, Christmas, Easter, and Thanksgiving dinner, plus various birthdays and the Fourth of July. When Moira complains that she'd rather not share Jed's family with his ex-wife, Jed—a why-can't-we-all-get-along kind of guy—will not take on his family and, Moira says, "has never really stood up to Bev."

After almost five years of marriage, Moira has had to accept the fact that "I'm dead meat. I'll never find my place in this

crowd. This family is going to always give Bev their first loyalty."
And although she has been well behaved at family gatherings,
she feels "great sadness and pain and loss"—and anger—at
being marginalized by Jed's family, and "furious at Jed for not
protecting me.

"I'm committed to the premise," she says, "that I want this
marriage to last," and she has been doing her best to make that
happen. "I'm strategizing"—arranging for her and her husband
and the children to be out of the city for at least some of the holidays. "I've resigned myself to the reality that his mother will never
accept me, so I'm not pounding anymore on a door that won't
open." And "I've been trying to appreciate the blessings that I
have, trying to put the positive back in my marriage."

She also, until this year, went along with sharing the family
holidays with Bev, but she says she will not do it anymore. "I gave
Jed an ultimatum—if he can't work it out with Bev and with his
family, I'm not showing up, I refuse to be at the table. He can't
keep overlooking how rejecting his family has been and how
wounded I am."

———————

Moira has plenty to deal with—a husband who can't seem to
understand how wounded she is, in-laws who are hostile to their
marriage, and a former spouse who will not go away. But as Karbo
notes in her book, many former wives and husbands will not go
away, even without the encouragement of ex-in-laws. Instead they
intrude, and they sometimes intrude outrageously, on an ex-
wife's or ex-husband's subsequent marriage.

A popular form of intrusion, which is repeated at frequent intervals, is the phone call, which often drives a new wife to despair. Karbo, making us laugh at what surely isn't one bit funny while it's happening, offers the following telephone-call taxonomy: The "*M'Aidez* Call," a plea for either money or assistance. The all-purpose, tell-me-what-I-should-do "Advice Call." The more highly focused, tell-me-which-one-to-buy "New Vehicle Inquiry Call." The "Venting Call." The "Shoulder to Cry On Call." The heartbreaking, oh-how-I'm-aching "Search for Pity Call." And the "Going Mental Call," which has two divisions, Karbo tells us—the "Fuck You" (for leaving me and destroying my life) and the "Fuck Me" (for making you leave because I'm a loser).

Karbo quotes Cindy, a second wife, about her husband's first wife's relentless phone calls: "She can't figure out how to turn up the temperature on the water heater. Or her wrist hurts, and she's worried it's a flare-up of her carpal tunnel problem. Doesn't Bernie remember . . . how he used to massage her wrists with Tiger Balm? . . . The pilot light is out in the stove. . . . This is a woman who played lacrosse in college and was an instructor for Outward Bound. Suddenly, she can't figure out about the pilot light?"

It's difficult not to assume that the former spouses who get such calls could, if they really wished to, find ways of stopping them. But guilt, compassion, a need to rescue, or simple spinelessness can sometimes prompt them not only to take the calls their exes keep making but to provide the money, advice, help, sympathy, or even the self-flagellation requested. The continuing over-involvement of these once-married, now-divorced partners has been given a wickedly perfect name by Karbo, who calls this kind of one-foot-in-and-one-foot-out relationship "divarriage."

Even when the exes aren't relentlessly working the phones, former husbands and wives will be ever entangled with each other if they have children. As for remarried partners trying to deal with each other's kids in what is now commonly known as the "blended family" and what Karbo calls the "extreme family," problems with these kids, according to medical writer Elaine Fantle Shimberg, "is a major reason the majority of parents in blended families give for breaking up."

I've heard about problems with kids in blended families that certainly justify the word "extreme."

Indeed, I know of two formerly quite contented second marriages in which each couple now shares its happy home with the wife's disturbed adult son from her first marriage—one of them an unemployed ex-junkie with some major medical problems, the other a compulsive gambler with debts in the high six figures and some very unfriendly collectors on his tail. I also know of a second marriage in which the schizoid daughter of the husband left her two little sons with her sixty-eight-year-old father and his new wife to raise. And I know many women and men who have acquired, along with a wonderful second marriage partner, the emotional, physical, legal, and educational difficulties of that partner's children. These do not tend to be, for the most part, tranquil marriages.

Even in first marriages, trouble with the children at any age can make for trouble between a husband and wife. Although it's pretty to think so, drawing closer when bad things happen to the children isn't always the way that spouses respond. Instead, they may fall apart, disconnect, get drunk, get depressed, or even decide "I've had it," walking out on children they're tied to by blood. In second marriages, in which the ties to the stepchildren are more tenuous, trouble with the kids will certainly shake up, and too often break up, the marriage.

Flo talks about the "back-breaking, mind-blowing effort to merge the five children from our two families," daughters and sons whose ages, when she and Jay married eighteen years ago, ranged from almost seven to sixteen. Says Flo sardonically, "My book, entitled *The Joys of Stepparenting*, is one-quarter of one page long," noting that the continuing difficulties of, and with, some of their kids—a partial list includes one psychotic break, one Hodgkin's disease, one out-of-wedlock granddaughter, and one indictment—still "create the most stress in our marriage."

Even the less apocalyptic difficulties of dealing with his and her children can threaten the survival of a second marriage.

Gladys, whose second marriage, to Wayne, has lasted for more than three decades, still can't bear looking back on their first several years, "which were so miserable I don't want to think about them." Having ended their marriages to be with each other, "we had a terrible, terrible time because we both were feeling so guilty about our own children and being so rotten to each other's kids." The four kids were what they fought about, and continued to fight about, till the kids left home, with Gladys angry at Wayne for "his indifference to my kids, for wishing they weren't living with us, weren't there," and with Wayne angry at Gladys for, as she frankly admits, "disliking his kids"—who spent weekends with them—"intensely." She says, with a great deal of lingering shame, "I never thought I could be such a horrible person."

What kept them together during those years "was the fact that we couldn't admit that we'd made a mistake" and a physical attraction that was "so dramatic, enormous, and dominant that we'd fight about the kids and then have great sex." Stubbornness and sex, she said, kept the marriage together even when "I wanted to kill him," even when "I hated and detested him." And although she says, with deep sorrow, that "our relationship was built at the children's expense," that relationship, now that the children are grown, is so companionable, so satisfying, so "excellent," that knowing what she knows now, knowing what all of them would go through, "I would do it again. And I'm confident he feels the same."

Ellis and Janet, one of the remarried couples discussed by Wallerstein and Blakeslee, say that the greatest challenge of their sixteen-year marriage was trying to blend their four kids—two of hers, two of his, all of them under the age of eleven—into some semblance of one big happy family.

"If I'd known how difficult it would be," says Janet, who remarried at age thirty-four, "I might not have undertaken it." "The weekends that my children came," says Ellis, who remarried at age thirty-seven, "were a living hell." "To be perfectly honest," Janet says, "sometimes I couldn't take it. I was ready to walk out." "It took time for it to sink in," Ellis says, "that we were not all going to be one happy family in an instant or even in a year or maybe ever."

While Flo and Jay, Wayne and Gladys, and Ellis and Janet have held their marriages together, not everyone with blended families can. As Wallerstein and Blakeslee note, "Except for babies and preschoolers, who are more easily integrated into a new family, children are almost always a threat to a second marriage." Why? Because often the interests of kids and couple collide. Because the couple comes with the kids, with no separate time to form a solid twosome. Because stepparents will not love their stepkids right away and may never love them the way they love their own children. Because the kids are often a handful, shaken by the divorce, or afraid of losing the love of the remarried parent, or hostile toward the person their parent remarried, or painfully torn between old and new family loyalties, or feeling excluded by the happy couple. Because the happy couple may be having unhappy fights about money and time—about who will pay how much for which of the kids and about whether they're dining alone for a change or going to yet another of those damn soccer games.

They may also be fighting over "How come you never take my side and tell your bratty children to shape up?"

One woman told Elaine Shimberg in *Blending Families* that she "tried to make it work for two years, but his teenage daughters would have no part of it. They were rude to me, made fun of my attempts to cook, and refused to help clean the house or share any other responsibilities. I felt like their maid, not a stepmother. I grew to hate them and, after a while, I hated him too, for not supporting me emotionally against their abuse. I'm getting a divorce."

Blended families raise the same question that nuclear families do: Who comes first, your children or your spouse? But that question becomes more urgent when a stepparent joins a household that used to be just mommy or daddy and kids and is forced to compete with the kids—as an interloper, as an outsider—for their parent's attention. As Leda ruefully notes in Arlene Heyman's splendid novel *Lovers and Ghosts*, "Although they had lived together many years, Gabe still seemed to regard Dan as the enemy, whom Leda had let slip into his lawful territory when he'd been too young to fight." Gabe is Leda's son with her former husband. Dan is her present husband, the "kind, industrious man who had wanted very much to be his stepfather."

In *Blending Families*, Shimberg answers the who-comes-first question by firmly saying your spouse does, arguing that when remarried parents focus too much of their energy on making their children and their stepchildren happy, they risk wrecking their marriage. On the other hand, in an interview with Francine Klagsbrun, author of *Married People*, a childless woman who married a man with three young daughters makes this sensible point: "You do not ask a father to choose between you and his children. One feels tempted to do just that, but . . . nobody wins that way." And so, while she has made sure that she comes first "enough of the time," she's aware that there are times "when the kids really should come first." Because "I am grown up," she says, " . . . I know that everybody can't come first all the time."

Although remarried couples with children at home can't come first all the time, they do have a right to stake out a life of their own. And they do, in my view, have a right to put their needs as a couple first—once the children have grown. But sometimes adult children, and maybe more often after a death than after divorce, deeply disapprove of the second marriage,

Saying, without saying it,

This is unseemly.

Devote yourself

To good works,

Educational cruises,

Your grandchildren,

And do not abandon

Your lost mate,

Your past life,

Or us.

Sometimes the opposition of disapproving adult children is vocal and vigorous.

One widow recalls being scolded by her daughters when, at the age of seventy-nine, she started seeing a widower, then eighty-one. She was shocked by their insistence "that I should not be going out with another man," but she was also, she says, "always clear that my children had no business telling me what to do." She adds, "If you have always been an affectionate, physical person in your marriage, what you miss most is the touching and the sharing." Having found that once again in this sweet new relationship, "I never wavered in my decision to be with him."

A widower in his late fifties was equally clear about his priorities when his younger daughter reproachfully said to him, "It's much too soon for you to remarry." "Maybe too soon for you," he replied, respectful of her feelings but not inclined to postpone his marriage to Zoe. "Maybe too soon for you—but not for me."

Married-with-children children were also resistant to the marriage of Tina and Warren, who had mourned their dead spouses and now were prepared to move on. In the face of their opposition, the sixty-plus widower gave this promise to the sixty-plus widow he had just made his bride: "I want you to know that there's nothing that is going to come between us. Not your kids. And not my kids. Not anyone."

All of these couples today manage acceptably, if not gloriously, with their grown children. And all of these partners are comfortable when their husband or wife makes references to the once beloved, now deceased, former spouse. While none of the partners admits to feeling competitive toward these spouses, Zoe concedes she became a serious cook—she had never loved cooking—because her husband's first wife had fed him so well, recalling the night when her husband informed her at the end of the meal, "A pear is a very nice thing, but it's not dessert," and "I said to myself, Oh, shit, she made dessert too!"

Sometimes the wife who died didn't just make dessert—she made every aspect of life so wonderful that the second wife can only be second best. And sometimes the husband who died was so appreciative, as Nathanael was, of his wife that the second husband can only look, as Dubin did, like an ingrate by comparison. Still, among the older remarried couples I have been speaking with, I haven't really encountered any ingrates. As the oldest of them, now close to ninety, contentedly agree, "There isn't a day that goes by that we don't say to one another how lucky we are."

When remarriages succeed, both of the partners, whether widowed or divorced, are often acutely grateful for their good luck: The luck of "having a second chance, a chance to get it right." The luck of "having found the love of my life." The luck of "being able to take care of each other, depend upon each other." The luck of "not being lonely any more."

These second husbands and wives, especially those who have married a long-married widow or widower, are also willing to do the difficult work that they often must do to graciously accommodate their spouse's first-marriage familial obligations. The "graciously" part can be a significant challenge. Sylvia, divorced for almost two decades before marrying a widower, sometimes groans at having to share her husband's enormous first-marriage obligations, obligations to his four children, their spouses, the seven grandkids, plus a stepdaughter by his dead wife's former marriage, plus his dead wife's brothers and sisters (who were, after all, his in-laws for almost thirty-five years), along with their spouses, children, and children's children. The demands on her can be huge, she says, but whenever she starts resenting yet another wedding, bar mitzvah, or family reunion, she never fails to remind herself, "Listen, schmuck! Remember alone? You want to be alone? I'll give you alone," after which her responsibilities to her husband's family start feeling less onerous.

"It's hard to be married," she tells me, and many other remarried wives and husbands agree. "But," she adds, and with this they also agree, "it's so much harder to be alone."

The more grown up we are, the more wisely we'll choose the second time around, the less likely we'll be to repeat our former mistakes, the better aware we'll be of our good fortune in finding someone to have and to hold, and the harder we'll work to nourish and keep what we've found. The more grown up we are, the greater will be our sense of, as Tina puts it, "having been blessed. Blessed that I could have this. Blessed that *we* could have this.

Blessed that, at our age, we could be so intimate, so playful, so attracted to each other, so utterly trusting of each other, so madly in love."

At one of the many parties for Tina and Warren several months after their wedding ceremony, a friend of Tina's asked her, "When are we going to stop celebrating your marriage?" Tina's answer was—and year after year continues to be—a joyful and profoundly grateful "Never."

CHAPTER ELEVEN

Growing Older Together

No man or woman really knows what perfect love is until
they have been married a quarter of a century.

—Mark Twain, *Notebook*

One of the nice things about aging is that after so many
years of coping you begin to see that problems aren't
insurmountable. You know you've solved them before....
No relationship is a bed of roses.

—Paula Doress and Diana Siegal,
Ourselves, Growing Older

AFTER TWENTY-FIVE or forty or more years of marriage, most of us know that it's no bed of roses. And few of us, maybe none of us, can claim a personal knowledge of perfect love. We've learned, over time, ways of working with the imperfections inherent in being married. We've learned, in our first or perhaps in a subsequent marriage, to live with the lulls of everyday married life. But as we grow older, and old, together we'll need to solve or surmount—or simply endure—an array of new marital problems that, along with a few new unexpected joys, are likely to characterize our later years.

Many of us, having benefited from a leap in life expectancy, will have lots of later years to spend with our spouse, years that begin when our children leave home and that end, if we don't divorce, when one of us dies. "Grow old along with me! The best is yet to be" can only evoke a skeptical "Yeah, right," as we contemplate the assorted assaults of age. But growing older together instead of separately, and holding each other's hand as we make the trip, can be—if not the best life has to offer—a good deal better than going it alone.

It is easier to grow older and old together if we're flexible, adaptable, open to change. It is easier if we recognize that, whether or not we're flexible and adaptable, our marriage won't stay the marriage it used to be. The children depart, we retire, we become in a number of small and large ways emeritus, and at each of these later-life stages, significant changes are forced upon us, ready or not. These changes, which we resist, accept, deny, or try to reshape to suit our own purposes, offer opportunities—not necessarily *welcome* opportunities—for growing up. These changes redefine us in ways that are sometimes good and sometimes bad news for our marriage.

Having more time for ourselves and each other now that the kids have moved on—though some adult children return, and some *never* leave home—may be a source of delight or trepidation. Not everybody suffers from empty-nest angst. "This is what I had in mind when I married you," a husband says to his wife after they've packed their youngest son off to college. "I've been waiting all these years for those strangers to leave so I could be here just with you." On the other hand, when another wife was asked what she planned to do when their last child was gone, she not-too-jokingly said, "Have a nervous breakdown." He imagines their being, again, the lovers they used to be before their first baby was born. She cannot imagine *who* she will be or what in the world they will talk about when they no longer are talking about their kids.

Some couples, like Milton and me, who started our families on our honeymoon and had kids around for the first twenty years of our marriage, revel in the freedom and spontaneity of childless marriedness. Indeed, I remember getting a call from our youngest, a freshman in college, announcing that he was coming home for the weekend, and my replying (before I could edit myself), "But honey, didn't you come home just last weekend?" Yes, of course we loved and missed our kids and were happy— well, almost always happy—to see them. Still, life after children held many pleasures too.

It doesn't for everyone. The departure of the children and the end of daily involvement with their needs and demands and difficulties and joys can be, for some parents, a painful, painful loss. And it sometimes can force a couple to confront the problems existing between the two of them, problems that their focus on their children had allowed them to avoid. "We're great as a family," I've heard in effect from several women and men in the difficult aftermath of their last child's departure. "It turns out we're not so great as a husband and wife."

Indeed, some couples may find it so hard to be a twosome again that they choose instead to be virtually full-time grandparents. Taking their grandchildren everywhere—to school, to after-school lessons, to the playground—they escape the strains of too much one-on-one closeness.

Another source of difficulty when the nest empties and he and she are alone at last is that she—if she's been devoting herself to full-time motherhood and full-time wifehood—may decide to pursue, or prepare to pursue, a career. Some husbands think this is great. Some husbands think this is great until they discover that their wives, at school or the office, have become far less available for business dinners or for fun and games. Some husbands never think this is great and may actively oppose a wife's wish to work because, as a therapist said of one such marriage, "he needs her to be there at his beck and call, and so he needs her *not* to blossom." And some wives, faced with a husband's opposition to their ambitions, may—like the woman whose husband needs her at his beck and call—put them aside and feel resentful and stifled or—like Julianne—defy him and set an ugly marital conflict in motion.

"During my three years of law school," Julianne told me, "he made every single day of my life a misery, picking at me, snarling at me, finding fault with everything I did. He hated that I was taking this time away from him. He also kept insisting he hated lawyers. He eventually got over it—it helped that I started making very good money—but our marriage suffered and almost didn't survive."

Retirement from work will, like retirement from parenting full-time, force important changes on us and our marriage. The happily retired among us may find ourselves busier than we were before—volunteering, working out, taking lessons in French or

piano or painting, and, with our spouses, traveling together, playing bridge or tennis or golf together, baby-sitting the grandchildren together, or spending a midweek afternoon at a movie or a
museum or a mall together, balancing individual time with couple time and making the most of our freedom and good health.

The short-story writer Alice Munro offers a glimpse of one
retirement marriage—the marriage of Fiona and Grant, who live
together contentedly in the country, until their cozy arrangements go awry. Following a pleasant daily ritual, they "usually
prepared supper together. One of them made the drinks and the
other the fire, and they talked about his work (he was writing a
study of legendary Norse wolves . . .) and about whatever Fiona
was reading and what they had been thinking during their close
but separate day. This was their time of liveliest intimacy, though
there was also, of course, the five or ten minutes of physical sweet-
ness just after they got into bed—something that did not often
end up in sex but reassured them that sex was not over yet."

Separate and together, many couples find much to enjoy in
their retirement, including—despite some slackening of desire
and less-than-reliable erections—a sufficiently satisfactory sexual
life. But for others among us, unhappily comparing what we have
with what we had, retirement can feel like a kind of death.

Maybe we've lost our confidence because we have no job to
confirm our competence. Maybe we feel diminished now that our
salary, our title, our secretary are gone. Maybe we're bored with
make-work work like clearing out the garage and mowing the
lawn. Maybe we're feeling as useless, depressed, and despairing as
poor Raymond, who told couples therapists Steve and Cathy
Brody, "I'm like an old bull elephant without any tusks. They
might as well shoot me."

Analyst Erik Erikson, writing about retirement, noted that "for those whose creativity and involvement in work has been of major importance and whose identity is largely derived from that work, there can be a bitter and deprived feeling of being expelled and depreciated." And psychiatrist Sidney Isenberg, addressing a group of aging high-level executives, warned them "to expect some depression and some strain on the marriage when they retire," noting that for many of them their identity was so tied up with their work that they were likely to "be lost for a while and to suffer from the pain of separation." He added that, in some instances, when a retired husband becomes depressed, his wife— "who has to put up with him"—may find herself becoming depressed as well.

When some wives try—and how they try!—to spur their retired husbands into some sort of gratifying, constructive activity, they may find themselves as thwarted as the fictional Enid was in Jonathan Franzen's novel *The Corrections*, who, "try as she might, she couldn't get him interested in life. When she encouraged him to take up his metallurgy again, he looked at her as if she'd lost her mind. When she asked whether there wasn't some yard work he could do, he said his legs hurt. When she reminded him that the husbands of her friends all had hobbies (Dave Schumpert his stained glass, Kirby Rood his intricate chalets for nesting purple finches, Chuck Meisner his hourly monitoring of his investment portfolio), Alfred acted as if she were trying to distract him from some great labor of his."

Retirement seems to pose more problems for husbands than for wives, who, when they retire, are more adept at finding non-career gratifications. And though they might agree with Monica's tart observation that "ever since I quit my job, I don't get as much respect at dinner parties," they aren't as bothered as men by their social demotion—at least, not yet; perhaps this will change. Furthermore, men are likely to be concerned that their wives will begin to lose respect for them when they're no longer big earners or big shots. They may be concerned that retirement will, one way or another, reduce the power and perks they enjoy in the marriage.

But if men seem to find retirement more worrisome and more difficult than women do, their problems very often become their wife's problems. As Esther confessed, "I have so little respect for him when I see him just hanging around in his sweats doing nothing." And Gloria, who needs her husband's importance to feel important, is terrified that now that he has retired as CEO of a big corporation, "all the lights will go out." A woman Erikson spoke with has had to deal, since her husband became a retiree, "with the new responsibility of boosting his confidence. He seems to require frequent reminding that he has not suddenly become incompetent—just retired." Other women admit to viewing their in-retirement husbands as somewhat less sexual, perhaps also seeing them as "an old bull elephant without any tusks." And several women, late bloomers who are starting to hit it big in their careers, have discovered they're out of sync with husbands who don't go to an office anymore.

The most common complaint, however, is that the wives of retired men want more time to be by themselves or with friends, but their husbands, having fewer projects and friendships and having become more emotionally needy, expect an "excessive" amount of married togetherness. Says Frankie: "If he wants to stay home and I want to go up to Boston for a few days, I'd like to be able to say, 'You stay and I'll go.' But I know he'd feel hurt and deserted even if I cooked him his favorite meals and froze them. He didn't used to be this way, but now he says he hates eating and sleeping without me."

She says his need for her presence has been making her feel both "flattered and confined." Some wives complain that they feel more confined than flattered.

> He's starting conversations with me when I'm reading.
> He's chiming in when I talk to my friends on the phone.
> He's coming with me when I shop at the supermarket
> So I won't have to shop alone. I like alone.

Along with the marital changes that accompany the empty nest and retirement, we may be unsettled by finding ourselves emeritus, defined by my dictionary as one who's received an honorable discharge from active service, and defined by me as someone who is sitting, or seen as sitting, on the sidelines while the younger and abler do what we once did. When the husband and wife who have always presided over the Thanksgiving dinner, surrounded by family, are pressed to surrender their roles—"because this is getting to be too much for you"—to their children, they're being relegated to emeritus. When their travel agent recommends a cruise instead of a trek—"because it's less demanding and, besides, they've got a doctor on the ship"—they're being relegated to emeritus. When several family members strongly urge them to stop driving their car after dark, they're being relegated to emeritus. And when people say of a husband and wife, when they're dancing the Lindy at their grandson's wedding, "Aren't they cute," they're being dismissed as a sexually viable couple and relegated to sexually emeritus.

Husbands or wives may sometimes resist being seen as sexually out of it by insistently displaying their sexuality—flirting, patting and pawing, injecting double entendres into conversations—sometimes with women or men their own age and some- times with the friends of their grown children. One man I know enraged his wife and terrorized the young women his daughter brought home because of his habit of "talking dirty" and pressing hugs and open-mouthed kisses upon them. On the other hand, a wife I spoke with is envious of her flirtatious age-seventy husband, "because women, the young ones, the old ones, still find him attractive and respond to him, or come on to him, while no one"—she says this wistfully and resentfully—"treats me like a sex object anymore."

Some elderly couples, notes Erikson, are able to make their peace with diminished degrees of "enterprise and involvement," accepting new self-definitions and new limitations, "new internal perceptions of themselves." One wife, expressing contentment with the current stage of her marriage, matter-of-factly and sensibly observed, "We've had most of life's experiences, and we've sort of settled back now to remember and to live out the rest of our life with a great deal less activity."

This woman and her husband are clearly ready to be emeritus. But some couples very passionately are not. And sometimes one partner is and one partner isn't.

A couple, for instance, may disagree about whether their family house is now a burden or whether even the weather is now a burden. Is it finally time to move to an apartment? Is it finally time to move to someplace warm? Surrendering a beloved home to a younger couple who can more easily walk up the stairs and shovel snow may make perfect sense at a certain point in life, but it can also make us feel discharged from active duty, sidelined, emeritus.

———————

In writer Tillie Olsen's classic short story "Tell Me a Riddle," selling the house is a matter of constant controversy, though it also serves as a stand-in for a lifetime of accumulated resentments. The husband and wife in the story engage in corrosively bitter battles: He wants to sell in order to move to a co-op for the aging. She won't hear of it. What do we need with all these rooms? he screams at her. Because I'm used to having them, she replies. You won't have to do any cooking or cleaning, he tells her. And then what would I do with myself? she replies. "After forty-seven years," her son Sammy insists when the family tries to resolve the matter, "there's surely some way you can find to live in peace." His mother's answer summarizes her present and past unhappiness: "There is no help, my children. Different things we need."

This brilliant and terrible story uses the argument over moving to explore all the ways in which a marriage has withered, reminding us that staying married and growing older and old together doesn't mean that we got or will ever get the many "different things we need." It also reminds us, however, that sometimes even in tortured marriages like this one, long-married couples have moments of tender connection. And so this husband sleeps badly when he's not sleeping next to his wife because there have been all those years of the "old harmonies and dependencies deep in their bodies; she curled to him, or he coiled to her, each warmed, warming, turning as the other turned, the night a long embrace."

And yet he feels he is "chained with her, bitter woman."

And yet she lives with a "bellyful of bitterness and every day . . . a different old grievance."

Literature and life are full of unhappy couples growing older together, slouching into the sunset finding fault with each other every step of the way. We've met the vituperative Martha and George of Albee's *Who's Afraid of Virginia Woolf?* True story: When some neighbors of mine saw the play, the husband looked at his wife and said, in all sincerity, "They call *that* fighting?" (They're no longer either my neighbors or still married.) And then there are Alice and Captain, the miserable couple of August Strindberg's *The Dance of Death,* who share "a groundless hate, without cause, without purpose, but also without end," who have tried to leave each other many times but are "welded together and can't get free," who wait for death as for "a liberator."

Some dance-of-death marriages last because the wife and husband are welded together by hate, a bond at least as powerful as love. Some crazy marriages last because of the couple's perfectly meshed neurotic needs. Some mean little marriages last because both he and she feel at home with the bickering and badgering, the put-downs and gotchas they constantly engage in, exactly as their parents did before them. And some deadened marriages last because one or both partners want to hold on to the comforts of marriage, or because they feel too guilty or frightened to leave, or because—even though the marriage is arid and empty—they aren't sure that leaving would be an improvement. Many of these angry, lonely, joyless, loveless, sniping wives and husbands remain unhappily married for decades and decades until they are liberated by death. But some of them may decide on a late-life divorce.

When women and men initiate divorces late in life—and there's been a substantial increase in recent years—they tend to do so for very different reasons. The women, says Kate Vetrano, head of the American Bar Association's elder-law committee, have had it with being the caregivers who "give, give, give . . . without the proper acknowledgment or respect" and are looking to live, at last, on their own terms. The men see divorce as "their second wind, their second chance at a new woman, a new life." In the old days, says Vetrano, you married young, you raised your children, and then you died. But today older people, many of whom are living vigorously well into their eighties, "see many healthy years ahead of them. They decide, 'I'm going to make those years happy.'" They decide to divorce.

For those who don't divorce, however, happiness may have to wait for death, the waiting sometimes accompanied by the painful knowledge of all that has been missed, the grievances sometimes nursed in bitter silence and sometimes tirelessly expressed. Enid, in the final years of her husband Alfred's life, felt compelled to repeatedly tell him, "while she still had time, how wrong he'd been and how right she'd been. How wrong not to love her more, how wrong not to cherish her and have sex at every opportunity, how wrong not to trust her financial instincts, how wrong to have spent so much time at work and so little with the children, how wrong to have been so negative, how wrong to have been so gloomy, how wrong to have run away from life, how wrong to have said no, again and again, instead of yes." And when Alfred finally dies, she walks out into the spring night feeling, after almost five decades with this difficult man, "that nothing could kill her hope now, nothing. She was seventy-five and she was going to make some changes in her life."

A marriage may be troubled for most of a couple's married life, or real problems may arise only in later years—when we return to being two people instead of two parents and find how little we have in common; when retirement leads to depression or too much togetherness; or when our emeritus status leaves us socially, emotionally, and—often—geographically dislocated. Money difficulties may also stir up marital unhappiness late in life, especially if the income we had counted upon to cushion these later years isn't sufficient, or has to be used to help our adult children, or is eaten away by medical expenses, generating constraints on spending and where-has-our-money-gone recriminations and feelings of disappointment and deprivation. But perhaps the biggest impediments to happiness as we grow older and old together are the illnesses and impairments that inevitably accompany the aging process.

His back gives out, and sex gets complicated. Her knees give out, and ski vacations are through. Arthritis puts an end to the gardening that, for decades, was a mutual pleasure. Or he desperately needs, but refuses to use, a hearing aid. As always, we continue to discuss the state of the world and the charms of our grandchildren, but now we often discuss how we slept last night too, in addition to such matters as palpitations, the prostate, reflux, and colonoscopies. Indeed, the state of our health has become, alas, as important to us as the state of the world, for even less-than-life-threatening medical problems will alter the way we live, day by day, with each other.

Then there's the tougher stuff: a severe depression that turns the golden years gray with misery, or one of the major diseases that, either suddenly or progressively, makes a massive assault on the body and brain, all of which will teach us, for better and worse, what we and the person we've married are made of.

Sy and Hallie, married forty-five years, can teach all of us what the very well married are made of.

Sy, in the past four years, has gone through three different kinds of cancer, requiring hospitalizations, operations, chemotherapy, and radiation. In addition, the money which he and Hallie had counted on to retire disappeared when their stocks became worthless. At ages sixty-six (Sy) and sixty-three (Hallie), they were forced to sell their dream house and start all over again, minus the hefty pension plan and life-insurance policy that were also lost in their vast financial disaster.

Such reverses could ravage a marriage and tear a couple apart, but Sy and Hallie continue to stand together, anchored by their love for each other, by their shared delight in their children and grandchildren, and by their shared capacity both to enjoy life's highs and to deal with life's lows. "She's a trouper. She rolls with the punches," Sy says of Hallie. "We're on the same track. She's

with me all the way." As for the future, both of them believe that Sy will recoup their losses one day—and already, he says, he's starting to do just that, citing the return of his chemo-shorn hair, their sex life, his golf game, and, thanks to the new business he started, some money. He adds, "We've always been aware that, good as things can be, nothing's forever. We've seen many bubbles burst, and we know that when a bubble bursts, we need to get busy and blow another bubble."

Sy doesn't praise his wife for being so steadfast and so supportive—he says that's who she is, that's what she does. Nor does Hallie praise him for being so resolute, so resilient, and so strong. However, he confides with a smile, she keeps a Superman figurine on her night table and on the face of this utterly indomitable hero of our childhood she has pasted a photograph of . . . Sy.

Sy and Hallie, two grown-ups who are putting their life back together in their sixties, know that they can count on each other through medical and economic hard times and know that they can count on themselves to do whatever it is they have to do. Jess, married over sixty years, is clearly a grown-up too as he tends to a wife whose mind, these past few years, has been relentlessly deteriorating. A vigorous man in his eighties, he spends half a day, every day, still practicing law, and the other half at home babysitting Mae, relinquishing vacations, travel, and most of his social life in order to be with her. He has money enough to pay for the very finest around-the-clock-care, but he doesn't choose to take care of her that way, "because she likes being with me, and because, detached as she is today, she still is always looking around for Jess." He adds that, to his surprise, he's "feeling more tender toward her than I have in all our years together and I'm

kissing her more often too." Refusing to see his patient, protective caretaking of Mae as anything special, he says that it isn't that difficult to do and that "she would have done the same for me. Besides," he adds, "I think I've been pretty damn lucky in my life. What's happening now is just a part of the voyage."

Disability and caretaking may indeed be part of the voyage, but some couples find it hard to be philosophic. As one glum husband puts it, "We've been a good balance to each other in the past. But there's not a good balance now." In the past his wife was a competent, energetic mother of five and a wonderfully supportive marriage partner who encouraged and took pride in his professional achievements and fashioned a happy household in which he flourished. But the now that he and she live in has been redefined by her medical ills, which require him to take care of an often ungrateful and no-longer-supportive invalid "who is frustrated and embarrassed at being helpless," who is "frightened and furious" when he sometimes "passes the buck" by hiring outside help, and who—because she's so needy and so terrified—"ties him to her with a very short rope," preventing him from seeing friends by refusing any assistance from paid workers.

Erik Erikson, writing of this sad couple, says that each "feels wronged, isolated, and abandoned." The current state of their marriage, he says, "represents a poignant extreme in the kinds of adjustments old age and its deteriorations can force long-term partners to make."

Moving from a beautiful home to two rooms in an old-folks facility that offers meals and extensive medical care, to live with a disabled spouse who grows more and more demanding and who dozes off in the middle of conversations, isn't merely grim—it can also be heartbreaking, especially if you're watching the

woman or man that you have loved being taken apart, bit by bit, by a brutal disease.

"I can't remember your name, but I know that I love you," a man tells his wife of sixty years when Alzheimer's has stripped him of most of his memory. And here is the brave, wrenching letter that my valiant friend Selma Anne wrote to her husband, preparing him for the darkness that was about to descend on their fifty-nine years of marriage:

> *Dear Paul,*
> *The wife you once had and whom you loved dearly, whose skills made you proud, and who fed you well in many ways, unfortunately has been stolen by Dr. Alzheimer's fatal horror. . . . I am not what I was. There is no question but that my skills are leaving me, my mind is failing me, and any pretense of healing is false. As I know from watching my mother* [who had the same disease], *the day will come when I will be so angry with fate that I will throw things at you. Please forgive me ahead of time, and try to remember me the way I was.*

Try to remember me the way I was. Try to remember me. Remember. In a poem by Stanley Kunitz, the speaker recalls being "wild with love" over forty years ago, and asks,

> Darling, do you remember
> the man you married? Touch me,
> remind me who I am.

Having a wife or a husband who remembers, and reminds us, who we once were is one of the sweetest aspects of long-term marriage.

A woman of seventy tells me that her husband, who fell in love with her when she was a sexy, playful twenty-three, has never forgotten how hard it was to win her away from all the guys who were after her. She says, "He looks at me and still sees the red curly hair and the young body in the bikini, and he can't get over how fortunate he is that he was the man I finally chose."

And she can't get over how fortunate she is that the man she chose over forty years ago still holds the girl she once was in his heart today.

I sit with a man as he muses upon his fifty-seven years of married life: "We've been so lucky," he says to me. "So lucky. We loved raising children together, and we loved the later years, bowling and going on cruises, enjoying the grandchildren. I met her when she was nineteen and fell in love with her at first sight and I'm still in love with her."

This man was reminiscing at the hospice bedside of his dying wife. Her eyes were closed, her face pale, her breathing shallow. And yet, when I asked him how soon after their fateful, romantic meeting they had married and he said that he was having trouble remembering, his wife's eyes fluttered open and she softly but clearly answered, "Four months."

She was helping him remember the way they were.

Erikson's study of couples who have grown old together has found that most of the husbands and wives describe "marriages of lifelong mutual affection, supportiveness, understanding, companionship, and ever-increasing appreciation." However, when he checked his files, he was startled to discover that some of these very same husbands and wives had—several decades earlier—complained at length about their marital difficulties. Perhaps, Erikson speculates, they prefer to believe, and do believe today, that they were "devoted from the very beginning." Perhaps their later-life intimacy has transcended and colored their earlier marital history, allowing them to forget past discontents and recall only a "long lifetime of marital satisfaction."

Perhaps, when it comes to marital satisfaction, forgetting can be as important as remembering.

As for what satisfies us—what makes us happy after decades and decades together—here is what some wives and husbands have told me, and whether or not they're recasting the past in an overly rosy glow, they speak from the heart:

From a woman in her sixties, married thirty-two years: "I like to hear the sound of his voice. I like the security of his sleeping next to me. I am happy when I hear the garage door open and I know that he is home. I feel safe with him—I know he'd never hurt me. I got married at age thirty-three because I was madly in love—and I adore him still."

From a woman in her seventies, married forty-two years: "He's sweet and strong and masculine. He's my rock of Gibraltar. He's my family and my buddy and the best company—I like having him around. We know each other's crazinesses and we've figured out how to live with them. And he smells delicious—I love the way he smells."

From a woman in her eighties, married sixty years: "I've always felt benignly toward men. I've only known kindly men, and my husband hasn't ever disappointed me. I have never once put my hand out"—when she's in need, when something goes wrong—"that he hasn't taken it. And if what he sometimes offers me isn't always exactly what I want, I know it's the best he can do and I give him credit, I'm willing to give him full credit, for trying."

From a man almost ninety, married sixty-five years: "We were like two halves of one entity, two separate people blended into one. It was almost as though heaven had mandated that her life and mine be intertwined."

Growing older and old together, our lives may become increasingly intertwined, as even the most self-reliant among us discover the virtues of mutual dependence. We learn to watch over each other, to help each other, to lean on each other, hard as the giving and taking sometimes can be. We even learn that accepting his dependence, her dependence, our dependence, can be another kind of maturity, if, like Jess, we can put it within the context of our whole life and understand that it's "just a part of the voyage."

In the movie *On Golden Pond*, with Katharine Hepburn as Ethel and Henry Fonda as Norman, we watch a long-married couple—in the summer months of Norman's eightieth year—coming to some kind of terms with his poignant dependencies. Although Norman is, and must always have been, irascible, ornery, tactless, his failing heart and memory have made him angry and frightened and even more difficult. Ethel's relentless optimism can't jolly him out of his gloom. Marriage to Norman requires a lot of hard work.

Ethel sees all his faults, but she also sees beyond his faults to the man she loves, to the man she knows "would walk through fire for me." She is also able to recognize that when her husband yells, "he is yelling at life," an "old lion" reminding himself "that he can still roar." Teasing him, cajoling him, protecting him, defending him, she's determined to bring what pleasure she can to his days. And when she's afraid he might die, and prays, "Dear God, don't take him now. You don't want him. He's just an old poop," her prayer conveys the depths of her exasperated love and how much, how very much, she needs him too.

Married for decades, she knows, as all of us long-time marrieds know, what it takes to stay married and why it's worth the effort. Not perfect love, and no bed of roses, marriage can nonetheless be the best place to be as we grow older together.

CHAPTER TWELVE

Staying Married

*I mean you're given all these lessons for the unimportant
things—piano-playing, typing . . . how to balance equa-
tions, which Lord knows you will never have to do in normal life. But how about parenthood? Or marriage, either,
come to think of it. Before you can drive a car you need a
state-approved course of instruction, but driving a car is
nothing, nothing, compared to living day in and day out
with a husband.*

—Anne Tyler, *Breathing Lessons*

WE WHO ARE LIVING, day in and day out, with a husband or a wife, did not take marriage lessons before being married, even though being married is sure to be more complicated
than driving a car. There were things that we weren't prepared for
and didn't know that we didn't know until we married, things
that we had to learn on the job, through experience, through trial
and plenty of error. A therapist friend of mine says that "there is
nothing that can prepare us for marriage but marriage." I both
agree with her—and disagree. Even without a state-approved
course of instruction in matrimony, we are able to get some sense
of what marriage can be. As for how to stay married, day in and

day out, through decades and decades of married life, here are some thoughts from this book that might bear repeating.

Much as we yearn for certainty, we can never know in advance that we've made the right choice. Picking a partner who suits us now and forever is mostly a matter of dumb luck. The less luck we have, the harder we will need to work at making our marriage work, although every marriage is "work, day labor, day labor." We marry in absolute ignorance and stay married by being lucky and doing the work.

Says a wife, married thirty-five years, "Eternal vigilance is the price of a good marriage. Pay attention. Never stop paying attention. Take care of your marriage."

The work we do, the attention we pay, the sacrifices we make are on behalf of something bigger than both of us. In order to build it together, we have to give over some portion of our self, give it not to our husband or wife but to our joint creation, our "third thing." We stay married through the darkest of days because our deepest commitment, our shared commitment, is to this third thing, this marriage we are creating.

Says Mrs. Antrobus in Thorton Wilder's *The Skin of Our Teeth*, "I married you because you gave me a promise. That promise made up for your faults. And the promise I gave you made up for mine. Two imperfect people got married and it was the promise that made the marriage. . . . And when our children were growing up, it wasn't a house that protected them; and it wasn't our love that protected them—it was that promise."

The promise we make to each other is that we'll protect and preserve our marriage, that we'll feed and watch over our marriage, that we'll defend it against attacks—even our own. The promise we make to each other, and to ourselves, is that our marriage will endure.

From time to time, however, in spite of the promises we make, we're going to find ourselves wondering, "What am I doing here?" From time to time we will find ourselves hating—not merely disliking but hating—the husband or the wife we usually love. From time to time and sometimes for painfully long stretches of time, we will look around at our spouse, at our kids, at our passable but oh-so-prosaic marriage, appalled that we have signed on for this for life. From time to time we will wonder whether this is as good as it gets, and is that good enough.

We stay married because we promised to stay married. Because we want to raise our kids with the only person who loves them as much as we do. Because we have fashioned, through daily routines and special celebrations, "rituals of emotional connection." And because, as the years go by, we have created and shared an irreplaceable history.

Says a wife, married sixty years, "All that I was went into my marriage, grew and matured in it. I am its creator and its product. All of my activities have been in it, with it, around it. My friendships and my work have been woven into it. I have known love, caring, parenthood, loss, pockets of human illumination, layers of knowledge. My marriage is my life."

But the history of our marriage, whether or not it is our life, and in spite of all those rituals of connection, is not only, as one woman put it, "not the Fourth of July every day." It often, too often, slogs rather than sparkles. In our efforts to stay married through the disenchantments of couplehood, through the disarrays of parenthood, through the rut and routine of everyday married life, we might try to embrace and enjoy domestic dailiness. Through marriage's "soars and slumps," we might try to discover a few sonnets at the supermarket. And when romantic passion succumbs, as it must, to the mundane, we might consciously choose to see married love not merely as what we possess at the start of our marriage, but as a heroic adventure, a magnificent accomplishment that we strive to achieve together over the years.

We might choose to cultivate "a romance of the ordinary."

Says Michael Vincent Miller in *Intimate Terrorism*, "After all, don't husbands and wives have to go to heroic lengths to make a marriage work these days? Perhaps marriage in the modern world, with all its restless energy, its labyrinths of complex meanings to negotiate, its ordeals and setbacks to overcome, could be our next arena for heroic deeds."

The lengths we go to to stay married might include attempting to live by the following precepts, which tend to be more heroic (and a hell of a lot more difficult) than they may sound: Try to be nice to each other even if you don't particularly feel like it. Try to give to each other without being asked. Remember that, like charity, courtesy and charm begin at home. Offer a little more praise and a lot less criticism than you think your spouse deserves. Honor each other's goodwill and good intentions, even when you don't get what you need. Don't expect to get all that you need from each other. Figure out how intimate you can be without suffocation and how separate you can be without alienation. When possible, laugh. When possible, say yes to having sex—with the husband or wife to whom you are married. Keep in mind that fidelity is not in the lap of the gods but a choice that you consciously make, again and again. Compromise. Compromise some more.

Says Jo, in Sue Miller's novel *While I Was Gone,* "There are always compromises, of course, but they are at the heart of what it means to be married. They are, occasionally, everything."

It helps, in our efforts at compromise, if we can distinguish injuries to our soul from injuries merely to our sensibilities. It helps if we can stand, for a minute or two, in our partner's shoes and look at the view from his or her perspective. It's easier to compromise if we can dispense with Mars-Venus combative polarities and see our husband or wife as what one therapist likes to call "the other half of the suffering human race." It's easier to compromise if we recognize that, when we do, the winner's the marriage.

But sometimes we cannot compromise. Sometimes a resolution cannot be found. Sometimes we end our discussions, negotiations, chilly hostilities, or screaming fights with neither of us giving up an inch of ground. Sometimes we cannot be moved because our differences are simply irreconcilable.

Faced with the tough reality that, in this or that regard, he'll never change, she'll never change, that's how it is, we stay married by reminding ourselves what we like about, and connects us to, our partner, and by letting the emphasis fall on what is right instead of what is wrong in our marriage. Some may call this selling out or merely making do; we can choose to call it mature acceptance, saying to ourselves with far less bitterness than rue, "That's how it is."

Says a wife, married twenty-six years, "I also try to remember it's not about me. He isn't doing this"—whatever it is that is making her crazy—"to torture me." Knowing he'll never change whatever it is that she wishes he'd change, she tries to work around it or bear with it or ignore it but confesses that she sometimes still gets mad. Not being a saint, she doesn't expect to ever be totally tolerant of his failings, but she more and more often can tell herself, "That's how it is."

We stay married by making some peace with what can't be changed. We also stay married by adapting to change, to the changes that—with or without our consent—occur in us, in our spouse, and in our marriage. These changes will require us to be flexible and adaptable and sometimes to endure substantial pain. They also will require us, if we wish to stay *happily* married, to keep revising our definition of happiness, revising it to reflect the shifting realities of our life and of our age.

And so we might view the heart-pounding tumult of falling madly in love as one kind of happiness, the definitive happy experience of our youth. But reading the Sunday papers in the silent, sustaining intimacy that flows between partners who've shared a lifetime together can, if we are willing to revise our definition, surely be defined as happiness too.

And on Saturday nights
When my husband and I have rented
Something with Fred Astaire for the VCR,

And we're sitting around in our robes discussing
The state of the world, back exercises, our Keoghs,
And whether to fix the transmission or buy a new car,
And we're eating a pint of rum-raisin ice cream on the grounds that
Tomorrow we're starting a diet of fish, fruit, and grain,
And my dad's in Miami dating a very nice widow,
And no one we love is in serious trouble or pain,
And our bringing-up-baby days are far behind us,
But our senior-citizen days have not begun,
It's not what I called happiness
When I was twenty-one,
But it's turning out to be
What happiness is.

All happily married couples seem to take pleasure in each other's company and cherish marriage's rootedness and connectedness. They enjoy being central to each other's life. But some happy couples do not require what other couples find crucial to marital happiness, like straight-down-the-line equality, or joined-at-the-hip shared interests, or passionate sex. There are, as I've been told by the married women and men I've talked with, many ways to define being happily married:

Being happily married means hanging out with each other and never—well, hardly ever—being bored with each other. It means knowing each other well enough to know what lies within the other's heart, and trusting each other deeply enough to, sooner or later, allow ourselves to be known. It means, as one wife told me, "being loved and valued by the person we married for what we love and value in ourselves." It means, as one husband told me, "being honored and appreciated, and having such a good time while we're doing it."

Says a wife, married twenty-one years, "I love our friendship and all the little things we share. I love the funny and endearing names we call each other. I love knowing that he is totally reliable. I love discussing ideas with him. I love when he gets sentimental and his eyes well up."

Says a husband, twelve years into his second marriage, "I love to look at her, and the sound of her. I want to live out the rest of my days being near her, to know more of the joy of that, a joy that I had never known before."

Says a wife, married twenty-three years, "What could be better than finding my best friend, soul mate, true love, domestic partner, co-parent, dream date, and everything else all in the same person and having him live with me in my very own house."

Says a husband, married sixteen years, "I've married the most decent human being I've ever known. The warmth and humor and love and appreciation she brings to this marriage is beyond my imagining. It's a continuing process of discovery and reaffirmation."

Being happily married means regarding the person we've married as our lover and source of joy, our comrade and comforter. It means knowing, when times are tough, that we won't be alone. It means, as one husband told me, that "my pain makes her hurt, that my happiness makes her happy." It means, as one wife told me, that "I've found my safe haven, my sanctuary, my home."

Being happily married means seeing our marriage as the best of all possible lives.

But not all the time.

For we need to view married life, as Michael Vincent Miller warns us, not as eternally blissful but as "bittersweet." We need to view it ironically, our dreams of romance tempered by a practical recognition that marriage encompasses disappointment and hardship and hurt. We need to recognize, as Stanley Cavell points out, how very difficult it is "to domesticate sexuality without discouraging it." We need to keep reminding ourselves—when we look with displeasure upon the person we married—that nobody's perfect.

We need to grow up.

It's important to say—and I know that I probably haven't said this enough—that growing up doesn't mean always beige, always moderate. We can be playful, ecstatic, goofy, intemperate, and unreasonable. Grown-ups needn't be sensible all the time. Nor, when we look at our marriage and at the person we married, are we required to cast off *all* our illusions. If he still thinks he hit the jackpot when she said yes to him, if she still thinks he's the sexiest man on earth, well . . . lucky them.

But still, we need to grow up—and that's not always easy.

Having relinquished oneness for twoness, the wild for the tame, freedom for obligation, having renounced surprise for predictability, we may feel that we became grown-ups simply by virtue of having made the choice to marry. But we've yet to learn how much patience, perseverance, tolerance, sacrifice, and generosity marriage will ask of us. We've yet to learn how hard we'll have to work, together and separately, day in and day out throughout our married life.

After forty-two years, my husband and I are still learning, though we seem to have figured out a thing or two.

John Updike writes about "the living moment awash with beauty ignored in the quest for a better moment, slightly elsewhere, with some slightly differing other." We've learned to embrace those moments, those living moments awash with beauty, whenever we can. We attend to the living moment and we're grateful to be sharing it together, though there surely are times when my husband would prefer any "differing other" to this pesty woman, though there surely are times when I would prefer any "differing other" to this maddening man. As for those terrible moments when children fall ill or towers implode, we're grateful to be holding each other's hand. Hard though we work to stay married, we're still grateful for the dumb luck that brought us together.

Give us forty more years or so and we'll probably grow into a grown-up marriage.

NOTES

CHAPTER 1: WHY WE GET MARRIED

Page 5   "The dread of loneliness": Connolly, *The Unquiet Grave*, in *The International Thesaurus of Quotations*, compiled by Rhoda Thomas Tripp, p. 383.

Page 6   "A young college-educated bourgeois male": Roth, *My Life as a Man*, pp. 169–170.

Page 7   45 percent: Wallerstein et al., *The Unexpected Legacy of Divorce*, p. 295, is the source for the figures on divorce rates for first and second marriages.

Page 8   two to three times greater: The figure on the divorce rate of children whose parents have been divorced comes from The National Marriage Project, *The State of Our Unions 1999*, p. 8.

Page 8   "we didn't want to make": Lois Smith Brady, "Ulcca Joshi and Christopher Hansen," *New York Times*, August 5, 2001, section 9, p. 9.

Page 8   twenty-seven for men, twenty-five for women: The National Marriage Project, *The State of Our Unions 1999*, p. 19.

Page 10   civil solidarity pact: Suzanne Daley, "French Couples Take Plunge That Falls Short of Marriage," *New York Times*, April 18, 2000, pp. A1, A4.

Page 10   "sex without strings": The National Marriage Project, *The State of Our Unions 2000*, p. 6.

Page 11   *Lebensabschnittgefährte*: Roger Cohen, "Is the Frankfort Stock Exchange a Place for Sex?" *New York Times*, February 16, 2000, p. A4.

Page 11   "covenant marriage": Francine Russo, "Bridal Vows Revisited," *Time*, July 24, 2000, pp. G1–G3.

Page 12   "Will I ever get married?": Viorst, "Will I Ever Get Married?" in *When Did I Stop Being Twenty and Other Injustices*, p. 11.

Page 15   *Before You Say "I Do"*: Outcalt, *Before You Say "I Do."*

Page 17   grew from less than half a million: Popenoe and Whitehead, The National Marriage Project, *Should We Live Together?* p. 3.

Notes

Page 17   More than half of all first marriages: Ibid.

Page 17   46 percent higher: Ibid., p. 4.

Page 17   Although this finding doesn't apply: Ibid., p. 6.

Page 18   "It is reasonable to speculate": Ibid., p. 5.

Page 19   the rate of marriages has declined: The National Marriage Project, *The State of Our Unions 1999*, p. 18.

Page 19   a mere 23.5 percent: This figure comes from the 2000 census.

Page 19   "marriage . . . no longer looms": Ibid., p. 12.

Page 19   "a permanent sleepover": Whitehead and Popenoe, The National Marriage Project, *Why Wed?* p. 15.

Page 21   "purple-haired, tattooed": Ingall, "Going to the Temple," in Chasman and Jhee, eds., *Here Lies My Heart*, p. 27.

Page 21   "I want to say": Ibid., p. 29.

Page 21   "We have looked at": Jennifer Steinhauer quotes Waite in "Fewer Take Journey to the State of Wedlock," *New York Times*, January 9, 2000, pp. 21–22, quote on p. 22.

Page 22   "wonderful dream man": Heimel, "Beware of Mr. Right," in Chasman and Jhee, eds., *Here Lies My Heart*, p. 18.

Page 22   "I'd been traveling": Fussman, "How I Bought My Wedding Ring," in Chasman and Jhee, eds., *Here Lies My Heart*, p. 35.

Page 23   "Marry" and "Not Marry": Darwin, "This Is the Question," *The Autobiography of Charles Darwin*, pp. 232–234.

Page 25   "There is scarcely": Rilke, "Letters on Love," in Kass and Kass, eds., *Wing to Wing, Oar to Oar*, p. 283.

Page 26   "For one human being": Ibid., p. 284.

CHAPTER 2: THE FIRST SHOCKS OF MARRIAGE

Page 29   "Marriages, after all": Darling, "For Better or Worse," in Chasman and Jhee, eds., *Here Lies My Heart*, p. 188.

Page 30   "The honeymoon is over": Viorst, "The Honeymoon Is Over," in *It's Hard to Be Hip Over Thirty and Other Tragedies of Married Life*, p. 14.

Page 34   "Shortly after the wedding": Perutz, *Marriage Is Hell*, pp. 13–14, 15.

Page 36   "I must affirm": Franklin, "Reflections on Courtship and Marriage," in Kass and Kass, eds., *Wing to Wing, Oar to Oar*, p. 412.

Page 39   "What did he do?": Waite and Gallagher, *The Case for Marriage*, p. 13.

Page 41   "to the possibilities": Dicks, *Marital Tensions*, p. 63.

Page 41   "may persecute in their spouses": Ibid.

Page 42   "Nadine thrived on defiance": Trollope, *Other People's Children*, p. 9.

Page 42   "Dwayne: People told us": Gottman, *Why Marriages Succeed or Fail*, p. 129.

Page 43   "all hell may": Dicks, *Marital Tensions*, p. 81.

Page 43   "I am discussing couples": Ibid.

Page 46   "Any marriage worthy": Kramer, *Should You Leave?* p. 51.

CHAPTER 3: MARRIAGE AND THE FAMILIES

Page 47   "If . . . I quit inviting": Viorst, "Maybe We'll Make It," in *It's Hard to Be Hip Over Thirty and Other Tragedies of Married Life*, p. 18.

Page 50   "requires leaving home": Beavers, *Successful Marriage*, p. 152.

Page 51   "loyalty to one's parents": Ibid., p. 153.

Page 52   "emotionally grow up": I don't have the exact source for this, but it comes from something written by Carl Whitaker for *The Bulletin of the Menninger Clinic*, around 1960.

Page 56   "more often a wish": Boszormenyi-Nagy and Spark, *Invisible Loyalties*, p. 223.

Page 56   "value system and way of life": Ibid.

Page 57   "marriage represents an encounter": Ibid., p. 32.

Page 57   "demands on both spouses": Ibid., p. 103.

Page 57   "form a solid loyalty team": Ibid., p. 105.

Page 58   "many married persons": Ibid., p. 49.

Page 61   "that they not only live": Ibid., p. 218.

Notes

Page 61   "If his mother was drowning": Viorst, "True Love," in *It's Hard to Be Hip Over Thirty and Other Tragedies of Married Life,* p. 70.

Page 68   "most impressed at": Beavers, *Successful Marriage,* p. 80.

Page 68   "even the intrusive in-laws": Boszormenyi-Nagy and Spark, *Invisible Loyalties,* p. 21.

Page 69   "This was her family": Colwin, *Family Happiness,* p. 270.

Page 69   "Therefore a man": Genesis 2:24.

CHAPTER 4: HOW KIDS CHANGE THE COUPLE

Page 71   "Last year I had a shampoo": Viorst, "Nice Baby," in *It's Hard to Be Hip Over Thirty and Other Tragedies of Married Life,* p. 20.

Page 72   "parents who become": Wallerstein and Blakeslee, *The Good Marriage,* p. 79.

Page 72   "children add to a family": Betcher and Macauley, *The Seven Basic Quarrels of Marriage,* p. 233.

Page 72   "primary maternal preoccupation": Winnicott, see chapter on "Primary Maternal Preoccupation," in *Collected Papers.*

Page 73   "mother and daughter cocooned": Frayn, *Headlong,* p. 48.

Page 73   "His love for that baby": Block, *Motherhood as Metamorphosis,* p. 253.

Page 73   "There are times": Rubin, *Intimate Strangers,* p. 201.

Page 76   "Once I notice": Ibid.

Page 76   "The baby wakes up": Ephron, *Heartburn,* p. 158.

Page 79   "there is no exit": Block, *Motherhood as Metamorphosis,* p. 231.

Page 81   "refer to making love": Klass, "Intimacy," in *Love and Modern Medicine,* p. 55.

Page 84   "It is fatherhood": Kass and Kass, eds. *Wing to Wing, Oar to Oar,* p. 17.

Page 84   "a jolt into adulthood": Block, *Motherhood as Metamorphosis,* p. 228.

Page 90   "There is simply no question": Ibid., p. 247.

Page 92   "adults don't make children": I love the line, but I don't know where it came from.

Notes

CHAPTER 5: ORDINARY EVERYDAY MARRIED LIFE

Page 95 "Love begins as a sonnet": Achenbach, "Homeward Bound," in Chasman and Jhee, eds., *Here Lies My Heart,* p. 52.

Page 97 "I'd planned": Viorst, "Anti-Heroine," in *People and Other Aggravations,* p. 40.

Page 98 "The rain had stopped": Yates, *Revolutionary Road,* p. 182.

Page 98 "I was thinking": Sue Miller, *While I Was Gone,* pp. 8–9.

Page 99 "We sometimes go out": Achenbach, "Homeward Bound," in Chasman and Jhee, eds., *Here Lies My Heart,* p. 54.

Page 100 "In July 1965": Shapiro, *After Moondog,* pp. 1, 2, 8.

Page 100 "the puzzlements": Yates, *Revolutionary Road,* from the introduction by Richard Ford, p. xvii.

Page 100 "take heed": Ibid., p. xxvi.

Page 102 "a rude, a withering remark": Johnson, *Le Mariage,* p. 119.

Page 103 "one of the first things": Gottman, *Why Marriages Succeed or Fail,* p. 65.

Page 103 "even newlyweds": Ibid., p. 66.

Page 105 "I made him swear": Viorst, "Nothing But the Truth," in *How Did I Get to Be Forty and Other Atrocities,* p. 38.

Page 106 "Now you've said things": Updike, *Too Far to Go,* p. 40.

Page 106 "not untrue": Larkin, "Talking in Bed," in *Collected Poems,* p. 129.

Page 106 "I'm not one of these": Rubin, *Intimate Strangers,* p. 80.

Page 108 "Too many are eaten alive": Kramer, *Should You Leave?* p. 239.

Page 109 "Awareness of trespass": Ibid.

Page 110 "Alone I could own": Viorst, "Alone," in *How Did I Get to Be Forty and Other Atrocities,* p. 50.

Page 110 "*togetherness* between two people": Rilke, "Letters on Love," in Kass and Kass, eds., *Wing to Wing, Oar to Oar,* pp. 286–287.

Page 110 "a good marriage": Ibid., p. 286.

Notes

Page 112 "He needs someone": Ken Auletta, "The Last Tycoon," *The New Yorker,* April 23 and 30, 2001.

Page 113 An image sticks in my mind: The following four paragraphs, slightly modified here, appeared in Judith Viorst's article "An Open Letter to My Son and Future Daughter-in-Law," *Redbook,* May 1988, pp. 28, 32.

Page 114 "apathy and renewal": Updike, *Too Far to Go,* p. 74.

Page 114 "is both too fierce": Michael Vincent Miller, *Intimate Terrorism,* pp. 145–146.

Page 114 "a romance of the ordinary": Ibid., p. 221

Page 114 a "willed performance": Ibid., p. 229.

Page 115 "rouse ourselves": Muldoon, "Long Finish," in *Paul Muldoon Poems 1968–1998,* pp. 438–441.

Page 115 "the soars and slumps": Ibid.

CHAPTER 6: MARITAL SIBLING RIVALRY

Page 117 "What is a troubled marriage": Michael Vincent Miller, *Intimate Terrorism,* p. 95.

Page 117 "We have a healthy": From Joseph Barbato's interview with Collins, "Poet on a Roll Takes Stock," *Publishers Weekly,* September 17, 2001, p. 48.

Page 117 My husband has been: The following several paragraphs, enlarged upon here and ending with the words "Ingmar Bergman," appeared in Judith Viorst's article "The Marriage Superbowl: When Husbands and Wives Compete," *Redbook,* April 1975, pp. 9, 12.

Page 119 "When we ate": This Joanne-William exchange appears in Shapiro, *After Moondog,* p. 320.

Page 120 "that beautiful people": Blumstein and Schwartz, *American Couples,* p. 251.

Page 122 "I overheard": Sue Miller, *While I Was Gone,* p. 157.

Page 125 "an issue between": Block, *Motherhood as Metamorphosis,* p. 266.

Page 125 "I want him to be important": Rubin, *Intimate Strangers,* p. 197.

Page 125 "not looking to beat": Ibid., pp. 197–198.

Page 126   "I get into": Ibid., p. 199.

Page 127   "Where there is sibling rivalry": Michael Vincent Miller, *Intimate Terrorism,* p. 94.

Page 131   "most modern-day egalitarian": Blumstein and Schwartz, *American Couples,* p. 162.

Page 131   "Even when couples": Wallerstein and Blakeslee, *The Good Marriage,* p. 198.

Page 132   "I feel terrible": Rubin, *Intimate Strangers,* p. 26.

CHAPTER 7: MARRIED SEX

Page 137   "Why is it like this?": Sue Miller, *While I Was Gone,* p. 146.

Page 140   "I have grown accustomed to your face": Viorst, "Familiarity Breeds Content," in *When Did I Stop Being Twenty and Other Injustices,* p. 41.

Page 142   "You want to be": Erica Jong, "Can Sensuality, Tantric Sex Take the Mind off Bad Prose?" *New York Observer,* April 23, 2001, p. 15.

Page 146   "naked at the head": Updike, *Too Far to Go,* p. 117.

Page 147   almost 50 percent of husbands: Pittman, *Private Lies,* p. 34. According to Brody and Brody, *Renew Your Marriage at Midlife,* p. 207, the figures are more than one third of all husbands and almost as many wives.

Page 147   "ten years of monogamy": Blumstein and Schwartz, *American Couples,* pp. 272–274.

Page 151   "I cannot convey": Lawson, *Adultery,* p. 199.

Page 152   "I felt ten feet tall": Ibid.

Page 152   "I have learned to live": Ibid., p. 217.

Page 152   "novel and uncomplicated sex": Ibid.

Page 152   "pleasure in conquest": Ibid.

Page 152   "Marriage tames adventure": Ibid., p. 26.

Page 152   "the chance to play": Ibid., p. 264.

Page 152   "I felt sick": Ibid., p. 199.

Page 152   "The whole affair made me": Ibid.

Page 152   "By everything I'd been taught": Ibid., p. 200.

Page 153   "worried about the spreading dishonesty": Malamud, *Dubin's Lives*, p. 238.

Page 154   "He is playing around": These and the subsequent "Henry" lyrics in this chapter are from the musical *Love and Shrimp*, words by Judith Viorst, music by Shelly Markham.

Page 155   "Every affair": Lawson, *Adultery*, p. 235.

Page 155   "a deep knowledge": Ibid., p. 260.

Page 156   "*benign* infidelity": Dicks, *Marital Tensions*, p. 168, for this and all other Dicks quotes in this paragraph except "when the unfaithful spouse," which appears on p. 167.

Page 159   "There is a guy": O'Neill, *The Marriage Premise*, pp. 177–178.

Page 160   "The man who resides": Ellis is quoted in Barash and Lipton, *The Myth of Monogamy*, p. 184.

Page 160   "is not natural": Ibid., p. 191.

Page 160   "the desire to have": Wallerstein and Blakeslee, *The Good Marriage*, p. 258.

Page 160   "The opposite of monogamy": Phillips, *Monogamy*, entry 98.

Page 161   "perhaps monogamy": Barash and Lipton, *The Myth of Monogamy*, p. 191.

CHAPTER 8: MAKING WAR, MAKING UP, MAKING DO

Page 163   "The law says": Sandburg, "Two Strangers Breakfast," in *Complete Poems*, p. 242.

Page 163   "Poor Georgie-Porgie": Albee, *Who's Afraid of Virginia Woolf?* p. 12.

Page 163   "It's your smugness": Updike, *Too Far to Go*, p. 40.

Page 164   "I can't even see you": Albee, *Who's Afraid of Virginia Woolf?* pp. 16, 17, 101.

Page 164   "He who is not arguing": Mack and Blankenhorn, eds., *The Book of Marriage*, p. 403.

Page 164   "Quarrels are the dowry": Ovid, from *The Art of Love*, in *The*

Notes

International Thesaurus of Quotations, compiled by Rhoda Thomas Tripp, p. 386.

Page 164   "If married couples": Nietzsche, from *Human, All Too Human,* in *The International Thesaurus of Quotations,* p. 386.

Page 166   "Most loving couples": Quoted by Kramer, *Should You Leave?* p. 237.

Page 167   "My mother's technique": Viorst, "Striking Back," in *It's Hard to Be Hip Over Thirty and Other Tragedies of Married Life,* p. 30.

Page 167   "avoidant couples": Gottman, *Why Marriages Succeed or Fail,* p. 44.

Page 167   "I CANNOT STAND IT!": Albee, *Who's Afraid of Virginia Woolf?* p. 152.

Page 167   "volatile couples": Gottman, *Why Marriages Succeed or Fail,* p. 40.

Page 167   "volcanic arguments": Ibid., p. 41.

Page 168   "On the way home": Viorst, "Postmortems," in *Forever Fifty and Other Negotiations,* p. 18.

Page 169   Some marital fights: The next several pages, extensively modified and elaborated on here and ending with the words "as a huge victory," appeared in Judith Viorst's article "Fight Together But Stay Together," *Redbook,* June 1984, pp. 106–107, 167.

Page 176   While it's all very nice: The next several pages, extensively modified here and ending with the words "admitting, and then there's *admitting,*" appeared in Judith Viorst's article "Fight Now, Apologize Later," *Redbook,* May 1975, pp. 31, 33, 34.

Page 182   And then there's the time: The following paragraph, modified here, appeared on p. 18 of Judith Viorst's article "What My Husband and I Are Still Learning About Staying Married," *Redbook,* September 1982, pp. 16, 18.

Page 183   "We would rage": Banville, *Eclipse,* p. 139.

CHAPTER 9: THE DIVORCE OPTION

Page 187   "Every Day a Little Death": Sondheim, *A Little Night Music,* song title.

Page 187   "You're such a nice woman": Updike, *Too Far to Go,* p. 63.

Page 192   "Can even dying": Ibid., p. 232.

Page 193   "When the grandfather": Jane Smiley, "There They Go, Bad-Mouthing Divorce Again," *New York Times,* September 12, 2000, op-ed.

Page 193   "Marriage is a bloodbath!": Heimel, "Beware of Mr. Right," in Chasman and Jhee, eds., *Here Lies My Heart,* p. 19.

Page 199   "see what was out there": Connie Collins, "Try, Try Again," *More,* November/December 2000, p. 70.

Page 199   "Basically," she says: Ibid.

Page 199   "were with her all the time": Ibid., p. 72.

Page 200   "mercilessly . . . two mutual tormentors": Lewis, *The Four Loves,* p. 160.

Page 201   "spoiled, impatient, selfish, and lazy": Paul, *The Starter Marriage,* p. 130.

Page 201   "truly believe": Ibid., p. 6.

Page 201   "we're less willing to tolerate": Ibid., p. 130.

Page 201   "if it's not meant": Ibid., p. 30.

Page 201   "unwilling or unable": Ibid., p. 130

Page 201   "Even though *every single person*": Ibid., p. 172.

Page 201   "would wish a starter marriage": Ibid., p. 258.

Page 202   "one marriage per lifetime": Ibid., p. 208.

Page 202   "tidal wave of divorce": This and the other quoted material in this paragraph can be found in Blaine Harden, "Bible Belt Couples 'Put Asunder' More, Despite New Efforts," *New York Times,* May 21, 2001, pp. A1, A14.

Page 206   "The more monumental": Michael Vincent Miller, *Intimate Terrorism,* p. 80.

Page 207   "the rescue marriage": Wallerstein and Blakeslee, *The Good Marriage,* p. 92.

Page 209   "the assumption that change": Otto Kernberg, "Boundaries and Structures in Love Relationships," *Journal of the American Psychoanalytic Association,* vol. 25, no. 1, 1977, p. 85.

Page 209   "forced to conclude": Ibid., p. 84.

Notes

Page 209   So when Brenda: The following paragraphs, with some additions and deletions and ending with the words "without it," appeared in Judith Viorst's article "We Didn't Divorce," *Redbook*, September 1984, p. 89.

Page 211   "As a therapist": Kramer, *Should You Leave?* p. 55.

Page 211   *"There are limits":* Ibid., p. 129.

Page 211   "Change enough": Ibid., p. 143.

CHAPTER 10: MARRYING AGAIN

Page 213   Almost everyone who: Karbo, *Generation Ex,* p. 17

Page 213   There ought to be: Trollope, *Other People's Children,* p. 141.

Page 214   60 percent: Wallerstein, Lewis, and Blakeslee, *The Unexpected Legacy of Divorce,* p. 295.

Page 214   "ephemeral as spring": Darling, "For Better and Worse," in Chasman and Jhee, eds., *Here Lies My Heart,* p. 198.

Page 215   "she's not in his face": Karbo, *Generation Ex, p. 72.

Page 216   "Nathanael thought": Malamud, *Dubin's Lives,* pp. 254, 255.

Page 216   "we aren't sufficiently": Ibid., p. 336.

Page 217   "the hope": Trollope, *Other People's Children,* pp. 73, 74.

Page 218   "excited, triumphant love": Ibid., p. 78.

Page 219   "We all have a tendency": Mitchell, *Can Love Last?* p. 82.

Page 220   "Surely you know": Tolstoy, *Anna Karenina,* pp. 146–147.

Page 220   "Vronsky . . . was not": Ibid., pp. 496–497.

Page 221   Some 70 percent: Karbo, *Generation Ex,* p. 110.

Page 223   The *"M'Aidez* Call": Karbo offers a hilarious discussion of the *M'Aidez* and other phone calls in chapter 7 of *Generation Ex.*

Page 223   "She can't figure out": Ibid., p. 115.

Page 223   "divarriage": Ibid. See Karbo's chapter 10.

Page 224   "extreme family": Ibid., pp. 227–228.

Page 224   "is a major reason": Shimberg, *Blending Families,* p. 136.

Notes

Page 226 "If I'd known": Wallerstein and Blakeslee, *The Good Marriage*, p. 299.

Page 226 "The weekends": Ibid., p. 301.

Page 226 "To be perfectly honest": Ibid., p. 292.

Page 226 "It took time": Ibid., p. 301.

Page 226 "Except for babies": Ibid., p. 302.

Page 227 "tried to make it work": Shimberg, *Blending Families*, p. 137.

Page 228 "Although they had lived": Heyman, *Lovers and Ghosts* (unpublished manuscript).

Page 228 "kind, industrious man": Ibid.

Page 228 "You do not ask": Klagsbrun, *Married People*, p. 219.

Page 229 "Saying, without saying it": Viorst, "Late Love," in *Suddenly Sixty and Other Shocks of Later Life*, p. 66.

CHAPTER 11: GROWING OLDER TOGETHER

Page 233 "No man or woman": Twain, from *Notebook*, in *The International Thesaurus of Quotations*, compiled by Rhoda Thomas Tripp, p. 387.

Page 233 "One of the nice things": Doress and Siegal, *Ourselves, Growing Older*, p. 136.

Page 234 leap in life expectancy: The average life expectancy was forty-seven years at the end of the nineteenth century and is now seventy-nine for women and seventy-two for men.

Page 234 "Grow old along with me": Robert Browning, "Rabbi Ben Ezra," in Stephens, Beck, and Snow, eds., *Victorian and Later English Poets*, pp. 353–354.

Page 237 "usually prepared supper": Munro, "The Bear Came Over the Mountain," in *Hateship, Friendship, Courtship, Loveship, Marriage*, p. 284.

Page 237 "I'm like an old bull elephant": Brody and Brody, *Renew Your Marriage at Midlife*, p. 29.

Page 238 "for those whose creativity": Erikson, Erikson, and Kivnick, *Vital Involvement in Old Age*, p. 299.

Page 238 "try as she might": Franzen, *The Corrections*, pp. 4–5.

Notes

Page 239   "with the new responsibility": Erikson, Erikson, and Kivnick, *Vital Involvement in Old Age*, p. 118.

Page 240   "He's starting conversations": Viorst, "About His Retirement," in *Suddenly Sixty*, p. 45.

Page 241   "enterprise and involvement": Erikson, Erikson, and Kivnick, *Vital Involvement in Old Age*. All the quoted material in this paragraph appears on p. 175.

Page 242   "After forty-seven years": Olsen, "Tell Me a Riddle," in *Tell Me a Riddle*, p. 76.

Page 243   "old harmonies": Ibid., p. 75.

Page 243   "chained with her": Ibid., p. 79.

Page 243   "bellyful of bitterness": Ibid., p. 74.

Page 243   "a groundless hate": Strindberg, *The Dance of Death*, in *Strindberg: Five Plays*, p. 131.

Page 243   "welded together": Ibid., p. 130.

Page 244   "give, give, give": Karen Springen, "Feeling the 50-Year Itch," *Newsweek*, December 4, 2000, p. 56.

Page 244   "their second wind": Ibid., p. 57.

Page 244   "see many healthy years": Ibid., p. 56.

Page 244   "while she still had time": Franzen, *The Corrections*, p. 568.

Page 248   "We've been a good": Erikson, Erikson, and Kivnick, *Vital Involvement in Old Age*, p. 115.

Page 248   "who is frustrated": Ibid. All the quoted material in this sentence appears on p. 116.

Page 248   "feels wronged, isolated": Ibid.

Page 248   "represents a poignant": Ibid.

Page 249   "wild with love": Kunitz, "Touch Me," in *The Collected Poems*, p. 266.

Page 250   "marriages of lifelong": Erikson, Erikson, and Kivnick, *Vital Involvement in Old Age*, p. 110.

Page 251   "devoted from the very beginning": Ibid., p. 111.

Page 251   a "long lifetime": Ibid., p. 113.

Chapter 12: Staying Married

Page 255   "I mean you're given": Tyler, *Breathing Lessons*, p. 182.

Page 256   "work, day labor": Rilke, "Letters on Love," in Kass and Kass, eds., *Wing to Wing, Oar to Oar*, p. 283.

Page 256   "I married you": Wilder, *The Skin of Our Teeth*, in *Three Plays*, pp. 200–201.

Page 257   "rituals of emotional connection": John Gottman and Julie Gottman, "Seven Principles for Making Marriage Work—The Masters and Disasters of Marriage," *The Art of Marriage*, December 1999, p. 20.

Page 258   "soars and slumps": Muldoon, "Long Finish," in *Paul Muldoon Poems 1968–1998*, pp. 438–441.

Page 258   "a romance of the ordinary": Michael Vincent Miller, *Intimate Terrorism*, p. 221.

Page 258   "After all, don't": Ibid., p. 237.

Page 259   "There are always": Sue Miller, *While I Was Gone*, p. 95.

Page 260   And so we might view: Viorst. This paragraph is a paraphrase of some lines from an article on happiness written for *Family Circle*.

Page 260   "And on Saturday nights": Viorst, "Happiness (Reconsidered)," in *Forever Fifty and Other Negotiations*, pp. 24–25.

Page 263   "bittersweet": Michael Vincent Miller, *Intimate Terrorism*, p. 218. On that same page he discusses the ironical perspective.

Page 263   "to domesticate sexuality": Cavell, *Pursuits of Happiness*, p. 31.

Page 264   "the living moment": Updike, "How Was It, Really?" in *Licks of Love*, p. 150.

BIBLIOGRAPHY

Albee, Edward. *Who's Afraid of Virginia Woolf?* New York: Signet Books, 1962.

Banville, John. *Eclipse.* New York: Alfred A. Knopf, 2001.

Barash, David P., and Judith Eve Lipton. *The Myth of Monogamy.* New York: W. H. Freeman, 2001.

Beavers, W. Robert. *Successful Marriage.* New York: W. W. Norton, 1985.

Betcher, William, and Robie Macauley. *The Seven Basic Quarrels of Marriage.* New York: Villard Books, 1991.

Block, Joyce. *Motherhood as Metamorphosis.* New York: A Dutton Book, 1990.

Blumstein, Philip, and Pepper Schwartz. *American Couples.* New York: William Morrow, 1983.

Boszormenyi-Nagy, Ivan, and Geraldine M. Spark. *Invisible Loyalties.* New York: Harper & Row, 1973.

Brody, Steve, and Cathy Brody. *Renew Your Marriage at Midlife.* New York: G. P. Putnam's Sons, 1999.

Cavell, Stanley. *Pursuits of Happiness.* Cambridge, Mass.: Harvard University Press, 1981.

Chasman, Deborah, and Catherine Jhee, eds. *Here Lies My Heart.* Boston: Beacon Press, 1999.

Colwin, Laurie. *Family Happiness.* New York: Harper & Row, 1982, 1990.

Darwin, Charles. *The Autobiography of Charles Darwin.* 1876. New York: Harcourt, Brace, 1958.

Dicks, Henry V. *Marital Tensions.* London: Karnac Books, 1967, 1993.

Doress, Paula Brown, and Diana Laskin Siegal. *Ourselves, Growing Older.* New York: Simon & Schuster, 1987.

Ephron, Nora. *Heartburn.* New York: Vintage Books, 1983.

Erikson, Erik H., Joan M. Erikson, and Helen Q. Kivnick. *Vital Involvement in Old Age.* New York: W. W. Norton, 1989.

Franzen, Jonathan. *The Corrections.* New York: Farrar, Straus & Giroux, 2001.

Frayn, Michael. *Headlong.* New York: Henry Holt, 1999.

Bibliography

Gottman, John. *Why Marriages Succeed or Fail.* New York: Fireside, 1994.

Graff, E. J. *What Is Marriage For?* Boston: Beacon Press, 1999.

Gurman, Alan S., and David G. Rice, eds. *Couples in Conflict.* New York: Jason Aronson, 1975.

Heyman, Arlene. *Lovers and Ghosts* (unpublished manuscript).

Johnson, Diane. *Le Mariage.* New York: A Dutton Book, 2000.

Karbo, Karen. *Generation Ex.* New York: Bloomsbury, 2001.

Kass, Amy A., and Leon R. Kass, eds. *Wing to Wing, Oar to Oar.* Notre Dame, Indiana: University of Notre Dame Press, 2000.

Klagsbrun, Francine. *Married People.* New York: Bantam Books, 1985.

Klass, Perri. *Love and Modern Medicine.* Boston: Houghton Mifflin, 2001.

Kramer, Peter. *Should You Leave?* New York: Penguin Books, 1997.

Kunitz, Stanley. *The Collected Poems.* New York: W. W. Norton, 2000.

Larkin, Philip. *Collected Poems.* New York: Farrar, Straus & Giroux, 1988, 1989.

Lawson, Annette. *Adultery.* New York: Basic Books, 1988.

Lewis, C. S. *The Four Loves.* New York: Harcourt, Brace & World, 1960.

Mack, Dana, and David Blankenhorn, eds. *The Book of Marriage.* Grand Rapids, Mich.: William B. Eerdmans, 2001.

Malamud, Bernard. *Dubin's Lives.* New York: Farrar, Straus & Giroux, 1977, 1979.

Miller, Michael Vincent. *Intimate Terrorism.* New York: W. W. Norton, 1995.

Miller, Sue. *While I Was Gone.* New York: Ballantine Books, 1999, 2000.

Mitchell, Stephen A. *Can Love Last?* New York: W. W. Norton, 2002.

Muldoon, Paul. *Paul Muldoon Poems 1968–1998.* New York: Farrar, Straus & Giroux, 2001.

Munro, Alice. *Hateship, Friendship, Courtship, Loveship, Marriage.* New York: Alfred A. Knopf, 2001.

The National Marriage Project. *The State of Our Unions 1999.* New Brunswick, N.J.: Rutgers University, 1999.

———. *The State of Our Unions 2000.* New Brunswick, N.J.: Rutgers University, 2000.

Olsen, Tillie. *Tell Me a Riddle.* New York: Delta/Seymour Lawrence, 1989.

O'Neill, Nena. *The Marriage Premise.* New York: Bantam Books, 1978.

Outcalt, Todd. *Before You Say "I Do."* New York: A Perigee Book, 1998.

Paul, Pamela. *The Starter Marriage.* New York: Villard, 2002.

Perutz, Kathrin. *Marriage Is Hell.* New York: William Morrow, 1972.

Bibliography

Phillips, Adam. *Monogamy.* New York: Pantheon Books, 1996.

Pittman, Frank. *Private Lies.* New York: W. W. Norton, 1989, 1990.

Popenoe, David, and Barbara Dafoe Whitehead. The National Marriage Project. *Should We Live Together?* New Brunswick, N.J.: Rutgers University, 1999.

Roth, Philip. *My Life as a Man.* New York: Holt, Rinehart & Winston, 1970, 1971, 1973, 1974.

Rubin, Lillian B. *Intimate Strangers.* New York: Harper & Row, 1983.

Sandburg, Carl. *Complete Poems.* New York: Harcourt, Brace, 1950.

Shapiro, Jane. *After Moondog.* New York: Warner Books, 1992, 1993, 1999.

Shimberg, Elaine Fantle. *Blending Families.* New York: Berkley Books, 1999.

Stephens, James, Edwin L. Beck, and Royall H. Snow, eds. *Victorian and Later English Poets.* New York: American Book Company, 1934.

Storr, Anthony. *Solitude.* New York: The Free Press, 1988.

Strindberg, August. *Strindberg: Five Plays.* Berkeley: University of California Press, 1981, 1983.

Tolstoy, Leo. *Anna Karenina.* 1876. Translated by Joel Carmichael. New York: Bantam Books, 1960.

Tripp, Rhoda Thomas, ed. *The International Thesaurus of Quotations.* New York: Thomas Y. Crowell, 1970.

Trollope, Joanna. *Other People's Children.* New York: Berkley Books, 2000.

Tyler, Anne. *Breathing Lessons.* New York: Alfred A. Knopf, 1988.

Updike, John. *Licks of Love.* New York: Ballantine Books, 2000.

———. *Too Far to Go.* New York: Fawcett Crest, 1956, 1979.

Viorst, Judith. *Forever Fifty and Other Negotiations.* New York: Simon & Schuster, 1989.

———. *How Did I Get to Be Forty and Other Atrocities.* New York: Simon & Schuster, 1973, 1974, 1976.

———. *It's Hard to Be Hip Over Thirty and Other Tragedies of Married Life.* New York: World, 1968.

———. *People and Other Aggravations.* New York: World, 1971.

———. *Suddenly Sixty and Other Shocks of Later Life.* New York: Simon & Schuster, 2000.

———. *When Did I Stop Being Twenty and Other Injustices.* New York: Simon & Schuster, 1987.

Waite, Linda J., and Maggie Gallagher. *The Case for Marriage.* New York: Doubleday, 2000.

Bibliography

Wallerstein, Judith S., Julia M. Lewis, and Sandra Blakeslee. *The Unexpected Legacy of Divorce*. New York: Hyperion, 2000.

Wallerstein, Judith, and Sandra Blakeslee. *The Good Marriage*. Boston: Houghton Mifflin, 1995.

Whitehead, Barbara Dafoe, and David Popenoe. The National Marriage Project. *Why Wed?* New Brunswick, N.J.: Rutgers University, 1999.

Wilder, Thorton. *Three Plays*. New York: Harper & Row, 1957.

Winnicott, D. W. *Collected Papers*. New York: Basic Books, 1958.

Yates, Richard. *Revolutionary Road*. New York: Vintage Books, 1961, 2000.

ACKNOWLEDGMENTS

My husband, my children, their wives, my friends, and the excellent therapists whose brains I picked have made their contributions to this book. So have the women and men who—in exchange for my promise to protect their privacy— were willing to answer my questions about their marriages. I thank them all.

I want to give a special thanks to the psychoanalysts, psychologists, and one civilian who read and critiqued various drafts of this book: Joan Willens Beerman, Barbara Breger, Lou Breger, Ruth Caplin, Harvey Rich, and Sheila Rogovin. I am grateful to them for their insights and expertise, and for their friendship.

I also want to thank, for the sustenance they provide, my friends Hanna Altman, Sunny Aurelio, Patsy Davis, Joy Dunkerley, Margot Hahn, Phyllis Hersh, Arlene Heyman, Elinor Horwitz, Silvia Koner, Elaine Konigsburg, Martha Nelson, Leslie Oberdorfer, Patricia O'Brien, Betty Ann Ottinger, Sally Pitofsky, Shay Rieger, Barbara Rosenfeld, Lisbeth Schorr, and Judy Silber. And I want to offer a separate thanks for all the help I received from my friend Nell Minow, a perceptive and articulate and deeply dedicated marriage-watcher.

And as long as I'm thanking, I certainly want to include my agent-for-life, Robert Lescher, and his wonderful associate, Michael Choate, and my editor-for-life, Fred Hills, and *his* wonderful associate, Burton Beals, and—again—my beloved family: Tony and Hyla, Nick and Marya, Alexander and Marla, our almost-daughter Jeannette and Steve, and my husband, Milton, without whom this book would not exist.

INDEX

Index

Index

finances *(cont.)*
    fights about, 165
    of older couples, 245, 246
    professional rivalry and, 131–32, 133
    as reason for marriage, 5, 7
    as responsibility of new fathers, 75
first marriages, 211
    ending in divorce, 7, 200–202, 213, 214
    preceded by living together, 17
Follies (Sondheim), 192
Fonda, Henry, 252
Fonda, Jane, 112
"For Better or Worse" (Darling), 29
Ford, Richard, 100
forgiveness, 179, 183, 193, 215
Franklin, Benjamin, 36–37
Franzen, Jonathan, 238
freedoms, personal, 109, 111
friends
    of retired couples, 239
    rivalry over, 127–29
Fussman, Cal, 22

Gallagher, Maggie, 21
Generation Ex (Karbo), 213, 214–15, 222–24
Good Marriage, The (Wallerstein and Blakeslee), 131–32, 160, 207, 226–27
Gore, Al, 23
Gore, Tipper, 23
Gottman, John, 42–43, 103, 167
grandparents, 78–79
    older couples as, 235–37
    rivalry between, 126
grievances, bottled up, 171
guilt, 32
    in blended families, 225
    child-neglect, 89, 90
    about obligations to parents, 49, 57, 58

habits, annoying, 31
Havens, Leston, 166
health
    effects of marriage on, 22
    problems with, of older couples, 245–49
Heartbreak Kid, The (movie), 9–10
Heartburn (Ephron), 76
Heimel, Cynthia, 22, 193
Hepburn, Katharine, 252
Heyman, Arlene, 228
Hinderliter, Cathryn, 202
"Homeward Bound" (Achenbach), 95
honesty
    about feelings toward in-laws, 53–54
    hurtful, 105–8

I Love Lucy, 102
illnesses, coping with, 46, 245–49
inattention, 100–102
infidelity, *see* adultery
Ingall, Marjorie, 21
injuries, overstatement of, 174
in-laws, *see* families of origin
inner work, 26
Institute for Family Values, 21
"Inimacy" (Klass), 81
Intimate Terrorism (Miller), 114, 117, 206, 258
Invisible Loyalties (Boszormenyi-Nagy and Spark), 56–58, 61, 68
Isenberg, Sidney, 238

jealousy
    father's, of new baby, 75
    see also rivalry
Jerome, St., 164
Jong, Erica, 141–42

Karbo, Karen, 213, 214–15, 222–24
Kass, Amy, 84
Kass, Leon, 84

Index

Index

Index

Index

ABOUT THE AUTHOR

Judith Viorst is the bestselling author of *Suddenly Sixty, Forever Fifty, Necessary Losses,* and several other books for adults. She is also the author of sixteen children's books, including the classic *Alexander and the Terrible, Horrible, No Good, Very Bad Day.*

She was born and brought up in New Jersey, graduated from Rutgers University (and, later, from the Washington Psychoanalytic Institute), lived in Greenwich Village—where she worked as a garment-district model, unappreciated secretary, and children's book editor—and has spent the last forty-two years in Washington, D.C., after marrying Milton Viorst, a political writer. (They have achieved the almost-impossible: working in adjoining offices at home and eating three meals a day together for most of those years.) They have three married-with-children sons—Anthony, a lawyer; Nick, in law school; and Alexander, who does community development lending at a bank. They also have, so far, four grandchildren: Miranda, Brandeis, Olivia, and Nathaniel.